A YEAR OF
Grace,
Healing
and Hope

A DAILY
DEVOTIONAL

D1025978

by best-selling author

ROD PARSLEY

A YEAR OF GRACE, HEALING AND HOPE BY ROD PARSLEY

Published by Results Publishing
Columbus, OH

World Harvest Church
P.O. Box 100
Columbus, OH 43216
www.rodparsley.com

Compiled and edited by Inspired Direct, LLC, Nashua, NH.
This book or parts thereof may not be reproduced in any form, stored in
a retrieval system or transmitted in any form by any means—electronic,
mechanical, photocopy, recording or otherwise—without prior permission of
the publisher, except as provided by United States of America copyright law.

Scripture taken from the HOLY BIBLE, NEW INTERNATIONAL VERSION.
Copyright © 1973, 1978, 1984 International Bible Society. Used by permission of
Zondervan Bible Publishers.

International Standard Book Number: 1-933336-93-5 (paperback)

Printed in the United States of AmericaPrinted in the United States of America

A YEAR OF
Grace,
Healing
and Hope

TO MIRNA, A SWEET GUATEMALAN CHILD—
MAY YOUR SHORT LIFE BE A REMINDER TO US TO
LOOK AFTER "THE LEAST OF THESE."

When our *Bridge of Hope* team first saw Mirna, she was sitting on the dirt floor, staring off vacantly. Her arms were like broomsticks, and at nine years old she weighed only 25 pounds.

We have seen some heartbreaking things around the world, but tiny, sweet Mirna broke our hearts. She died not 48 hours after we arrived. We prayed for her, hugged her and watched over her as the medical team scrambled to save her. But we were too late...we were just too late. Here is the saddest part of all: if we had been there one week earlier, we could have saved her.

There is nothing more painful than the sight of a child dying from hunger, especially when it doesn't have to happen! I've seen it all over the world. You don't forget things like this.

No child should ever be forced to suffer like Mirna did. God never intended for His precious children to waste away. He says in Isaiah 58:6, *"Is not this the kind of fasting I have chosen: to loose the chains of injustice and untie the cords of the yoke, to set the oppressed free and break every yoke?"*

I have dedicated this devotional to her as a reminder to myself to never forget "the least of these." Experts tell me there are more than one billion people starving right now and that every six seconds, someone dies of starvation and related diseases.

To ensure that more children are saved from a fate like Mirna's, I want to do everything I can to provide 10 million meals for hungry families around the world in 2010. As Christians, we are called to be salt and light to the world. Will you join me?

*"To God's elect...who have
been chosen according to the
foreknowledge of God the Father,
through the sanctifying work
of the Spirit, for obedience to
Jesus Christ and sprinkling by
his blood: Grace and peace be
yours in abundance."*

— I PETER I:I-2

Dear Friend,

Thousands of people watch our program every month for the first time. They need God's touch, and they write or call and ask me to pray. We pray faithfully over every prayer request and need, and we see miracles happen, from dramatic healings to financial breakthroughs.

But thousands of people don't get their miracle and we never hear from them again. Why? They look at Rod Parsley to make it happen. Instead, they need to look to Christ Jesus. The Bible says, *"I lift up my eyes to the hills— where does my help come from?"* (Psalms 121:1).

With God anything is possible. I am trusting God that this will be your year to see His grace, healing and hope manifest in your life. God is not hampered by any forces of this world. He can do all things. He desires abundance for His children.

Proverbs 4:20-22 says, *"My son, pay attention to what I say; listen closely to my words. Do not let them out of your sight, keep them within your heart; for they are life to those who find them and health to a man's whole body."*

I want to share a word with you each day to challenge and inspire you to all God has for you. A life of blessings is waiting for you. Now.

Yours in Christ,

Pastor Rod Parsley

January 1

Make Disciples of All Nations

*"Therefore go and make disciples of all nations,
baptizing them in the name of the Father and of the
Son and of the Holy Spirit, and teaching them to obey
everything I have commanded you. And surely I am
with you always, to the very end of the age."*

—MATTHEW 28:19-20

The commandment that Jesus gave to His disciples is an urgent call to all born-again believers.

As we start this new year, we need to be reminded that we are in the last days of our time on earth, and the kingdom of heaven is at hand. As born-again believers this is wonderful news! It means that we don't have long to wait until that glorious day when we will see God and walk heaven's streets of gold.

It also means that our time is growing short to act on Jesus' commandment to make disciples of all nations. We cannot delay any longer. Too many are at risk of dying without Jesus!

We can no longer just sit within the walls of the church on Sunday mornings—we must step out in faith and spread the Gospel message in a great end-time harvest of souls. Our job as believers is not to stay in, but to go out to a lost and hurting world with the Gospel of Jesus Christ! We can go out in confidence, knowing that God's Holy Spirit is empowering us.

FURTHER READING:
Matthew 24:14
Mark 16:15
2 Corinthians 4:5

January 2

Walk in the Spirit

"I have been crucified with Christ and I no longer live,
but Christ lives in me. The life I live in the body,
I live by faith in the Son of God, who loved me and
gave himself for me."

—GALATIANS 2:20

Have you been merely existing in the Christian life, and not experiencing the power of the everlasting God?

Then I want you to grab hold of this new year—it's time to let God work in a new you! This year you are going to refuse to allow your future to be dictated by the world...this is the year you're going to walk in the Spirit!

The Christian life is not complicated, but it is sometimes difficult. Why? It is not your natural life...it's your super-natural life. And that means to live abundantly in Christ, you must let go of your own will and instead depend on the supernatural power of God and the induement of His Holy Spirit!

Unless you let the Holy Spirit direct your life, you will become controlled by your own desires and live according to the changing whims of the world.

This year, refuse to be dominated by the flesh. This year, set your mind on the things of the Spirit so that you can walk in the fullness of His power.

FURTHER READING:
Romans 8:1
Galatians 5:16-18
Galatians 6:8

January 3

A Cord of Three Strands

"Though one may be overpowered, two can defend themselves. A cord of three strands is not quickly broken."

—ECCLESIASTES 4:12

Little Penny held onto the one thing she owned; a white cord. She was thin and dirty like the other children at the orphanage, and she clutched this frayed scrap of ribbon as though it were the most important thing in the world. This baby girl had barely survived the hurricanes. But God was with Penny and the other children in this orphanage.

These children in the orphanages own nothing but the clothes on their backs... and Penny's precious strand of cord that had once held her hair. When I saw her guarding her frayed cord I couldn't help but recall the scripture in Ecclesiastes about the cord of three strands.

Penny and thousands of other orphans like her lack so many basics that most of us take for granted.

All around the world thousands of orphans like Penny are waiting for someone to care—for someone to offer them hope. What these children need is a cord of three stands... a partnership between you, me, and our heavenly Father... a partnership that will offer hope and a future...a partnership that is not easily broken.

FURTHER READING:
Deuteronomy 10:18
Deuteronomy 24:7
Psalms 140:12

January 4

Streams of Living Water

*"If anyone is thirsty, let him come to me and drink.
Whoever believes in me, as the Scripture has said,
streams of living water will flow from within him."*

—JOHN 7:37-38

God created mankind to know Him and to have a relationship with Him. We need Him. We have been created with an innate hunger and thirst for God that nothing else can possibly satisfy.

In those times when you feel like your life is empty or lacks direction, it may be that you are trying to quench that thirst for God with something else.

Sometimes we mistake that need for God with another type of need, and attempt to fill it with possessions or success or drugs or alcohol. But no matter how attractive those things might appear, they cannot possibly satisfy us and soon we'll thirst again.

But God offers us a way to quench our thirst so that we thirst no more. God invites us to drink of the water that He provides through His Word. Every day, set aside time to study the Bible, and let His Word guide your life. When you fill yourself with His goodness, the Bible promises us that streams of living water—true Spirit-filled life—will flow from us.

FURTHER READING:
Romans 8:14
Psalms 1
John 4:13-14

January 5

Fruit of the Spirit

"But the fruit of the Spirit is love, joy, peace, patience, kindness, goodness, faithfulness, gentleness and self-control. Against such things there is no law."

—GALATIANS 5:22-23

What does the Bible mean by the fruit of the Spirit? In the natural realm, fruit is a byproduct of the growth of the tree. When a tree produces fruit, it is evidence that a natural phenomenon is at work, and that the tree is "yielding fruit after his kind" (Genesis 1:11).

It's similar in the supernatural realm. If you are a born-again believer, the fruit of the Spirit is evidence of spiritual growth and maturity, and that a supernatural phenomenon is at work in you—the indwelling of the Holy Spirit! You cannot produce these qualities on your own—they can only be produced after you have received God's life and have been endued with power from on high!

The fruit of the Spirit is God's character. We receive the fruits of the Spirit when we accept Christ as the Lord of our lives. These are attributes of God that we are called to emulate, just as 3 John 1:11 says: "Dear friend, do not imitate what is evil but what is good. Anyone who does what is good is from God. Anyone who does what is evil has not seen God."

FURTHER READING:
Acts 1:8
John 14:16
James 3:17

January 6

Fruit of the Spirit: Love

"Love is patient, love is kind. It does not envy, it does not boast, it is not proud. It is not rude, it is not self-seeking, it is not easily angered, it keeps no record of wrongs. Love ... always protects, always trusts, always hopes, always perseveres. Love never fails."

—I CORINTHIANS 13:4-8

Love is a familiar word in our culture, and to most of us love is a powerful emotion that transcends all others. But in the Biblical sense, love is not merely a warm and fuzzy human emotion, but a choice of the will. This kind of love is a selfless love that always seeks the highest and best for another. It is an unconditional love that gives freely without asking anything in return.

God's love for us is the ultimate example of pure, selfless love—never-ending and all-encompassing. God's love for us is so great that He chose to send His son Jesus to die on the cross of Calvary to redeem us! And Jesus chose to bear our sins and die on the cross to redeem us and restore us to God's favor. Oh, that we could possibly emulate the love that God has for us! Romans 5:8 says, "But God demonstrates his own love for us in this: While we were still sinners, Christ died for us."

As Christ has shown us, biblical love is not what we feel but what we do.

FURTHER READING:
Matthew 5:44
John 3:16
1 Corinthians 13:1

January 7

Fruit of the Spirit: Joy

"But let all who take refuge in you be glad; let them ever sing for joy. Spread your protection over them, that those who love your name may rejoice in you."

—PSALMS 5:11

You might think of joy as happiness. But don't be confused; joy is not an emotion—it is a supernatural expression given to us by the indwelling of the Holy Spirit.

Unlike happiness, which is a fleeting emotion that often depends on our circumstances, joy is a deep and abiding sense of contentment that provides a foundation for our lives in Christ. Unlike fragile happiness, which can wither during times of testing, joy grows and blossoms in the hard soil of tough times.

The Bible is replete with examples of those who continued to rejoice even in the face of persecution. For example, the apostle Paul wrote his letter to the Philippians while he was imprisoned, yet his letter is one of joy, exhorting the people of Philippi to rejoice (Philippians 4:4).

We will never find joy by seeking self-centered excitement and pleasure. True joy results when we give ourselves to God, wholly and completely, and yield to His will and purpose. True joy is the gift of knowing that our loving heavenly Father holds our future in His hands.

FURTHER READING:
Psalms 51:12
James 1:2-4
1 Peter 1:8

January 8

Fruit of the Spirit: Peace

"And the peace of God, which transcends all understanding, will guard your hearts and your minds in Christ Jesus."

—PHILIPPIANS 4:7

Everyone's searching for peace—peace of mind, inner peace, world peace. But as born-again believers, we want to know the peace that Jesus promised us in John 14:27: "Peace I leave with you; my peace I give you. I do not give to you as the world gives. Do not let your hearts be troubled and do not be afraid."

The peace of God is an inner calm that we can experience only when we put everything—our lives, our worries, our future—in His hands and fully trust Him for the result. When we face trials we know He is in control. "I have told you these things, so that in me you may have peace. In this world you will have trouble. But take heart! I have overcome the world." (John 16:33)

When we utterly submit to His will for us, we can rest in Him knowing that our sins are forgiven, that we are reconciled to God, and that soon we will leave this earth to share in His glorious kingdom!

FURTHER READING:
Psalms 29:11
Colossians 3:15
Ephesians 2:14

January 9

Fruit of the Spirit: Patience

*"Be patient then, brothers, until the Lord's coming.
See how the farmer waits for the land to yield its
valuable crop and how patient he is for the autumn
and spring rains. You too, be patient and stand firm,
because the Lord's coming is near."*

—JAMES 5:7-8

In the Biblical sense, patience requires an entirely new attitude toward life and toward our dealings with others.

As we face the difficulties of life, we must remember that as born-again believers our faith is rooted in the belief that we will spend eternity walking heaven's streets of gold. And once we realize that every situation on earth is just temporary, it changes our attitude. No matter what difficulties life throws our way, we can persevere. "Blessed is the man who perseveres under trial, because when he has stood the test, he will receive the crown of life that God has promised to those who love him." (James 1:11-13)

Patience toward others is grounded in another fruit of the Spirit: love—the kind of love that puts others' needs above our own and does not seek personal gain. Romans 12:10 says: "Be devoted to one another in brotherly love. Honor one another above yourselves."

FURTHER READING:
Psalms 37:7
Psalms 40:1
Romans 5:3

January 10

He Lifts Up the Needy

"Defend the cause of the weak and fatherless; maintain the rights of the poor and oppressed. Rescue the weak and needy; deliver them from the hand of the wicked."

—PSALMS 82:3-4

Maggie was found half-alive in a burning trash pile in Haiti. Mercifully, she was pulled out just in time. Her rescuers learned of the trauma that had been forced upon this poor girl. She'd been sexually abused and she'd been beaten almost to death.

In time, Maggie's body healed and she learned to smile again, leaving behind her painful past. More importantly, Maggie came to learn about a Savior who loved her. She embraced Him with all her might and radiated with hope for her future. In the orphanage that took her in, she was loved by the younger children. She cooked for them and helped them in any way she could. Her future was bright and full of hope. But one day she got sick...and there was nothing anyone could do to make her better. Maggie died shortly before I left Haiti.

The Bible instructs us to look after the poor, the needy and the oppressed: "Administer true justice; show mercy and compassion to one another. Do not oppress the widow or the fatherless, the alien or the poor" (Zechariah 7:9-10). Will you follow the Lord's command to help those in need?

FURTHER READING:
1 Samuel 2:8
Psalms 113:7-8
Job 30:25

January 11

Fruit of the Spirit: Kindness

"When the kindness and love of God our Savior appeared, he saved us ... because of his mercy."

—TITUS 3:4-5

As a Christian, once you are grafted into the vine of Jesus Christ, you will begin to see yourself bearing God's fruit in your life. The way you look and act will begin to change as you become more like your Father in heaven.

One of the fruits that will grow in your life will be kindness. This word denotes a mellowing of a disposition that was once harsh and austere. It is the divine attribute that makes God loving yet righteous.

It doesn't take away from God's goodness, but rather, it makes God's goodness accessible to us. Kindness is the patient love of God that would allow Him to humble Himself and leave the portals of heaven to meet us where we were, so He could gently share His love with us.

By bearing God's kindness through your life, you will be sharing the love and patience that God bestowed upon mankind (Ephesians 2:1-9).

It's not human nature to love others who are unloving toward you—or to put the needs of others before your own—but it is the fruit of His Spirit alive and working within your heart.

FURTHER READING:
Colossians 3:12-17
Titus 3:3-8
Ephesians 2:1-9

January 12

Fruit of the Spirit: Goodness

"Who is wise and understanding among you? Let him show it by his good life, by deeds done in the humility that comes from wisdom."

—JAMES 3:13

God has given us all good things and one of the best ways we can thank Him is by being good and doing good works.

Goodness is defined as moral excellence, virtue and excellence of quality. Goodness is not just appearing to be good; it is the essence of a person's character.

However, we will never be good on our own. As sinful humans, we can only be good through the work of the Holy Spirit. If we are to be good, we must spend time with the source of all goodness—God. Do not engage in evil activities but seek to honor the Lord in your words, actions, and even your thoughts.

The 23rd Psalm says, "You prepare a table before me in the presence of my enemies. You anoint my head with oil; my cup overflows. Surely goodness and love will follow me all the days of my life, and I will dwell in the house of the Lord forever."

If we give love, love will be given to us. If we espouse good, then good will come to us. Be active in doing good, in thinking good and in being good, through the encouragement of the Holy Spirit inside you.

FURTHER READING:
Ephesians 5:8-10
Romans 15:14
2 Peter 1:3

January 13

Fruit of the Spirit: Faithfulness

*"If we are faithless, he will remain faithful,
for he cannot disown himself."*

—2 TIMOTHY 2:13

There are times we actually think we are the ones hanging onto God. The truth is that God is the One hanging onto us! He is the faithful One.

That's why we sing: "Great is Thy faithfulness! Morning by morning, new mercies I see. All I have needed Thy hand hath provided; great is Thy faithfulness, Lord unto me!"

You can trust Him, for He is faithful. If we allow His Spirit to bear fruit in our lives, He actually increases our ability to trust and have faith in Him. As the Spirit reminds us of God's promises, our heart is renewed—and we find we have the faith to step out and obey for His kingdom.

"Through these he has given us his very great and precious promises, so that through them you may participate in the divine nature..." (2 Peter 1:4).

He quickens the Word of God to our minds and shows us the way to go. "Consequently, faith comes from hearing the message, and the message is heard through the word of Christ" (Romans 10:17). Faithfulness to God is a fruit of the Spirit, and it increases as we draw closer to Him.

FURTHER READING:
*Matthew 25:14-23
1 Timothy 1:12-17
2 Timothy 2:22*

January 14

Fruit of the Spirit: Gentleness

"Be completely humble and gentle; be patient,
bearing with one another in love"

—EPHESIANS 4:2

When we are told that we will bear the fruit of the spirit called gentleness, what does that mean?

Gentleness is directly tied with God's kindness. Because God is kind, He is gentle. It is an attribute that flows directly out of God's disposition.

In the movies, Jesus is depicted as being this sad and long-faced fellow who slowly walks around and softly touches people...as if that is meekness. But that's not meekness at all!

Meekness is power under control. Meekness is having the hands of a carpenter—hammering large planks of wood together—and yet gently holding a baby in His hands.

Just think of the wonder of these statements: "Jesus reached out and touched the man...immediately he was cured" (Matthew 8:3) or "He touched her hand and the fever left her" (Matthew 8:15). This was more than just a carpenter who was touching these people—it was the God who created the heavens and the earth. Now, that's meekness!

That's the power of God's love in gentle action...and that's the fruit of the God's Spirit of gentleness alive in you!

FURTHER READING:
Isaiah 40:1-11
1 Peter 3:1-12
Proverbs 15:1-4

January 15

Fruit of the Spirit: Self-Control

*"And to knowledge, self-control; and to self-control,
perseverance, and to perseverance, godliness"*

—2 PETER 1:6

There is no other sporting event like the Olympics. It thrills our
senses as we watch the top athletes in the world going head to
head in competition.

And yet, the sensation for us as spectators goes far beyond
that. We realize we are watching each individual battle against
time and themselves as they strive to be the best they can be at
that single moment of glory.

That is what "self-control" is all about.

That is what the apostle Paul was describing when he said,
"Do you not know that in a race all the runners run, but only
one gets the prize? Run in such a way as to get the prize.
Therefore I do not run like a man running aimlessly...No,
I beat my body and make it my slave so that after I have
preached to others, I myself will not be disqualified for the
prize." (1 Corinthians 9:24-27). There's something inside
Olympic athletes that causes them to rise up early in the
morning and train.

For you and I, that "something" is the Holy Spirit. Self-
control is the fruit of the Spirit that rises from within and
calls us to live a holy life with God's power in control.

FURTHER READING:
1 Corinthians 9:19-27
2 Timothy 2:1-19
2 Peter 1-11

January 16

God Cares

"The thief comes only to steal and kill and destroy..."

—JOHN 10:10

People often blame God when bad things happen. A hurricane or a tornado occurs and it's called "an act of God." An innocent person dies and people ask, "Why would God let this happen?"

Our society has given God a bad name He doesn't deserve.

Get this truth in your spirit: God is a good God. He cares for you. God isn't waiting to hurl lightning bolts at you whenever you make a mistake. Instead, God tells us to cast all our cares upon Him, because He cares for us. God is full of blessing, mercy, abundance, strength, healing, victory and security. He sent His Son to die so we might have eternal life with Him!

Satan is the one that wants to harm you. Satan comes to steal, kill and destroy—but Jesus says, "I have come that they may have life, and have it to the full" (John 10:10). The cross stands as your memorial that God wants to make peace with you. He wants to save you. One of the key provisions through Calvary is healing for our physical bodies. "He himself bore our sins in his body on the tree...by his wounds you have been healed" (1 Peter 2:24).

Remember that Satan is the cause of pain on this earth; not God. God wants you to prosper and live in abundance.

FURTHER READING:
1 Peter 5:5-9
James 4:7-10
1 John 4:1-5:15

January 17

Declare His Word

"He was pierced for our transgressions...
and by his wounds we are healed."

—ISAIAH 53:5

Declaring God's Word is important to your healing. Your words speak volumes into the spiritual realm. By speaking His Word aloud, you declare with your mouth how it shall be and force the darkness away with His light.

Speak these words out loud, right now. Let this truth penetrate your soul: "But he was pierced for our transgressions, he was crushed for our iniquities; the punishment that brought us peace was upon him, and by his wounds we are healed" (Isaiah 53:5). When you speak His Word, God begins to work inside you. Through His blood shed upon the cross, Jesus Christ invades the area of your affliction.

On Calvary, at the cross of Christ, the price for your healing was paid. The blood from Jesus' wounds flowed against the bark of the tree. A crimson stain marked the post where God's redemption of all humanity occurred.

The Bible declares: "Now is the time of God's favor, now is the day of salvation" (2 Corinthians 6:2). Salvation means healing, deliverance, and prosperity—making you whole. Speak His Word aloud and let Him heal you.

FURTHER READING:
3 John 2
Psalms 103
Psalms 139

January 18

Power to Heal

*"Jesus Christ is the same yesterday
and today and forever."*

—HEBREWS 13:8

Don't allow anyone to stop you from receiving your healing. Be like blind Bartimaeus who—as he sat by the roadside begging—heard Jesus passing by and shouted, "Jesus, Son of David, have mercy on me!"

Others rebuked him and told him to be quiet, but he shouted even louder. He wasn't going to let anything stop him from touching Jesus! "Have mercy on me," he cried...and Jesus did!

When the doubters start knocking at your door saying, "God doesn't heal today," you need to proclaim the truth of Hebrews 13:8, "Jesus Christ is the same yesterday and today and forever."

Then remind them of Romans 8:11, "If the Spirit of Him who raised Jesus from the dead is living in you, he who raised Christ from the dead will also give life to your mortal body through His Spirit, who lives in you."

Through the power of Jesus and faith in Him, you have the power to heal and be healed. "So is My word that goes out from My mouth: It will not return to me empty, but will accomplish what I desire and achieve the purpose for which I sent it" (Isaiah 55:11). Ask for it, and you will receive it.

FURTHER READING:
Psalms 107
Hosea 6:1-3
Psalms 118

January 19

Reach Out

"He said to her, 'Daughter, your faith has healed you.
Go in peace and be freed from your suffering.'"

—MARK 5:34

"Who touched me?" This question came from Jesus as He was crowded by the multitudes trying to get close to Him. One little woman reached out in faith and touched Him, expecting to receive a tangible transfer of His anointing.

When she did...she was healed! Why?

She believed what she heard about Jesus healing the sick. The thought of receiving a "touch" from Jesus sparked insight and faith. "When she heard about Jesus..." (Mark 5:27).

She spoke the truth again and again in her heart. Mark 5:27-28 says, "She came up behind him in the crowd and touched his cloak, because she thought, 'If I just touch his clothes, I will be healed.'"

She didn't give up...she pressed on. She could have given up, but she touched Jesus and received His healing. We are to act in faith just like this woman did. Do you need a tangible transfer of His anointing on your life? Reach out to Him in faith.

When the woman reached out, a tangible transfer of power took place. She came into the Lord's presence and touched His anointing and power...and was healed...all because of her faith!

FURTHER READING:
Mark 5:21-43
Mark 6:53-56
Mark 10:46-52

January 20

Fear or Faith?

"Do you want to get well?"

—JOHN 5:6

At the Pool of Bethesda, Jesus met a man afflicted for 38 years with a sickness. A condition this lasting becomes part of a person's identity and he thinks, "I will always be a cripple."

So Jesus asked the man a fascinating question: "Do you want to get well?"

"Sir," the man replied, "I have no man to put me into the pool." Do you see what the man said? He didn't answer Jesus' question! Jesus asked, "Do you want to get well?" There was something in the man's attitude holding him back from even thinking about receiving healing.

What makes you say, "I can't," "I won't," "It will never happen," or "I'm afraid"? Whatever the fear is—whatever the depression you've found comfort in—whatever keeps you from fulfilling God's purpose for your life—remember that those excuses are not of God. They nullify faith.

Fear is false evidence that masquerades as truth. Fear is the counterfeit of faith. They are mutually exclusive and cancel one another out.

I want you to agree with me that you will not lift your fear up before God, and instead you will lift Him up in praise and worship! You will say, "Yes, I want to get well!"

FURTHER READING:
John 5:1-18
Daniel 6
Matthew 8:1-13

January 21

What Are You Expecting?

*"Now faith is being sure of what we hope for
and certain of what we do not see."*

—HEBREWS 11:1

The Bible says, "Do not fear, for I am with you; do not be dismayed, for I am your God" (Isaiah 41:10). Fear is one of the tools our adversary uses to knock us off balance.

When the enemy comes with the first little problem, we must not allow ourselves to be caught off guard. What are you expecting right now? Some people expect nothing but the worst. They don't expect a raise or a breakthrough. They don't expect to be healed.

How do I know? Because if someone is expecting, that person makes changes. When my wife was expecting each of our children, she made some changes to prepare for the event to come. She waited with hopeful expectation. You and I are to likewise prepare to receive our answer from God.

After all, what is faith in God? Faith is expectation...and where there is expectation, there is preparation. And where there is faith, there can be no fear, for faith shoves fear out. Faith cancels your fear. Your victory will be won in the arena of expectation and expectation begins with hope.

So, I ask you: What are you hoping for?

FURTHER READING:
Hebrews 11
Matthew 11:20-25
Romans 5:1-5

January 22

Leaven of the Pharisees

"Be careful," Jesus said to them. "Be on your guard against the yeast of the Pharisees...."

—MATTHEW 16:6

The leaven of the Pharisees is a show of religion. They are like dead bones on the inside but on the outside they have the look and appearance of piety and spirituality. Their character lacks true love and devotion to God.

Everything they do is to be seen by men. "They make their phylacteries wide and the tassels on their garments long" (Matthew 23:5). They need to be placed in the seat of honor at gatherings. They enjoy being called by a title. They are blind guides. They are filled with greed and self-indulgence, hypocrisy and wickedness.

They pray out in the open to be seen by men. They babble and use many words in order to give a good impression, but Jesus knew that it was all a performance and he called them "hypocrites" (Matthew 6:5).

Jesus warned his disciples not to be like the Pharisees. He never intended for us to depend on the rudiments of religion—He wants to have a real relationship with us. Our trust is in the marvelous grace of God, not in our own religious works.

FURTHER READING:
Matthew 6:5-8
Matthew 23
Galatians 5:6-13

January 23

Unforgiveness

*"For if you forgive men when they sin against you,
your heavenly Father will also forgive you."*

—MATTHEW 6:14

If you have yet to receive your miracle...if God seems silent and far away from you...there is hope, but you will need to be honest with yourself and explore some areas of your heart.

During my 30 years as a pastor, I've known people who were angry because they didn't receive an answer to prayer. They heard me preach about how God is still working miracles today, (and He is!) but when those miracles didn't manifest in their own lives, they got angry. Some even left the church or stopped listening to God!

Oftentimes as I talked with them, I learned there was an area of wounding that went much deeper than the physical symptoms they were seeking prayer for. There was anger, bitterness and unforgiveness festering in their hearts.

That's dangerous, because unforgiveness stops the blessings of God. In fact, it stops the forgiveness of God! The Bible says we must first forgive others before God will forgive us—don't let a grudge stand in the way of your relationship with Him.

If you have unforgiveness in your heart, release it now to Jesus. Let the healing presence of God flow into your life.

FURTHER READING:
Matthew 5:17-26
Matthew 6:9-15
Matthew 18:15-35

January 24

Unbelief

*"And he did not do many miracles there
because of their lack of faith."*

—MATTHEW 13:58

Jesus went to His hometown and the people were amazed.
They asked, "Where did this man get this wisdom, and these
miraculous powers?" (Matthew 13:54). But then doubt entered:
"Isn't this the carpenter's son? Isn't His mother's name Mary...?
And they took offense at Him" (Matthew 13:55-57).

Jesus didn't do many miracles there "because of their lack
of faith" (Matthew 13:58). Their lack of faith prevented Him
from showering them with blessings. Do you have faith that
God will answer your prayer? Unbelief happens when we trust
ourselves and not God for the solutions.

The disciples once asked Jesus why a miracle didn't happen
for them. Jesus said, "Because you have so little faith. I tell
you the truth, if you have faith as small as a mustard seed, you
can say to this mountain, 'Move from here to there' and it will
move. Nothing will be impossible for you" (Matthew 17:20).

James 1:6 says that he who doubts is like a wave that is tossed
by the sea. Do not let unbelief prevent you from living His will
and experiencing His blessings.

FURTHER READING:
Matthew 13
Hebrews 11
Mark 10:46-52

January 25

Do You Know the Way?

"And if I go and prepare a place for you, I will come back and take you to be with me that you also may be where I am. You know the way to the place where I am going.' Thomas said to him, 'Lord, we don't know where you are going, so how can we know the way?'"

—JOHN 14:3-5

Do you know the way into the presence of God and to the place Christ has prepared for you?

Many believe that the way into the "prepared things" of God is through spiritual activities or being busy for the Lord—but that's not the answer. Thomas asked Jesus, "How can we know the way?"

Jesus' answer was clear and concise: "I am the way and the truth and the life. No one comes to the Father except through me" (John 14:6). It is not through positions or activities. It is not through good sermons or memorized scriptures. It is only through a personal relationship with Christ; through faith in the shed blood of the Lord Jesus.

There is only one route to the "prepared place" and that is through Christ Jesus—anything else will lead you to the outer court, the court gates or outside the city...but not into the presence of God. Do you know the way?

FURTHER READING:
Romans 5:2
Ephesians 2:18
Hebrew 10:20

January 26

God is Able

"Nothing is too hard for you."

—JEREMIAH 32:17

I have never seen such a season of the miraculous power of God.

Not just ordinary sicknesses, or folks who had a headache—I have seen folks afflicted with cerebral palsy walking out of wheelchairs. "Ah, Sovereign Lord, you have made the heavens and the earth by your great power and outstretched arm. Nothing is too hard for you" (Jeremiah 32:17).

It reminds me of the passage in Ezekiel 37 when God asked, "Son of man, can these bones live?" And Ezekiel said, "O Sovereign Lord, you alone know." Then God said, "Prophesy to these bones and say to them, 'Dry bones, hear the word of the Lord!'" Today, God is shouting with a resounding "Yes!" over the sapphire sill of heaven's gate.

"These bones can live! Nothing is too hard for Me!" Just like Ezekiel saw the breath of God bringing bones back to life, we've seen the resurrection power of God setting people free in their bodies.

"If the Spirit of him who raised Jesus from the dead is living in you, he who raised Christ from the dead will also give life to your mortal bodies through his Spirit, who lives in you" (Romans 8:11). We have the power of Jesus Christ living within us. Resurrection power means life!

FURTHER READING:
John 11
Ezekiel 37
Philippians 3:7-14

January 27

Healing is a Process

*"Blessed is the man who perseveres under trial;
because when he has stood the test, he will
receive the crown of life."*

—JAMES 1:12

Healings aren't always instantaneous. Sometimes they are a process. When Jesus was in Bethsaida a blind man begged Jesus to touch him. Jesus took him outside the village, spat on the man's eyes and laid hands on him. Then Jesus asked, "Do you see anything?"

The man looked up and said, "I see people; they look like trees walking around" (Mark 8:24). Jesus prayed a second time for this man's healing. It was a process!

It reminds me of Craig Demartino, a mountain climber who fell 10 stories off a cliff onto the forest floor. The impact shattered bones and broke his neck. The doctors gave him an hour to live. It was no less a miracle—11 surgeries and 18 months later—for God to have Craig up and climbing mountains again. Truly incredible! "It wasn't me," Craig says, "but God doing this through me, so people could say, 'Wow, look at what God did!'"

God made Craig a sign and a wonder for all to see the healing power of God—even though it was a process.

Will you trust God's process?

FURTHER READING:
Habakkuk 2:2-4
James 1:2-18
1 Peter 1:3-9

January 28

A God of Miracles

"Who among the gods is like you, O Lord?
Who is like you—majestic in holiness, awesome in glory,
working wonders?"

—EXODUS 15:11

I had a sister named Debbie, and we had always been close. When word came that she had been in a terrible car accident, I was shocked, frightened, and prayed the only way I knew how at that point in my life: "Lord, if it be Thy will, please heal her."

She lingered between life and death for weeks, had many surgeries and still the doctors had no hope. Finally, they sent her home to die.

I knew what the Bible said, but I knew nothing about divine healing. Miracles were foreign to my life until one incredible day in 1979. Some friends introduced me to a preacher named Norvel Hayes, who was holding a meeting. "Bring Debbie and God will touch her," he told me. Not only did God heal my sister at that Indianapolis meeting—but my life changed forever.

Have you ever witnessed a miracle? It changed me the same moment she was healed. "Now the Lord is the Spirit, and where the Spirit of the Lord is, there is freedom" (2 Corinthians 3:17).

God still heals today as He did in the Bible. He is still a God of miracles.

FURTHER READING:
Ephesians 3:14-21
John 15
Daniel 4:1-3

January 29

Signs and Wonders

"God also testified to it by signs,
wonders and various miracles..."

—HEBREWS 2:4

After my sister had been touched, Norvel Hayes called me up on stage the next night. "I'm going to show you that God can use anybody and He's going to use this young Baptist preacher under a healing anointing."

He took my hand and spread out my fingers and told me to gently touch each person on the forehead and say, "Be healed."

As I laid my hand on the first person's forehead, the whole group of 20 people went down. I was amazed! One woman had come in with a severely deformed jaw. When she got up, her jaw was straightened!

Another woman came up two nights later with an astonishing report. Her gynecologist told her she was three months pregnant. The woman said, "This is the gynecologist who gave me a complete hysterectomy. I had no womb when I walked in here. Now I'm three months pregnant."

After that, I traveled home knowing that anything written in the Book of Acts is possible. Christ gives us the power to do everything He said we would, if we have faith! Look for signs and wonders from God and you will surely see miracles.

FURTHER READING:
Acts 1:8
Acts 2
Hebrews 2:3-5

January 30

Leaven of the Sadducees

"How is it you don't understand that I was not talking to you about bread? But be on your guard against the yeast of the Pharisees and Sadducees."

—MATTHEW 16:11

The leaven of the Sadducees is the denial of the supernatural power of God. They reject the "traditions of the elders."

They only accept the first five books of the Old Testament and do not believe in tongues, heaven, hell, eternity, the resurrection or spirits, (including the Holy Spirit) angels or demons. Furthermore, the Sadducees are influenced by rationalism—if they cannot comprehend or understand it, they conclude that it cannot be. The Sadducees are not very knowledgeable about the Word of God—not even the portion that they believe in (Matthew 22:31-32).

If we believe the Bible is the Word of God, we must not accept only part of it and reject the rest. We must avoid the exhaltation of human reasoning and rationalization over divine revelation.

Refuse to embrace the traditions of men as Biblical doctrines. John 17:17 says, "Sanctify them by the truth; your word is truth."

Allow the Lord to sanctify you—for His Word is truth.

FURTHER READING:
John 17:17
Luke 12:1-4
Mark 4:22

January 31

Look after the Orphans

*"Religion that God our Father accepts as
pure and faultless is this: to look after the orphans
and the widows in their distress..."*

—JAMES 1:27

The little girl I held in my arms weighed less than a cat. Her arms were like matchsticks, but she was a toddler...and she was dying.

That's why I decided to come to Haiti. One in every five children in Haiti dies before his fifth birthday. Most often death comes from something we could easily treat with a few dollars and a little care.

Toddlers roam the streets of Haiti day and night, looking in trash bins for food. They eat dirt because it is all they have. It breaks my heart—and I know it breaks the heart of God. I believe what breaks God's heart even more is for His people to hear about such dire need and do nothing.

God commands us to help those who have nothing. Proverbs 19:17 says, "He who is kind to the poor lends to the Lord, and he will reward him for what he has done."

Most of us would be amazed at how little it takes to make a life-or-death difference in a Haitian child's life. Will you follow the commands of the Lord to help the hurting?

FURTHER READING:
Luke 12:48
Job 22:7-11
Isaiah 58:5-10

February 1

Help the Poor

*"One man gives freely, yet gains even more;
another withholds unduly, but comes to poverty."*

—PROVERBS 11:24

It is a sad indictment of the American Church today that, in the world's richest nation, poverty continues to suffocate people. Poverty is not the government's problem. God has given that charge to His people and His church. This sort of good cannot be done without the hand of God.

Leviticus 19:10 teaches that our excess belongs to the poor: "Do not go over your vineyard a second time or pick up the grapes that have fallen. Leave them for the poor and the alien."

These days very few of us have vineyards or wheat fields to tend, but all of us have excess.

Jesus said the way to perfection was to follow Him with a perfect heart. He showed love and compassion to the poor and the hurting—people that society had deemed unlovable—and commands us to cultivate this same attitude toward them.

Not only this, but when we help the poor and needy, we are helping Jesus. Matthew 25:40 says, "The King will reply, 'I tell you the truth, whatever you did for one of the least of these brothers of mine, you did for me.'" If we claim to love and follow Him, we must take each one of His messages to heart.

FURTHER READING:
Leviticus 23:22
Leviticus 25:35
Deuteronomy 15:11

February 2

Promises of God

"Oh Sovereign Lord, you are God!
Your words are trustworthy and you have promised
these good things to your servant."

—2 SAMUEL 7:28

King David had a desire that God did not allow him to fulfill. Yet the Lord had other great things ahead for David. David praised God after being told, "No." He knew the promises of God were real and trustworthy.

There are people today who would lead you to believe that the sign of God's favor is getting everything we want or desire.

The Bible simply does not support this notion. God places us where we need to be to do His will and reflect His glory. We can accept this with grace; using hard work, prayer, and faith to move us through the situations we do not enjoy.

In Philippians 4:12 Paul says, "I know what it is to be in need, and I know what it is to have plenty. I have learned the secret of being content in any and every situation, whether well fed or hungry, whether living in plenty or in want."

Cultivate Paul's secret today! It will get you through these hard times. The Lord will always answer your prayers. He promises to answer you when you call. Trust that His promises are steadfast and secure. He knows what is best for you.

FURTHER READING:
Luke 10:2
Luke 12:23
John 13:7

February 3

Leaven of the Herodians

"'Be careful,' Jesus warned them. 'Watch out for the yeast of the Pharisees and that of Herod.'"

—MARK 8:15.

The leaven of the Herodians is the craving of sinful man that comes from being of the world and under the power of the god of this world—the devil.

Herodians follow the lust of their eyes, they give in to the lust of the flesh and they boast of the things that they possess and what they have accomplished. They are governed by self—self-interest, self-desire, self-focus, and self-pleasure.

Every vice that is in the sinful nature of man is able to influence and exert control over a Herodian, for they follow the call of the world and not of God. Greed, gambling, sexual perversion, murder, lust, robbery, covetousness, lying, and all the other sins listed in the Bible (Romans 1:29) become the driving force behind a Herodian.

God expects us to live differently, now that we have been born again. Galatians 5:16 says, "So I say, live by the Spirit, and you will not gratify the desires of the sinful nature." Let us renounce the leaven of the Herodians and live the way God intends—according to His Spirit.

FURTHER READING:
Mark 6:14-29
1 John 2:16
Luke 12:1

February 4

Resisting Prejudice

*"There is neither Jew nor Greek, slave nor free,
male nor female, for you are all one in Christ Jesus."*

—GALATIANS 3:28

I am sorry to let you know that we still have a hearty dose of prejudice in America today. We don't have to look much further than our own churches to see segregation alive and well in the United States.

Don't believe the lie that we segregate by choice. We segregate because we do not offer the arms of love freely to every person who steps through our doors. God made one Church!

God is here for all people. He gave us distinctions not to divide us but so we would complement one another.

In Isaiah 56:6-7 He says, "And foreigners who bind themselves to the Lord to serve him, to love the name of the Lord, and to worship him, all who keep the Sabbath without desecrating it and who hold fast to my covenant —these I will bring to my holy mountain and give them joy in my house of prayer." It's time to search our hearts.

The Church of Jesus Christ must lead the way in eradicating racism in this nation. We must make known to the world that we are all equal in the sight of God. Only then can we fight the enemy of prejudice in our very midst.

FURTHER READING:
Acts 2:2-5
Revelation 5:9
Matthew 28:19-20

February 5

Desires of Our Hearts

"No one can serve two masters. Either he will hate the one and love the other, or he will be devoted to the one and despise the other. You cannot serve both God and Money."

—MATTHEW 6:24

Something begins to change us when we let materialism grip our souls. We start to justify things we know aren't right, things we know are going to hurt us, or hurt our families. "I've worked hard for this," we might say. "I deserve it."

But those are words Satan uses to deceive us. Satan tried to do the same thing to Jesus in Matthew 4:8-9.

"The devil took him to a very high mountain and showed him all the kingdoms of the world and their splendor. 'All this I will give you,' he said, 'if you will bow down and worship me.'"

The Lord God in heaven knows the desires of our hearts. He knows what we need and He does not withhold our rewards from us. He has promised all good things will come to us.

If you truly deserve something God will see it through to you. God wants you to have all you need to do His will. Matthew 6:8 tells us that our Father knows what we need before we even ask Him. Do not let the lust for worldly possessions rule your soul, but set your mind on the things of the Spirit.

FURTHER READING:
Ecclesiastes 5:10
Isaiah 55:2
Matthew 27:3-5

February 6

The Sleeping Giant

"Wake up, O sleeper, rise from the dead,
and Christ will shine on you."

—EPHESIANS 5:14

Some people are concerned about the current darkness America finds itself in—and I am concerned too. I also know that times of trial and struggle historically bring great seasons of revival, as men and women go to their knees and cry out to God for divine wisdom and help.

Scripture says, "If my people, who are called by my name, will humble themselves and pray and seek my face and turn from their wicked ways, then I will hear from heaven and will forgive their sin and heal their land" (2 Chronicles 7:14).

I've often referred to the Church of America as a sleeping giant. It's time for the Church to arise! Isaiah 60:1-2 says, "Arise, shine, for your light has come, and the glory of the Lord rises upon you. See, darkness covers the earth and thick darkness is over the peoples, but the Lord rises upon you and his glory appears over you."

We have been called to be light to this world. "Nations will come to your light, and kings to the brightness of your dawn" (Isaiah 60:3). Hang on! I believe we are on the verge of one of the greatest revivals the world has ever known!

FURTHER READING:
Isaiah 60:1-5
Matthew 16:18
Deuteronomy 30

February 7

Key Ingredients

"Suppose a brother or sister is without clothes and daily food. If one of you says to him, 'Go, I wish you well, keep warm and well fed,' but does nothing about his physical needs, what good is it? In the same way, faith by itself, if it is not accompanied by action, is dead."

—JAMES 2:15-17

Prayer and faith are key ingredients for change—but we still have work to do. We are called to impact the world for Christ and bring others to a saving knowledge of Jesus Christ. You can do this by preaching the Gospel message and by helping those in need. By doing so, you show Christ's love for others.

Doing something to create greater good in our world is an outward expression of our inward faith. We can effect change in the world because of our faith. Though works aren't how we are saved, works are how we serve the God who has saved us.

1 Corinthians 3:12-14 teaches us that on the Day of Judgment, Christ is going to test how we built on His foundation. He's going to show our work for what it is, test it and show its quality.

You do not know when your last day on earth will be. You do not know when you will lose the opportunity to labor in God's fields. So go out and spread the Good News each day!

FURTHER READING:
Matthew 9:37
John 9:4
Acts 20:34-36

February 8

Christian Civilization

"And they sang a new song: You are worthy to take the scroll and to open its seals, because you were slain, and with your blood you purchased men for God from every tribe and language and people and nation."

—REVELATION 5:9

Our nation's founding document, the Declaration of Independence, declared that we are endowed by our Creator with inalienable rights to life, liberty and the pursuit of happiness.

Since our nation's founding, America has decided some lives matter more and some lives don't matter as much.

We need to be the nation God has asked us to be. Ezekiel 22:2 asks us, "Son of man, will you judge her? Will you judge this city of bloodshed? Then confront her with all her detestable practices." Verse 29 goes on to say, "The people of the land practice extortion and commit robbery; they oppress the poor and needy and mistreat the alien, denying them justice."

As Christians, our duty is to encourage other believers to join together and collectively advance our God-informed opinions. We have to move forward by acting like our Lord Jesus Christ does. Participating in our democracy is not optional for Christians. It is an important way to make a positive impact on our culture and create a more moral America.

FURTHER READING:
Matthew 27:24
Isaiah 5:20
Deuteronomy 19:20

February 9

All Religions Are Not Equal

*"In fact, the law requires that nearly
everything be cleansed with blood, and without
the shedding of blood there is no forgiveness"*

—HEBREWS 9:22

Many believers today are confused when it comes to other religions. They have bought into the notion that all religions are the same and that there is a universal god to which we can all pray and be blessed. This is deception.

Christianity is not a religion, but a way of life based on the Holy Bible, God's eternal Word. Other religions have their sacred books too, but only Christianity had a Savior who died for us so we could be delivered from the wages of sin and reap the blessings and promises of God.

Buddha didn't die on the cross for his followers. Salvation can't be found in a Hindu cow, a Buddhist temple, or a Shinto shrine. It can't be found in the church doctrines of any Christian tradition, either.

The only thing that matters is whether you accept what Christ did for you on the cross. Jesus gave us redemption and forgave our sins (Colossians 1:14). Do you believe that He died so you may live? Will you confess with your mouth that Jesus is Lord...will you lay down everything to follow Him?

FURTHER READING:
Mark 8:34
Galatians 6:14
1 Corinthians 1:18

February 10

Responsibility to Charity

"Who gave himself for us to redeem us from all wickedness and to purify for himself a people that are his very own, eager to do what is good."

—TITUS 2:14

The responsibility for charity lies with the Church—and not the church as an institution. The Church is you and me and all who believe in Jesus Christ. Again and again our Lord calls us to acts of charity. We were never meant to toss it into the lap of the government.

In Proverbs 14:21 God tells us, "He who despises his neighbor sins, but blessed is he who is kind to the needy."

Many times the problem of poverty is hidden from us in our insulated lifestyles. If we're not in want ourselves, it's too easy to ignore the problem. Yet we can find it if we look, and we can help if we make helping a priority in our hearts and minds.

Perhaps there is a need in your nearby community. Perhaps there's a homeless shelter that needs to be built, or a faith-based charity hospital that needs funding. Perhaps there's just a struggling family that needs a single bill paid to survive one more month. If you pray, God will show you where the opportunities are, and He will honor your desire to fulfill the responsibility to bless those less fortunate.

FURTHER READING:
Psalms 41:1-3
Proverbs 11:25
Psalms 35:10

February 11

Atonement

"All have sinned and fall short of the glory of God, and are justified freely by his grace through the redemption that came by Christ Jesus. God presented him as a sacrifice of atonement, through faith in his blood."

—ROMANS 3:23-25

Many Christians lack a basic understanding of what atonement really means—it is the blood of Jesus making amends for our sins.

It is the preordained reconciliation that came forth because of the work that Christ did on the cross (1 Peter 1:19-20).

The amazing thing is that while you and I were still sinners Christ died for us—He did not wait until we paid penance; He did it while we were still in the clutches of sin—while we knew Him not (Romans 5:8).

Christ is our high priest who entered the holy of holies on the behalf of mankind. He followed the procedure that God the Father laid out. The sacrifice of His life fulfilled the requirements that God demanded.

Christ's atonement was perfect—it was complete. We can now boldly approach the throne of grace with confidence. God will have mercy on us in our time of need (Hebrews 4:16). Seek Him today; your sins have been atoned for, now and forever.

FURTHER READING:
Leviticus 16:4
Galatians 4:4
Leviticus 23:27-28

February 12

Watch With Me

"Then he returned to his disciples and found them sleeping. 'Could you men not keep watch with me for one hour?' he asked Peter."

—MATTHEW 26:40

Jesus asked His disciples to keep watch with Him, for His soul was crushed with grief. He was in deep agony and pain, yet His faithful few could not stay awake. They were tired and fell asleep, leaving Christ to watch and pray alone.

Today, many believers are slumbering when they should be watching and praying. There is a lack of spiritual heat. Cold embers now reside where fiery souls once burned.

Yet Christ is still asking us to "stay here and keep watch" with Him, because we do not know the day or the hour he will return (Matthew 26:38).

Are you willing to watch? Are you willing to pray? Are your prayers in line with the expressed will of God, or are they in accordance to your own will and desires? Are you willing to set aside time to press on in prayer? Or are other things more important?

Christ expects that His Church will be one that watches and prays. It is time to re-dig the well of prayer. Will you watch and pray?

FURTHER READING:
Matthew 6
Matthew 26:41
John 12:23-27

February 13

Doubt Verses Unbelief

"Immediately the boy's father exclaimed,
'I do believe; help me overcome my unbelief!'"

—MARK 9:24

There is a distinct difference between doubt and unbelief. That difference can mean the difference between answered and unanswered prayer.

Doubt is when you wonder "if" something could be, while unbelief is declaration that "I know it's not" or "It can't be." When Jesus went to His hometown to preach, He desired to perform miracles and to do great wonders, but He could not. The people had a spirit of unbelief and that prevented Him from doing "mighty works" (Mark 6:5-6).

The passage in Mark tells us that He was only able to lay hands on a few sick and heal them. Mark 6:5 tells us that healing the sick was not the "mighty works" Christ wanted to do—but He was blocked from doing the "big stuff."

Verse 6 tells us that He marveled at their unbelief. I believe He does the same when we choose to walk in unbelief rather than believing in our God.

If you have doubt, ask Jesus to help you. If you have unbelief, you need to bind up that spirit, and replace it with confidence and faith in God.

FURTHER READING:
Mark 9:22-25
Isaiah 53:5-6
Matthew 8:2-3

February 14

Faith is the Gift of God

"For by the grace given me I say to every one of you:
Do not think of yourself more highly than you ought,
but rather think of yourself with sober judgment, in
accordance with the measure of faith God has given you."

—ROMANS 12:3

All gifts are given to us by God and they are distributed by the Spirit of God—not for our own benefit but for the benefit of the body of Christ.

Each gift is to help build, restore, counsel, strengthen, enlighten, encourage or to bless the Church and her members.

Too often the gifts in the house are used to exalt "self," which is pride and haughtiness wrapped in the cloak of religious work, piety or duty.

Our faith is not for ourselves nor should it be rooted in us—it is about God. Without faith it is impossible to please Him. Hebrews 11:6 says, "And without faith it is impossible to please God, because anyone who comes to him must believe that he exists and that he rewards those who earnestly seek him."

God did not call us to have faith in ourselves, but to have faith in Him. He has given us a measure of faith to believe in Him, and as we grow in the knowledge and understanding of God our faith will grow as well.

FURTHER READING:
1 Corinthians 12:7-11
Romans 12:6-8
Matthew 17:19-20

February 15

Faith Through Impartation

"I have been reminded of your sincere faith, which first lived in your grandmother Lois and in your mother Eunice and, I am persuaded, now lives in you also. For this reason I remind you to fan into flame the gift of God, which is in you through the laying on of my hands."

—2 TIMOTHY 1:5-6

Paul reminds Timothy of his lineage of faith. He counsels him to fan into flames the gift of God, which was already in him.

Like Timothy, you have a gift of faith, because God gives to each of us a measure of faith (Romans 12:3). Faith can be imparted through the laying on of hands—a transference in the spirit.

Before Smith Wigglesworth went home to be with the Lord, he laid hands on Lester Sumrall and prayed, "Let the faith that is in me come into this young man." Before Dr. Sumrall went to heaven he did the same to me. Faith through impartation is real my friends... it is real!

If you are struggling with faith...let us pray together: "Lord Jesus, as we join our hearts and minds together in faith, let an impartation come into our spirits from the Holy Spirit, so when we speak a thing according to your will it shall be established. In Jesus' name, Amen."

FURTHER READING:
1 Timothy 4:14
Acts 6:6
Acts 8:17

February 16

Faith Pleases God

*"In the beginning God created
the heavens and the earth."*

—GENESIS 1:1

From the very first line of the Bible, God requires us to have faith. He doesn't go into elaborate detail about who He is or how He created everything. God doesn't lay out His case as a logical legal brief. He just states plainly, "In the beginning God created the heavens and the earth."

Once you read these words you are compelled to either walk in faith and believe the Word of God or choose to dismiss it.

It's clear that it takes faith to believe the Bible, because there are many unanswered questions. God wastes no time trying to talk us into believing His Word. The ability to believe God's Word is a gift of faith from Him (Ephesians 2:8).

If you find yourself questioning the reality of God's Word, then you need faith. How can you get faith? "Faith comes from hearing the message, and the message is heard through the word of Christ" (Romans 10:17).

Read the Word of God, listen to the Word of God, repeat aloud the Word of God, meditate on the Word of God and sing God's Word. This will allow faith to come—for without faith, it is impossible to please God (Hebrews 11:6).

FURTHER READING:
Hebrews 11:6
Proverbs 3:5-6
Romans 8:24-25

February 17

Will You Let God?

"If you pay attention to these laws and are careful to follow them, then the Lord your God will keep his covenant of love with you, as he swore to your forefathers"

—DEUTERONOMY 7:12

There are many believers today who have received answers to their prayers and don't even know it. From the moment they prayed, the Lord sent the answer.

Yet when they were told what they needed to do they refused to listen. They had the attitude of Naaman, whose pride almost robbed him of his healing...or like Samson, they refused to give up their addictions and live a holy life.

God desires to heal His people in every instance. In fact, God desires that no sickness be among His people (Deuteronomy 7:15). Yet in many cases, people have illnesses because they fail to obey Him faithfully.

Obedience and faith are prerequisites to covenant fulfillment. Without them we cannot receive from God for He doesn't reward rebellion nor can He operate in disbelief.

Is there something that you desire from God? Are you willing to walk in faith? Are you willing to obey no matter what?

If you are willing to let Him, God will do all that He has promised to do for you according to His Word.

FURTHER READING
Kings 5:10
Isaiah 65:24
Exodus 15:26

February 18

God Values Life

"He will take pity on the weak and the needy and save the needy from death. He will rescue them from oppression and violence, for precious is their blood in his sight."

—PSALMS 72:13-14

We have a tendency to think of ourselves as being more civil than those who have come before.

However, God measures a society by what it does to uphold the integrity, dignity and sanctity of life. God cries out against oppression. God does not believe anyone is disposable or expendable. He issues commands in the Bible to ensure that His people knew how precious life is: Leviticus 24:17 says, "If anyone takes the life of a human being, he must be put to death."

The prophet Ezekiel speaks out against the people of Israel who have forgotten this truth. In Ezekiel 45:9 he says, "You have gone far enough, O princes of Israel! Give up your violence and oppression and do what is just and right!"

Because every life is precious to God, it must be precious to His people. Since 1973, we have lost an entire generation of Americans because some thought they weren't important.

Our job as Christians is to take a stand against such atrocities and pray that God will turn this nation back to the values upon which it was founded.

FURTHER READING:
Isaiah 5:7
Ezekiel 35:6
Habakkuk 2:12

February 19

Pray for Guidance

"Praise be to the God and Father of our
Lord Jesus Christ, the Father of compassion
and the God of all comfort."

—2 CORINTHIANS 1:3

In order for cultures to become violent, barbaric, and uncaring, they have to be trained in violence, barbarism and selfishness.

In Amos 1:11 God points out that when we "pursue with the sword" we "stifle all compassion." He was not pleased and "his anger raged continually and his fury flamed unchecked." He was speaking of the city of Tyre, but He could have been speaking of any of today's youth. In our movies, video games, television and music, the culture of fury is glorified. Violence is presented as the one and only solution to problems. Pursuing our neighbors with "swords" is glorified over compassion, forgiveness and understanding. Is it any wonder that our youth load guns instead of playing with one another?

Our nation was founded on positive values—life, liberty and the pursuit of happiness. It is important to return to these God-given pursuits, and we need to ask for His help.

As a society, we need to demonstrate love, not violence. Ask the Holy Spirit to guide you in choosing forms of entertainment that are pleasing to God.

FURTHER READING:
Ephesians 4:32
Philippians 2:1-3
Colossians 3:12-13

February 20

Fruits of Humility

"An unfriendly man pursues selfish ends;
he defies all sound judgment."

—PROVERBS 18:1

We have become a culture absorbed with self. Self-fulfillment and self-satisfaction, self-esteem and self-actualization are the battle cries of our day.

We use these cries to justify a multitude of sins. The sick, elderly, unwanted and disabled are easy to ignore in our quest for "self," yet these are the very people Jesus reached out to.

Philippians 2:3 tells us, "Do nothing out of selfish ambition or vain conceit, but in humility consider others better than yourselves."

The focus should not be on ourselves, but on Christ, who is the ultimate example of humility. The God of the universe came down to earth and humbled Himself by becoming subject to all the things human beings experience—fear, hunger, weariness.

In John 13:5, he even washes the feet of His disciples: "After that, he poured water into a basin and began to wash his disciples' feet, drying them with the towel that was wrapped around him." Follow His example of humility today. Ask Him to guide you in living a life that honors Him.

FURTHER READING:
James 3:14
James 3:16
Psalms 119:36

February 21

Fruits and Roots

"Blessed is the man who trusts in the Lord, whose confidence is in him. He will be like a tree planted by the water that sends out its roots by the stream…. It has no worries in a year of drought and never fails to bear fruit."

—JEREMIAH 17:7-9

We cannot separate actions from consequences. Why, then, do we allow our culture to tell us that we can plant seeds of one kind and bear fruits of another? The world tells us that we can plant seeds of promiscuity and carelessness and bear fruits of beauty, happiness and even love. But the results are disease, unwanted pregnancy and unhappiness.

Root and fruit are inevitably intertwined.

Isaiah 32:17 says, "The fruit of righteousness will be peace; the effect of righteousness will be quietness and confidence forever."

One of the surest ways to change your life for the better is to stop sowing seeds that bear bad fruit! Plant seeds of righteousness and put those roots in your life. Unlike the culture around us, the Bible takes a very clear position on right and wrong.

Ask Him to guide your actions so you will produce good fruit that is pleasing to God.

FURTHER READING:
Jeremiah 6:19
John 15:4
Galatians 5:22-23

February 22

Get the Leaven Out

"A little yeast works through the whole batch of dough."

—GALATIANS 5:9

Sin works just like yeast—a little of it will spread through your whole life. A little false doctrine can compromise a whole church, just like a little bit of alcohol can compromise your ability to think and function.

The truth is that sin doesn't announce its plan to destroy you or your life. It comes in like a thief...subtly waiting for the perfect opportunity to cause the most damage—like during times of stress and strain.

If you get the leaven out beforehand, sin cannot cause harm—it cannot destroy. How can you get the leaven out?

By making a diligent search for it! Where should we search? In the pews...the pulpit...and in our homes. Who should make the search? The deacons...the elders...the preachers...and you!

As you turn over every item, as you look in every crack and crevice, whatever is not of God or in alignment with His Word should be thrown out.

It is time to get the leaven out. Sin is not a pet...it is not cute...it cannot be managed...it cannot be counseled...it cannot be reasoned with. The only solution is to eliminate it through faith in Jesus.

FURTHER READING:
1 Corinthians 5:6
2 Corinthians 6:14
1 Corinthians 5:9

February 23

Faith Alone

"And without faith it is impossible to please God, because anyone who comes to him must believe that he exists and that he rewards those who earnestly seek him."

—HEBREWS 11:6

Do you have what it takes to please God? Don't get me wrong; there is nothing we can do to earn His love, but as James 2:17 says, "In the same way, faith by itself, if it is not accompanied by action, is dead."

Many think that God is impressed by works or by following the law in a legalistic manner. Some believe that if they show kindness or if they are "good," this will please God. God is clear about what will please him—FAITH.

Do you have faith in God? Do you believe that He will answer your prayers and will provide for your needs? Faith doesn't come without effort. To be faith-filled you must be in a place where you are growing in God.

Faith goes beyond just saying "God exists." Faith is following Him all the days of your life. Faith is trusting in Him even in the worst situations, and remembering Him in the best.

Believe that God will bless you as you seek Him and you will witness answered prayers as never before...because God is a rewarder of those who diligently seek Him.

FURTHER READING:
Hebrews 7:19
Hebrews 9:9-10
Hebrews 10:19-22

February 24

No Doubt

"I tell you the truth, if anyone says to this mountain, 'Go, throw yourself into the sea,' and does not doubt in his heart but believes that what he says will happen, it will be done for him."

—MARK 11:22-24

Have you ever wondered why some prayers don't seem to be answered? Have you ever thought that it was because the Lord didn't hear you?

The truth is that when you pray, doubt can't be in your heart. Doubt tears down what faith tries to build. Doubt nullifies what faith desires to bring to pass. The key to answered prayers is belief—in God and that your prayer request will be answered.

What is it you are asking God for? To save a family member? To get out of debt? To grow closer to Him? Do you believe that He can give you your heart's desire? Do you believe that it can happen just as you have asked? Do you truly believe He can do anything?

Jesus said that if you believe it, you shall have whatever you ask. As you pray, lift up faith and not the problem. Lift up faith and not the obstacles. Lift up your faith in God and not the circumstance. There is nothing greater than God (Psalms 135:5). With Him, nothing is impossible.

FURTHER READING:
Luke 1:37
Matthew 7:7
Luke 17:6

February 25

Take Up Your Shield

*"In addition to all this, take up the shield of faith,
with which you can extinguish all the flaming arrows
of the evil one."*

—EPHESIANS 6:16

Attacks from the adversary come to everyone— in your mind, in your home, at your job, in your finances. Are you feeling battered and bruised because of the constant assault of the evil one?

It is time to turn the tables on the enemy! It is time to quench his fiery darts. It is time for you to walk in victory. How? By picking up your shield of faith. Dust it off and use it daily, for the Word of God says it will quench all—not some— but all the fiery darts of the wicked.

Exodus 15:6 says, "Your right hand, O Lord, was majestic in power. Your right hand, O Lord, shattered the enemy." He will help you overcome the enemy that attacks you, if you trust in Him. If you are tired of being beaten...if you are tired of being used and abused by the enemy...take up your authority by faith and watch every attack, every hindrance, every stronghold, every blockage, every curse and every fiery dart be put out as you apply your faith in Christ Jesus.

In Him, you can defeat the enemy and prosper!

FURTHER READING:
1 John 5:4-5
Romans 8:37
John 16:33

February 26

Victory is Yours

"For everyone born of God overcomes the world. This is the victory that has overcome the world, even our faith."

—I JOHN 5:4

At times, the world confronts us as a mighty force, bombarding us with assaults or opposing us like an immovable fortress. The enemy would like you to believe that there is no hope, that you don't stand a chance.

Those who know God know that's a lie. God says that if we are born of Him, we overcome the world. Our victory has already been assured. It was won on the cross.

It was provided for with the shed blood of the Lamb of God.

Because of His blood, you are of God, which makes you an overcomer. How can you stand in times of difficulty? How can you keep your head held high? How can keep getting up when the world knocks you down?

By faith in Jesus...by believing that He provided all that you need to overcome on the cross. Declare it daily. Stand on it without wavering.

Your Bible says, "You, dear children, are from God and have overcome them, because the one who is in you is greater than the one who is in the world" (1 John 4:4). Being born of God through Christ is the victory that overcomes the world.

FURTHER READING:
Romans 8:37
John 16:33
1 Corinthians 15:57

February 27

Purpose

*"Because you know that the testing
of your faith develops perseverance."*

—JAMES 1:3

Have you ever asked yourself why the devil is always picking on you? One fact to consider is that Satan only attacks believers— why would he waste time on people who don't follow God? But let's go a step further and think about God's purpose.

Could it be because God is refining you and developing the fruit of the Spirit in you (Galatians 5:22-23)?

Nothing is wasted or without purpose in Him. God uses our mistakes to teach, to correct and to help us grow. Almighty God seizes every opportunity to direct us in His ways...if we are willing and if we obey.

When your home is attacked, choose to fill it with the faith-filled Word of God—walk in your God-given authority.

When change does not happen quickly, stand firm in your faith in Jesus and watch things turn around.

When you operate in faith and authority, Satan can't continue his work of discord, disharmony, hatred and confusion. All the other schemes and tactics of the enemy become "null and void" because of the provisions of the cross (Galatians 3:13).

God's ultimate purpose is your success and victory.

FURTHER READING:
1 Peter 1:7
Isaiah 48:10
Job 23:10

February 28

A Significant Life

"Jesus looked at him and loved him.
'One thing you lack,' he said. 'Go, sell everything
you have and give to the poor, and you will have
treasure in heaven. Then come, follow me.'"

—MARK 10:21

Do you ever read about men and women who have done acts of momentous significance and wish you could be like them?

We read of people like Soviet cosmonaut Yuri Gagarin, the first man to ever orbit the earth, or Mother Theresa, the saint of Calcutta. Perhaps we admire figures such as Sir Edmund Hillary, the first man to scale the heights of Mt. Everest, or Clara Barton, founder of the American Red Cross.

If you could save one child from starvation, would that be significant enough for you? How about a whole family?

In Sudan, in Haiti and in Guatemala, millions are starving. Children are dying from lack of medical care. They wait for people just like you to care.

You could become the most significant person in their lives. You could save the lives of so many men, women and children with what might seem to many Americans like a small gift.

Allow your aspirations for significance to make a life-determining impact on these people.

FURTHER READING:
Ezekiel 18:7-9
Deuteronomy 15:11
Psalms 82:3

March 1

Unity of the Body

*"How good and pleasant it is when brothers
live together in unity!"*

—PSALMS 133:1

Christians are all part of one body—the body of Christ. It is important to remember that as you speak with and about your fellow Christians. Jesus said the world would know the love of the Father through the way Christians treat each other.

Petty disagreements and quarrels can quickly turn into anger, resentment and long-held grudges within the church.

When forgiveness is withheld from one member, the whole body suffers. Gossip, slander and division tear apart the sacred community of brothers and sisters. The brotherly love Christians should be modeling for the world then becomes marred.

Proverbs 17:9 says, "He who covers a transgression promotes love, but whoever repeats the matter separates close friends."

If you have denied forgiveness to someone in the body, forgive them as Christ has forgiven you (Colossians 3:13). It doesn't matter if they haven't asked for forgiveness—Christ died for us when we were still His enemies (Romans 5:6-10).

Extend a hand of forgiveness to your brothers and sisters today, so the work of God may continue.

FURTHER READING:
Romans 12:3-8
Matthew 18:20-22
Luke 17:3

March 2

Without Condition

"And when you stand praying, if you hold anything against anyone, forgive him, so that your Father in heaven may forgive you your sins."

—MARK 11:25

Don't waste time holding onto anger toward someone who has wronged you. Forgive that person today.

John 20:23 warns, "If you forgive anyone his sins, they are forgiven; if you do not forgive them, they are not forgiven." If you withhold forgiveness, you will be denied forgiveness as well.

I know you have reasons for not forgiving—someone hurt you too deeply, they did it on purpose, or they haven't asked to be forgiven. Whatever your reason is, it isn't listed as a condition for forgiveness in the Bible.

God knows your situation and He has still called you to forgive—no matter the circumstances. No one is perfect—everyone needs to be forgiven. Do not stand in the way of your own relationship with God by denying forgiveness to someone else.

Luke 6:37 says, "Forgive, and you will be forgiven."

Offer forgiveness to those who have hurt you, even if they don't deserve it. It may not change how you feel about what they did, but it will change you. It's too important to your spiritual health to put off.

FURTHER READING:
Matthew 6: 9-15
Luke 23:34
John 13:35

March 3

Sin Against Brothers

"...there should be no division in the body, but that its parts should have equal concern for each other."

—1 CORINTHIANS 12:25

Being a Christian doesn't prevent you from sinning—it just gives you the power to resist and overcome it through the power of the Holy Spirit.

Romans 3:23 tells us, "All have sinned and fall short of the glory of God." It doesn't matter if you attend church faithfully, if you're a pastor or if you're the pope—everyone sins and everyone needs the forgiveness of God.

Christians in the church at Corinth were cheating and sinning against their brothers and sisters. Church members were taking advantage of other members, even though they were supposed to be demonstrating God's love to a lost world.

Paul rebukes them for these things in 1 Corinthians 6:7-8. There can't be true fellowship when there is church division.

Pray to God right now to show you when you've been guilty of hurting someone else. He may show you ongoing sin or wrongdoing from your past. Ask the Holy Spirit to convict you of the sin in that situation and ask the Lord for forgiveness.

Do not deny the existence of sin in your life but acknowledge it and repent, and you will be forgiven.

FURTHER READING:
1 Kings 8:50
2 Chronicles 7:14
James 2:10

March 4

You Are Forgiven

*"The Lord our God is merciful and forgiving,
even though we have rebelled against him."*

—DANIEL 9:9

Are you haunted by past sins? Perhaps Satan, the accuser, keeps reminding you of mistakes you've made in your life. If so, rebuke him right now with the truth that you, as a believer in Jesus Christ, have been forgiven.

Don't listen to the lies of the enemy. Instead, turn to the Word of God and read about Paul, who calls himself the chief of sinners (1 Timothy 1:15). In the book of Acts, a man named Saul was persecuting the church. He gave his consent to the martyrdom of Stephen and traveled around hunting believers of the Way and punishing them. After Saul met Jesus, however, he gave his life completely over to the Lord and became Paul, the apostle who wrote much of the New Testament.

Paul could have wallowed in despair over his past sins, but he didn't—he knew the only way to be effective in ministry was to accept God's Word as truth and stand on His promise.

2 Chronicles 7:14 says, "If my people, who are called by my name, will...turn from their wicked ways, then will I hear from heaven and will forgive their sin." You are forgiven.

Put the past behind you and walk in that truth today.

FURTHER READING:
Acts 8-9
Colossians 2:13
1 John 1:9

March 5

Faith of the Paralytic

"In him we have redemption through his blood, the forgiveness of sins, according to the riches of His grace."

—EPHESIANS 1:7

Imagine crowding into a small house to hear Jesus speak and standing on your tiptoes to see over the heads of the people in front of you.

All of a sudden a hole opens in the roof above your head and a man on a cot is lowered down. Jesus forgives the man's sins and heals him miraculously (Luke 5:17-26).

The friends of the crippled man in this passage do a lot to get Jesus' attention. They carry him to the house where Jesus is teaching.

Since they can't get close enough to Jesus, they climb onto the roof and lower the man down so that he can be healed. If you read the passage carefully, you see that it wasn't all the work they did to get him there that brought forgiveness to the paralytic; the text says, "When Jesus saw their faith, he said to him, 'Friend, your sins are forgiven'" (Luke 5:20).

No amount of work will earn God's forgiveness. It is given to you by God's grace through your faith in His Son, Jesus Christ.

Take a minute right now to give Him glory for granting you forgiveness, through His abundant grace.

FURTHER READING:
Nehemiah 9:17
Psalms 85:2
Luke 5:17-25

March 6

Take Out the Plank

"There is not a righteous man on earth who does what is right and never sins.."

—ECCLESIASTES 7:20

When was the last time you knelt and asked God to forgive your sins? Yesterday? Last week? Last month?

Are you in need of forgiveness today?

We live with sin every day. We see it on TV, in movies, in our neighbors, friends, co-workers and family. Sin is usually easy to spot in others, but with all of the exposure we have to sin, we frequently become blinded to our own sin.

You may have told a little white lie to your boss about being sick when you took the day off or accepted more change than you were due when the cashier handed you too much by mistake. Maybe these things didn't even feel like sin at the time.

Luke 6:42 asks how you can offer to remove a speck from your brother's eye "When you yourself do not see the plank in your own eye?" We all need to remove any planks in our eyes in order to see clearly.

Right now, ask the Holy Spirit to show you anything you've done wrong. Confess these things to God and ask for the forgiveness that can only come from Him through the blood of His Son, Jesus Christ.

FURTHER READING:
Psalms 32
Psalms 86:5
Matthew 7:3-5

March 7

Hope Lives

"For I was hungry and you gave me something to eat, I was thirsty and you gave me something to drink, I was a stranger and you invited me in, I needed clothes and you clothed me, I was sick and you looked after me, I was in prison and you came to visit me."

—MATTHEW 25:35-36

She lay in the palm of my hand—two months old, weighing less than three pounds. We rushed her from the stick house in Guatemala where her mother and siblings lived, to a medical clinic recently stocked with supplies—a donation made possible by *Bridge of Hope* partners. Only a couple of months ago, her limbs were thin as reeds, but today they are chubby and strong. The black circles under her eyes are gone. She smiles! She laughs! She lives, praise God, she lives!

Satan did not claim that little girl. But there are so many others who still need rescuing. There are so many other little ones that are as thin, weak and helpless as Elvira used to be. They need the things we take for granted every day.

Pray without ceasing for these children—the needy and the hurting. Give what you can so they might live and know of the love of the Father, for when we give a helping hand to "the least of these," we help Christ Himself.

FURTHER READING:
Jeremiah 22:16
Proverbs 11:25
Psalms 41:1

March 8

Treasured Possession

"Now if you obey me, and keep my covenant, then out of all nations you will be my treasured possession. Although the whole earth is mine, you will be for me a kingdom of priests, and a holy nation."

—EXODUS 19:5-6

We know as Christians that we are bound by faith and not the law. Yet we know that the Ten Commandments and God's law still hold an important place in our hearts, even if we've never stopped to contemplate this heavenly promise—the promise that those who obey God and keep the covenant of the Ten Commandments are "treasured possessions."

The Lord has made other promises to us concerning the law. Psalms 19:7 says, "The law of the Lord is perfect, reviving the soul. The statutes of the Lord are trustworthy, making wise the simple." If your soul is starting to flag and grow weary, if you are starting to feel overwhelmed and confused by the world, turn to the Lord's ten simple laws, the commandments He put forth to His people on Mount Sinai all those centuries ago.

That's why you must never think the Ten Commandments are obsolete. That's why it is still important to study them today, to make them a part of your heart, so that you too may be the Lord's "treasured possession."

FURTHER READING:
Psalms 1:2-3
Matthew 5:17
Romans 6:1-2

March 9

No Other Gods

"I am the Lord your God, who brought you out of the land of Egypt, out of the land of slavery. You shall have no other gods before me."

—EXODUS 20:2-3

There are dozens of "little gods" in disguise in our lives, even if we are Christians, worshipping the one true God.

People's opinions, our money, appearance, family, friends or entertainment can become other gods we put before God. The devil seeks to deceive us by trying to make us believe that having other gods is limited to worship of another deity instead of God.

God would not see fit to warn us about putting other gods before Him if there were no other gods to be worried about. Nor would He tell us, as He does in Deuteronomy 10:17, that He is the "God of gods and Lord of lords, the great God, mighty and awesome...."

Who or what is receiving the glory in your life today? Who or what is most important to you, and who or what do you seek to please above all else? If you cannot answer "God" to all of these, then I challenge you to sort through your priorities.

Place Him at the center of your life and bring yourself back into alignment with this blessed commandment.

FURTHER READING:
Jeremiah 25:6
Deuteronomy 6:14
Luke 10:27-28

March 10

Don't Bow Down

"You shall not make for yourself an idol in the form of anything in heaven above or on the earth beneath or in the waters below."

—EXODUS 20:4-6

Why did God give a command against making a form of things in the heavens above or the earth below?

It is because needing a physical form to bow down to and worship diminishes faith, even if that physical form is an attempt to represent God Himself. The need for the physical is of the flesh, but we are to live and know God in the Spirit.

Romans 8:13 teaches, "By the Spirit you put to death the misdeeds of the body." Our "religious" behavior can take our church buildings, our list of "ministries" and accomplishments and put them in place of a relationship with God.

God's primary commandment is that we love Him! Even in this commandment He is calling upon us to love Him, and in return He promises to love us to a thousand generations.

Have you forgotten God today in favor of the physical forms of worship? Don't get stuck on earthly things just because you can see them. Today, I challenge you to just spend some time with Him in quiet, putting aside all outward forms of worship and prayer. Allow Him to work within you during this time.

FURTHER READING:
Deuteronomy 6:5
Hosea 3:1
Jude 1:21

March 11

The Name of God

"You shall not misuse the name of the Lord your God, for the Lord will not hold anyone guiltless who misuses his name."

—EXODUS 20:7

Have you ever used the name of the Lord against someone out of hate rather than relationship? Have you turned someone away or hardened your heart against someone, saying it was in the name of God?

This commandment warns us, "Do not use the name of the Lord in vain," but it also includes using His name to sanction hatred, unforgiveness, or condemnation. Often this takes the form of Christians putting other people down, and then excusing themselves by saying they are just "hating the sin but loving the sinner."

You're not loving someone if you make them feel excluded, if you have chosen to tear them down or if your motivation isn't love. It is our job to love—let God and the Holy Spirit deal with sins and change lives. Focus on giving bread to the hungry and comforting the lonely.

Romans 3:10 says "there is no one righteous, not even one!" Today I challenge you to avoid using the name of God to put anyone down. I believe we can do better.

FURTHER READING:
Romans 3:23
Matthew 10:12
Isaiah 52:5-7

March 12

The Sabbath

*"Remember the Sabbath day by keeping it holy.
Six days you shall labor and do all your work, but the
seventh day is a Sabbath to the Lord your God."*

—EXODUS 20:8-10

In Mark 2:27 Jesus said, "The Sabbath was made for man, not man for the Sabbath." We live in a generation that works almost constantly, but God in His compassion knew that we needed to rest. He also knew that it would be increasingly difficult for us to slow down and spend time with Him with the many distractions of the world pressing in on us.

The Sabbath commandment is a wonderful example of the timeless truths that God handed down to establish walls of protection around our lives and to help us understand how best to interact with others and with Him.

God took centuries to boil the commandments down to "love" because we first had to be taught what love meant. The first commandments are about loving God—the commandments that follow are about loving one another and ourselves.

I challenge you to put your work down. Observe a Sabbath day. Rest. Don't push your body and mind to the point where it's impossible to listen to the Spirit any longer. God Himself has asked you to take a break!

FURTHER READING:
Exodus 16:23
Leviticus 26:35
2 Chronicles 36:21

March 13

Honor Your Parents

"Honor your father and your mother, so that you may live long in the land the Lord your God is giving you."

—EXODUS 20:12

Why is honoring your father and mother important? One of the reasons is because our mothers and fathers go through life before we do. If we honor them—honor their wisdom, honor what they learned through their mistakes and honor the history they wrote for us, then we will naturally benefit. We will live longer because we will not need to repeat those mistakes.

I recognize that perhaps you are growing up or have grown up in a home where the parents may have done things that were not worthy of honor. If that is the case in your life, you should find a spiritual mother and a spiritual father to teach and guide you—then honor them with all your might!

Sometimes we can find our spiritual parents by first serving as spiritual sons and daughters, offering honor before the position has been sealed. Ruth did this for Naomi (Ruth 1:16-17). As a result Naomi gave Ruth the advice and counsel that started a new life for her.

Through the faithfulness of Ruth to her spiritual parent Naomi, the line of David was established, a legacy of faithfulness that would ultimately bring us the love of Jesus Christ.

FURTHER READING:
Ephesians 6:1-4
Proverbs 20:20
Matthew 15:4-6

March 14

The Least of These

"My whole being will exclaim, 'Who is like you, O Lord? You rescue the poor from those too strong for them, the poor and needy from those who rob them.'"

—PSALMS 35:10

Simon is a little boy who saw his parents die before he was five years old. For the past two years, he's been on the street, begging for help, praying to a God he knows is there to help him.

Sudan has suffered tragedy upon tragedy. Millions of Sudanese are dead, and more than four million have been driven from their homes. They are being targeted for two reasons: They are black and they are not Muslims.

They are our brothers and sisters in Christ.

Through compassionate supporters over the last decade, *Bridge of Hope* has freed more than 29,000 men, women and children from slavery and provided food, medical aid and basic necessities.

It's the very least we can do, for as Jesus said in Matthew 25, whatever we do to these our brethren, we do to Him.

If Jesus were to cry out for help to us, would we turn our backs on Him? Right now Jesus is asking for our help...in the form of a little Sudanese boy named Simon.

Dare we turn our backs on Him?

FURTHER READING:
Matthew 25:37-40
Isaiah 58:6-12
Job 5:15-16

March 15

Speaking Life

"You shall not murder."

—EXODUS 20:13

Most people would never think of breaking this commandment by murdering someone.

In fact it's easy to skip right over this commandment, thinking, "Well I wouldn't do that, so, moving right along...."

Be careful! Jesus teaches us in Matthew 5:21-22 that unjust anger and refusing to forgive are acts of murder that we commit in our hearts. He says, "Do not murder, and anyone who murders will be subject to judgment. But I tell you that anyone who is angry with his brother will be subject to judgment."

How often have we "killed" one another by holding grudges, hatred and anger over them? How often have we worked to secretly tear down others with our words and our gossip, speaking death over their lives and over their works?

I challenge you to search your heart for signs that you are holding grudges or failing to forgive. I challenge you to ask God to forgive you and to help you speak life instead of speaking death. I challenge you to refuse to murder others with words just as much as you would refuse to commit murder by any other means.

FURTHER READING:
James 3:6
Proverbs 16:27
Romans 1:29-30

March 16

Not Ashamed

"But whoever disowns me before men,
I will disown him before my Father in heaven."

MATTHEW 10:33

Are you embarrassed to be seen in public with a Bible? Do you hide yours in your briefcase or in your purse? Would you sit in a restaurant with your Bible proudly displayed on the table, or would you rather keep it hidden from view?

We are called to be witnesses for God. Take your Bible from its hiding place and display it proudly. Many have suffered and died just so you could have that priceless book.

Christ paid the price for your freedom, and because of what He did you are able to claim each promise in the Bible. Why be ashamed to let the world know that you treasure the Word of God?

The Bible has an uncanny ability to stir up human emotions —love, joy, hatred or disdain. If you will allow Him, God will open a door of opportunity for you to witness—to plant a seed for the kingdom.

You do not have to beat people over the head with God's Word. All you have to do is be willing, ready and not ashamed to let the world know you are a believer.

FURTHER READING:
Mark 8:38
Luke 9:26
Acts 1:8

March 17

Theft

"You shall not steal."

—EXODUS 20:15

Like many of the commandments, theft is one of those commandments Christians are likely to read right past. After all, few of us are likely to go rob a bank, steal from the till at work or shoplift.

Yet how many of us might bring office supplies home from work that don't belong to us? How many of us fudge on our time clocks or spend paid time at work doing personal matters? These are all forms of theft.

We should be thankful to God for everything we have and trust Him to provide what we don't have and need. God reiterates this commandment throughout the Bible.

Jesus said, "You know the commandments: 'Do not murder, do not commit adultery, do not steal, do not give false testimony, do not defraud, honor your father and mother'" (Mark 10:19).

Rather than stealing—no matter if it is money from the register at work or a trinket from a friend's house—give. God will bless those who give, whether it is money, possessions, help, time or encouragement.

As Christians we are called to pour out the message of God's love to the world, without detracting a single thing from it.

FURTHER READING:
Jeremiah 23:30
Romans 2:21
Titus 2:9-10

March 18

False Testimony

"You shall not give false testimony about your neighbor."

—EXODUS 20:16

This commandment is often interpreted as "thou shalt not lie," and it is true that the Lord is no fan of falsehood.

Yet the ninth commandment deals specifically with lies about a neighbor.

Proverbs 26:28 helps us to understand how both bring harm: "A lying tongue hates those crushed by it, and a flattering mouth works ruin." Often these go hand in hand as one person is flattering to their neighbor's face and then tears him or her down behind his back.

So much damage can be inflicted by such a small part of our body (James 3:3-6). Lies destroy careers, churches, families, marriages and reputations.

Avoid words that seek to do harm so that you may stay in the spirit of this commandment. It is better to keep our mouths quiet than stumble into this sin.

Our emotions can sometimes carry us away and pull us into a swirling void of negativity that grows and grows, so today I challenge you to steer clear and speak only the truth.

FURTHER READING:
Proverbs 6:16-19
Psalms 119:29
John 8:44

March 19

Culture of Envy

"You shall not covet your neighbor's house. You shall not covet your neighbor's wife, or his manservant, or maidservant, his ox or donkey, or anything that belongs to your neighbor."

—EXODUS 20:17

Everything about our culture entices us to want more and to want better things than we already have.

We live in the most affluent yet the most unhappy nation in the world. This is the result of removing gratitude from our value system and writing a "more, more, more" attitude in. If we don't want more and strive for more, we're told we somehow don't measure up.

The cure for envy and covetousness is found in gratitude and praise to God. Colossians 3:16 tells us that we should "let the word of Christ dwell in you richly as you teach and admonish one another with all wisdom, and as you sing psalms, hymns, and spiritual songs with gratitude in your hearts to God."

Today I want to bring a word to you to find a new measuring stick for yourself and others—let us measure ourselves by our obedience to God and by the evidence of the fruit of the Spirit in our lives.

FURTHER READING:
Job 5:2
Proverbs 14:30
Ecclesiastes 4:4

March 20

Advocate in Heaven

"But if anybody does sin, we have one who speaks to the Father in our defense—Jesus Christ, the Righteous One. He is the atoning sacrifice for our sins, and not only for ours but also for the sins of the whole world."

—1 JOHN 2:1-2

One of the hard things about reading the Ten Commandments is that they put a spotlight on the places in our lives where sin still lives—even when we thought we were doing "pretty well."

Ephesians 2:8-9 says, "For it is by grace you have been saved, through faith—and this not from yourselves, it is the gift of God—not by works, so that no one can boast." We should never forget that our salvation does not hinge on our ability to "do well." Our salvation hinges on faith in Jesus Christ. Praise God we don't have to do it on our own!

"Whatever the law says, it says to those who are under the law, so that every mouth may be silenced and the whole world held accountable to God. Therefore no one will be declared righteous in His sight by observing the law; rather, through the law we become conscious of sin" (Romans 3:19-20).

Read the Ten Commandments to become conscious of the areas in your life that need improvement, and never lose sight of the fact that we are called to faith and love through Jesus Christ.

FURTHER READING:
Galatians 2:16
Acts 13:39
Hebrews 9:12

March 21

Freedom Bound

*"Remember those in prison as if you were
their fellow prisoners, and those who are
mistreated as if you yourselves were suffering."*

—HEBREWS 13:3

The highest price ever paid for a slave was the price Jesus paid
for you and me. He bought us out of the slavery of sin with His
own blood. We, of all people, should have compassion on those
who are still bound as slaves.

When we refer to someone as still being bound, we're usually
referring to a person who's spiritually bound: "My sins have
been bound into a yoke ; by his hands they were woven together.
They have come upon my neck and the Lord has sapped my
strength. He has handed me over to those I cannot withstand"
(Lamentations 1:14). But thousands of miles away in Sudan,
Christian people are physically enslaved in large numbers. In
the midst of the slaughter, a horrific slave trade is thriving, but a
ray of hope shines in the darkness.

Bridge of Hope alone has redeemed over 29,000 captives in
Sudan, enabling them to return home and begin anew. The cost
of their freedom is relatively low.

Jesus paid the highest price ever—His life—for our eternal
freedom. Romans 6:18 says, "You have been set free from sin..."

FURTHER READING:
Isaiah 61:1
Romans 6
Psalms 111:9

March 22

Rock of Ages

*"All Scripture is God-breathed and is useful
for teaching, rebuking, correcting and training
in righteousness, so that the man of God may be
thoroughly equipped for every good work."*

—2 TIMOTHY 3:16-17

The Bible contains all the guidance we need to live fruitful, prosperous lives. It is inerrant, infallible, undeniable and indestructible.

When everything and everyone else fails you, the Word of God will not. The Bible is the living Word of the only true and living God. Luke 6:38 says, "Give, and it will be given to you. A good measure, pressed down, shaken together, and running over, will be poured into your lap. For with the measure you use, it will be measured to you."

God had to tell us to give because our natural inclination is to keep. Whenever you give, do it with expectation that you will receive. Give knowing that it will be given to you with increase. God can only multiply your seed if you sow it.

If you believe the Word of God you will act according to its principles and you will prosper. Don't settle for less when you can have a good measure, pressed down, shaken together and running over, as God states in His Word.

FURTHER READING:
James 1:23-26
Luke 6:38
Matthew 24:35

March 23

God Has Stacked the Deck!

"Your word is a lamp to my feet and a light for my path."

—PSALMS 119:105

Followers of Jesus Christ have a tremendous advantage that allows us to navigate the peaks and valleys of this world. God in His infinite wisdom created a manual for living that encompasses life from its beginning to its end.

It tells us all the attributes of the God we serve, chronicles His walk on earth and prescribes our path to eternal salvation. His manual covers all aspects of life. It leaves us without any want for knowledge.

Yet in spite of God's best efforts, many believers are confused and disheartened. Our confusion comes from not reading the Scriptures for all they are worth.

The Lord urges us to meditate on His Word. It is a "lamp onto our feet and a light unto our path" (Psalms 119:105). When digested, His Word illuminates the path before us, allowing us to have insight and foresight.

Oh, what a blessing for the believer who spends time in the Word. There is no problem too difficult, no circumstance too overwhelming, no situation beyond comprehension. Get into the Word; God has already provided the answers. It's all in His book...the Bible. Study His Word today.

FURTHER READING:
Hosea 4:6
2 Corinthians 1:20
Mark 4:10-12

March 24

Healing is a Fact

"A man with leprosy came and knelt before him and said, 'Lord, if you are willing, you can make me clean.' Jesus reached out his hand and touched the man. 'I am willing,' he said. 'Be clean!' Immediately he was cured of his leprosy."

—MATTHEW 8:2-3

Many Christians are suffering needlessly with sickness and disease. They don't realize that healing has already been provided for them. Healing is not a promise from God but an established fact—for the Word of God says that "by his wounds we are healed" (Isaiah 53:5).

The problem is that perfect faith cannot exist where the will of God is not known. How can people have faith that God wants to heal them if they don't know the will of God concerning their healing? The truth is that unbelief will prevent you from being healed. If you desire to be healed there is only one thing that will counter unbelief—sound Bible teaching.

You have to immerse yourself in the Word of God. You need to know what God has said concerning your healing. Then decide that you will believe what God says above every other opinion. Healing is the ministry of every believer, and that includes you!

FURTHER READING:
Mark 6:5-6
Isaiah 53:5-6
Mark 16:17-18

March 25

Holiness Costs

*"Everyone who has this hope in him
purifies himself, just as he is pure."*

—I JOHN 3:3

There are many Christians who like the notion of being holy as long as it cost them nothing—no hardships, no difficulties, no scorn and no financial or property loss.

Men like Samuel Wesley dug the wells of holiness and suffered losses—burning of crops, continual threats of physical harm and false imprisonment—yet they stood their ground for holiness.

Though men hated him, Samuel continued to live a life of holiness before God. Though his house was set on fire and he almost lost his son, John, who was trapped on the second floor of the burning building—he stood for holiness.

God is expecting us to stand for holiness too.

There is a cost to live a life of holiness—people will scorn you, they will hate you, you could lose your property, your money, you could get injured and you could even lose your life.

Jesus says, "For whoever wants to save his life will lose it, but whoever loses his life for me will find it" (Matthew 16:25).

A life of holiness costs something...are you willing to pay the price? There is no better price to pay than living for God.

FURTHER READING:
2 Corinthians 7:1
1 Thessaloians 4:7
1 Peter 1:15-16

March 26

Holiness Is Not an Option

"But just as he who called you is holy, so be holy in all you do; or it is written: 'Be holy, because I am holy.'"

—PETER 1:15-16

Holiness is sanctification and separation unto God—which is what we are called to as believers.

Preachers of old like John Wesley knew that holiness was a command and not an option. They lived their lives in humble dedication to God. They served God, worked tirelessly, studied God's Word diligently and prayed without ceasing. Psalms 65:4 says, "Blessed are those you choose and bring near to live in your courts! We are filled with the good things of your house, of your holy temple."

Today many of the "successful" churches thrive on flowery sermons designed to appeal to intellectualism or materialism. They neglect talking about self-control, discipline or a life of holiness. The truth is that personal discipline and holiness before God go hand in hand.

In Leviticus 19:2 God says, "'Be holy because I, the Lord your God, am holy." What does that mean? Your life should be one of diligent Bible study, daily communication with God through prayer, fasting and service. As you do this, you will be set apart to be used by God.

FURTHER READING:
2 Corinthians 7:1
1 Thessaloians 4:7
1 John 3:3

March 27

Ignorance is not Bliss

"For the Lord gives wisdom, and from his mouth come knowledge and understanding."

—PROVERBS 2:6

The Bible is a manual for living. Christians need to read the Bible to discover the wells of truth flowing from its pages. The Bible tells us God's view of life. It tells us His desires and His promises for His children.

All the knowledge you need can be found within the pages of this precious book. God in his infinite wisdom gave us a manual on how to correctly apply knowledge God's way, and that is true wisdom. Those who fail to utilize the Bible rob themselves of divine wisdom and are filled with only man's limited knowledge.

Too often God's people perish because of lack of knowledge (Hosea 4:6). God doesn't want His children to be ignorant. Ephesians 4:18 says, "They are darkened in their understanding and separated from the life of God because of the ignorance that is in them due to the hardening of their hearts."

My friend, ignorance is not bliss! It is a ploy of the enemy to rob, steal and destroy you and your life.

But God has given you wisdom, knowledge and life—it's all explained in His book.

FURTHER READING:
Proverbs 11:2
Proverbs 4:7
1 Corinthians 1:30

March 28

A Different Kingdom

"Give, and it will be given to you.... For with the measure you use, it will be measured to you."

—LUKE 6:38

As a Christian, you are in a different kingdom now. God's kingdom is completely different from everything in the kingdom of the world. In this kingdom, in order to get, you must give.

The instruction you choose to obey determines the future you will create. God won't make you give but He will bless you when you do. It doesn't make sense to trust your soul to God and not your pocketbook.

Jesus gave numerous instructions on what to do with your money and we ignore them at our peril. Everything God instructs you to do is for your own good.

God is your Father. Trust Him to provide for all your needs according to His riches in glory by Christ Jesus.

Faith without works is dead. Choose this day whom you will obey. You are surrounded by a great cloud of witnesses who have decided to believe God regardless of their opposition.

Follow their example and lay aside every weight and the sin which so easily ensnares you, and run with endurance the race that is set before you, looking unto Jesus, the author and finisher of your faith (see Hebrews 12:1-2).

FURTHER READING:
Matthew 10:29-31
Philippians 4:19
Hebrews 12:1-2

March 29

Promised Land

"The Lord said to Moses, 'How long will these people treat me with contempt? How long will they refuse to believe in me, in spite of all the miraculous signs I have performed among them?'"

—NUMBERS 14:11

Are you at the threshold of your promised land? Has God brought you to Canaan—your place of blessing? Are you secretly longing to return to that old familiar place of Egypt, or will you go forward, trusting God?

God told the children of Israel, "I am the Lord your God who brought you out of the land of Egypt, out of the house of bondage" (Deuteronomy 5:6). Yet when it was time for them to go into Canaan and cast out the giants, they refused because they saw themselves as grasshoppers.

As a result they wept all night, wanting to die, blaming God and crying out to go back to Egypt (Numbers 14:1-4). But if they had just believed God and gone into the Promised Land they would have had victory.

Are you willing to stand outside the Promised Land weeping, wanting to die, blaming God and deciding in your heart to return back to Egypt, the house of bondage? Or will you go into the land of milk and honey? God is waiting on you to decide.

FURTHER READING:
Numbers 13:33
Isaiah 44:17
Exodus 32

March 30

Stand Firm

*"If you do not stand firm in your faith,
you will not stand at all."*

—ISAIAH 7:9

Sometimes we hold on to that which is unsure, afraid to reach out for the thing that is sure. You cannot have both. You must leave the shaky house to move into the house built on the rock. You can't live in two houses or kingdoms at the same time.

There are only two kingdoms: Fear and FAITH. If you are walking in fear you are not in faith. Faith in God will cause the impossible to manifest in your life. Faith says that "it will happen" while fear says, "it will never happen."

Without faith it is impossible to please God, for he who comes to God must believe that He is, and that He is a rewarder of those who diligently seek Him (Hebrews 11:6).

Your heart is purified by faith, you are sanctified by faith, you live by faith, you are justified by faith, you have access by faith, and you stand by faith. It would be a foolish farmer who sowed seeds not expecting a harvest. For he has faith that because he sowed seeds, he will reap crops.

To seek is to search out, investigate, crave, demand and worship. How do you seek God? God honors those who actively and persistently pursue Him—in faith.

FURTHER READING:
Acts 15:9
Romans 3:28
Romans 11:20

March 31

Prayer

"Jesus looked up and said, 'Father, I thank you that you have heard me. I knew that you always hear me, but I said this for the benefit of the people standing here, that they may believe that you sent me.'"

—JOHN 11:41-42

Jesus—the only perfect man—prayed consistently. He prayed to give God thanks and He prayed when He was afraid (Luke 22:42-44). We should follow His example and pray continuously as well.

Philippians 4:6 says, "Do not be anxious about anything, but in everything, by prayer and petition, with thanksgiving, present your requests to God." When we pray, we open the door for God to work within us and in our lives. He promises to give us what we need. Matthew 7:7 says, "Ask and it will be given to you; seek and you will find; knock and the door will be opened to you." God can't make you enter into His kingdom, but He can stand at the door and knock.

Peter walked on the water until his focus turned away from Jesus to himself. As long as he kept his eyes on Jesus he did not sink. When he looked at his circumstances he started to sink.

Get your eyes off yourself and your problems and get them on Jesus. Put your faith in Him; He will not let you down.

FURTHER READING:
Matthew 13:11
Matthew 13:45-46
John 6:35

April 1

Seed of Faith

"For in the gospel a righteousness from God is revealed, a righteousness that is by faith from first to last, just as it is written: 'The righteous will live by faith.'"

—ROMANS 1:17

Are you secure in His promise to never leave you or forsake you? When we feel fear or uncertainty we should stand on

God's promises in His Word: "Peace I leave with you; my peace I give you. I do not give to you as the world gives. Do not let your hearts be troubled and do not be afraid" (John 14:27). Is your testimony one of faith or of fear?

My mentor Lester Sumrall said, "Faith is to be a constant dominating experience in your life—not something that comes once in a while...continually test yourself...when you start to make a decision or do something ask, 'Is this faith's road I'm walking? or is it unbelief's?' If it is unbelief's, get off that road! You don't belong there. 'Is this faith's choice? or is it fear's choice?' I'm not making that choice. I don't want fear dominating my life. That's living by faith. That's the eternal quest for faith. You must do it all the time. Don't quit. Just pursue it."

Put your trust in God and get a spirit of faith. He has never let anyone down and He won't start with you.

FURTHER READING:
Matthew 7
Psalms 23
Luke 6:48

April 2

Sow Your Seed

*"Seek the Lord while he may be found;
call on him while he is near."*

—ISAIAH 55:6

"Listen to me, Judah and people of Jerusalem! Have faith in the Lord your God and you will be upheld; have faith in his prophets and you will be successful" (2 Chronicles 20:20).

When God calls we must answer. The resurrection season is a cause for celebration. Celebrate with me when God sowed His best seed so that you might have eternal life. This is the season, the moment for your miracle. God sowed His best seed on Resurrection Sunday, and that seed changed everything.

God has always delivered with the power resident in a seed. Through the ages, God used a seed to accomplish His purpose. He instructed Adam and Eve in the principles of seedtime and harvest and spoke to the prophets about the ultimate seed He would sow—Jesus Christ, the seed that died to create a harvest of souls for the Lord!

Jesus also used many examples of seed in His teachings. When God wanted to redeem us, He sowed a seed—the prophesied redeemer, the Lord Jesus Christ we celebrate on Resurrection Sunday. As we're celebrating God giving His best, He speaks to us to give our best. There is power resident in a seed.

FURTHER READING:
Genesis 1:11
Song of Songs 2:1-20
Ecclesiastes 3

April 3

Fear the Lord

"The fear of the Lord is the beginning of knowledge,
but fools despise wisdom and discipline."

—PROVERBS 1:7

Some people still think they can figure out this life on their own, but it is foolish to think that they can rely on their own understanding to live this gift of life God has designed.

I am not instructing you to turn off your mind and set yourself on autopilot. Christians sometimes think they need to disengage their brains to come to God. We all received knowledge about God that convinced us of our need for Him even when we didn't understand.

What happens when we obey?

The Bible says, "All these blessings will come upon you and accompany you if you obey the Lord your God" (Deuteronomy 28:2).

Oh that this generation would learn the fear of the Lord! Is God merciful? Yes. Is He holy? Yes. Don't despise His instruction; it is not free. In everything we are commanded to trust God and we ignore Him at our own peril.

Will you trust Him today?

FURTHER READING:
Revelation 12:11-12
Matthew 10:28
Deuteronomy 28:2

April 4

First and Best

"Did Israel not understand? First, Moses says, 'I will make you envious by those who are not a nation; I will make you angry by a nation that has no understanding.'"

—ROMANS 10:19

Have you ever been in church and a family gets blessed again and again and you think to yourself, "Why do they always get blessed? Where is my blessing?"

God doesn't play favorites, so the only difference between you and them is the instruction you each chose to obey: "Sow your seed in the morning, and at evening let not your hands be idle, for you do not know which will succeed, whether this or that, or whether both will do equally well" (Ecclesiastes 11:6).

A regular Sunday night at World Harvest Church would be considered a revival in most churches. What is our secret? We know one seed changes everything.

God had a need. How did He set in motion the miracle that gave Him His heart's desire? He planted a seed—in the person of His own precious Son. God didn't just sow any old seed. No, He sowed His first and best seed—His only Son, Jesus.

The result? The family of God was born and you and I were given eternal life. Here God gives us the example to follow when we need a miracle. Give your first and your best seed!

FURTHER READING:
2 Samuel 22:3
Exodus 15:2
2 Chronicles 6:41

April 5

Restore the Bridge

"For the wages of sin is death, but the gift of God is eternal life in Christ Jesus our Lord."

—ROMANS 6:23

There is a huge separation between God and His creation, man. Satan has done his best to alienate us from our God, and has left a trail of broken planks on the bridge to Him. We are in the midst of the worst scenario the world has seen, as chaos, war, promiscuity, murder and drug use prevail.

In other words, sin.

Why is it that we have now decided sin is an obsolete idea whose usefulness has long ago vanished? Why do we now think that living a fairly good life is enough to "save" us? What makes us think we can dismiss sin as irrelevant in our times?

Satan's strategy is to get us to deny that sin and our sinfulness exist, thereby eliminating our need for a Savior.

Jesus came to save people from their sins (Matthew 1:21); that was His ultimate purpose.

We are under a terrible illusion if we really believe sin does not exist, or that it doesn't matter. Jesus gave His life so that we could have a relationship with God. His death has spanned the chasm between man and God, and now we can all come to Him in repentance.

FURTHER READING:
Galatians 6:1
Acts 2:38-39
Acts 16:31

April 6

Too Busy for God?

"For what is seen is temporary,
but what is not seen is eternal."

—2 CORINTHIANS 4:18

A woman who attended church occasionally was asked by a friend from her church what she thought about eternal life. She replied, "Are you serious? I don't have time for that. I have a business to run and three children to raise and believe me, that keeps me hopping."

Satan's influence can surely be seen here. He has made us disregard God in all areas of our lives, and the distance between God and man increases every day. We are too busy, too tired, or too anything else to take the time for communion with Him.

The saddest part about this is that communion with God is the most important part of each day; He is the reason why we have life, and He wants to give us life to the full. Why do we insist on focusing on all the other things instead?

We need to rebuild the bridge to God that Satan has torn down. Start today to live the life God has planned for you—a life that includes all the glory of His bounty...eternal life!

Ask Jesus into your heart today and forever "leave your life of sin" (John 8:11). Let Satan know that he does not hold sway over your human life or your eternal life. To God be the glory!

FURTHER READING:
1 Timothy 6:12
1 John 2:25
1 John 5:11-12

April 7

God is Great

"They have become filled with every kind of wickedness, evil, greed and depravity. They are full of envy, murder, strife, deceit and malice."

—ROMANS 1:29

We live in a world that has forgotten God. The latest best-selling books set out to discredit God. References to God are disappearing from many public institutions, and liberal activists want to remove His name from the Pledge of Allegiance.

God's people should be shouting from the rooftops, "God is great!" The absence of any kind of rebuttal is the result of the insidious work of Satan. Satan wants to destroy all communication between God and man, and we help him every time we do not speak up.

Forget what is 'politically correct' and praise God. Some may ridicule you for praising His name, but His Word will stand forever, long after the present fads have passed from this earth. Praise God constantly. Help to repair the breach between God and man.

The old hymn says it all: "I'll praise my maker while I've breath; and when my voice is lost in death, praise shall employ my nobler powers. My days of praise shall ne'er be past..." Praise Him today.

FURTHER READING:
Psalms 150:1
Luke 18:43
Hebrews 13:15

April 8

Good People

"For just as through the disobedience of the one man the many were made sinners, so also through the obedience of the one man the many will be made righteous."

—ROMANS 5:19

When Adam and Eve disobeyed God and ate that fateful fruit at the urging of the serpent, they received knowledge of all evil things. Things completely unknown to them—disease, wickedness and death—were released onto the earth.

They did not receive the things Satan had promised. Instead, they became clothed in the filthy apparel of unrighteousness. They had sinned and broken the intimate connection between God and man.

Why do we now think that living a good life is enough to save us? Why do we try to "earn" our salvation by doing good deeds and looking like "good people"? The Bible clearly states, "all our righteous acts are like filthy rags" (Isaiah 64:6).

Jesus said, "I am the way, the truth and the life. No one comes to the Father except through me" (John 14:6). He is the only way into God's presence.

We can't earn our salvation. Eternal life is only offered through faith in our Savior Jesus Christ.

FURTHER READING:
Galatians 6:1
Acts 2:38-39
Acts 16:31

April 9

Demons are Loose!

*"The Spirit clearly says that in later times
some will abandon the faith and follow
deceiving spirits and things taught by demons.
Such teachings come through hypocritical liars,
whose consciences have been seared as with a hot iron."*

—I TIMOTHY 4:1-2

Demonic forces have tainted the ministry of the gospel. Demons are regular attendants at church and sit next to us on pews. Some demons are so bold that they even speak to us from the pulpit and we listen. The Holy Spirit told Paul that this would happen—so we shouldn't be surprised or frightened.

God has provided the remedy for the demonic problem!

We have a God who is mighty...a King who reigns supreme... the Spirit of the Lord in and among us. Jesus Christ, the Lamb of God, still bears the marks of sacrifice and there's still the victorious and triumphant Church of Jesus Christ against which the gates of hell shall not prevail!

Matthew 16:18 says, "And I tell you that you are Peter, and on this rock I will build my church, and the gates of Hades will not overcome it."

There may be demons loose, but we have the power to bind and cast them out wherever we find them. Are you ready?

FURTHER READING:
Luke 10:19
Acts 28:3-5
Matthew 24:37-39

April 10

We Need to go Further

"And I tell you that you are Peter, and on this rock I will build my church, and the gates of Hades will not overcome it."

—MATTHEW 16:18

Did you know that the Church is to confront demons of darkness wherever we find them? We are to cast them out in the name of Jesus as a sign to unbelievers! This may sound radical to you but it is not—it is what Christ Jesus said we would do!

"And these signs shall follow them that believe; in my name they cast out devils" (Mark 16:17).

The Church has been slothful in deliverance. We have been lazy, for we don't want to pay the price to live holy lives, we do not study the Word of God the way we ought to, we do not spend the time before God's presence as we should and we do not exercise our authority as we are directed to do. So as a Church how can we know the Father's heart?

As believers our lives and actions are to testify that we belong to Christ Jesus. We are to spread the Word of God, cast out demons, set the captives free, take care of the needy and poor, and demonstrate the love of God continually.

It is time for the Church to be about the Father's business... it's time for us to go further.

FURTHER READING:
Luke 10:19
Mark 16:17
John 3:17

April 11

Preach the Truth

"My message and my preaching were not with wise and persuasive words, but with a demonstration of the Spirit's power."

—I CORINTHIANS 2:4

The Gospel message is full of the love, grace and power of God.

1 Peter 1:8-9 says, "Though you have not seen him, you love him; and even though you do not see him now, you believe in him and are filled with an inexpressible and glorious joy, for you are receiving the goal of your faith, the salvation of your souls."

Today's preaching often ignores sin and its results. We still need the food of the Spirit, not secular humanism and denial of the existence of God. If you are what you eat, make sure you receive good spiritual food. 1 Corinthians 10:3-4 says, "They all ate the same spiritual food and drank the same spiritual drink; for they drank from the spiritual rock that accompanied them, and that rock was Christ."

Some "new" thinkers tell us that God is outmoded and irrelevant in today's highly industrial and scientific world.

It is time now to bring back the salvation message to the Body of Christ. God will never be "out of date." In these last days, God is calling us to harvest souls for Him. Revival starts within the faithful hearts of individuals who seek Him.

FURTHER READING:
1 Corinthians 1:21
1 Thessalonians 2:13
2 Corinthians 2:17

April 12

Leaven of the Corinthians

"Therefore let us keep the Festival, not with the old yeast, the yeast of malice and wickedness, but with bread without yeast, the bread of sincerity and truth."

—1 CORINTHIANS 5:8

The leaven of the Corinthians is the believer who is immoral, greedy, indulges in idolatry, slander or sexual sins, who is a drunkard or a swindler.

These wayward believers reject spiritual authority and have the yeast of malice and wickedness (1 Corinthians 5:8). They lack self-control and are self-indulgent. They are indifferent to the plight of fellow believers. They are impatient—considering only their needs.

They fail to curtail their thoughts, which are the forerunners to their deeds. Jesus said in Matthew 5:28, "Anyone who looks at a woman lustfully has already committed adultery with her in his heart." The way you think tells who you really are (Proverbs 23:7).

Is all hope lost if you notice the leaven of the Corinthians in your own life? No! What should you do? Judge yourself so that you will not be judged (1 Corinthians 11:31). Get the leaven out by replacing it with sincerity and truthfulness (1 Corinthians 5:8).

FURTHER READING:
1 Corinthians 11:17-33
1 Corinthians 5
Romans 3:7

April 13

Leaven of the Galatians

"You foolish Galatians! Who has bewitched you?
Before your very eyes Jesus Christ was
clearly portrayed as crucified."

—GALATIANS 3:1

The leaven of the Galatians is that they are bewitched and foolish. They deny the necessity of grace.

They believe you can be a good person and be saved. They discount the experience they had with the Spirit of God and trade it for God's Book of the law, which puts them under a curse (Galatians 3; 10) if they do not keep all of it.

Furthermore, they embrace the law and reject faith—even though God says that without faith it is impossible to please Him (Hebrews 11:6).

The Galatians have become blind. They try to become perfected by their own human effort, so they no longer have a need for Christ since they believe their own works can save them.

No one can ever be right with God by keeping the law (Galatians 3:11). The righteous are to live by faith—and faith alone.

Christ rescued us from the law and from the curse pronounced by the law when He hung on the cross. Why go back to the condemnation, judgment and the death sentence of the law? Put your trust in God's grace—it will never fail you.

FURTHER READING:
Galatians 3
Galatians 5:7
1 Corinthians 1:23

April 14

Stand up for Jesus

"Simon, Simon, Satan has asked to sift you as wheat. But I have prayed for you, Simon, that your faith may not fail. And when you have turned back, strengthen your brothers."

—LUKE 22:31-32

It's no secret that evil permeates our world today, influencing our young people and our relationships. Infidelity runs rampant, divorce is ever on the increase, and one-third of all babies born in America live with a never-married parent. The devil is breaking down our moral fiber and offering tawdry earthly substitutes for the Word of God.

Satan must be overjoyed when he sees what his work has done to the world, that so many people have forgotten or turned away from God.

Instead of despairing, do what Ephesians 6:11 commands: "Put on the full armor of God so that you can take your stand against the devil's schemes."

Satan may be active in the world, but as long as Christians hold onto the Word of God, standing firm in righteousness, evil shall not prevail! The battle has already been won by Christ.

His death and resurrection defeated evil once and for all. You can and will prevail over evil in the name of Christ Jesus.

FURTHER READING:
1 John 5:18
1 Peter 5:8
Ephesians 6:11-18

April 15

Re-dig the Well

"That night the Lord appeared to him and said,
'I am the God of your father Abraham. Do not
be afraid, for I am with you; I will bless you
and will increase the number of your descendants
for the sake of my servant Abraham.'"

—GENESIS 26:24

Are there areas in your life that you have been trying to reclaim for God? Areas that once were His but over time you let down your guard and the enemy was able to infiltrate? If so, it is time to re-dig your wells!

We are told in Genesis 26:19-20 that Isaac had to re-dig wells that his father had dug earlier. These wells were filled with dirt that the Philistines had thrown in after Abraham died. Isaac could have decided to allow those wells to stay dormant because it was hard work, but instead he embraced the promises of God.

As you re-dig your wells for the Lord, you may encounter opposition, discomfort, challenges or strife. Just know that the Lord will do all He has promised for you. He will give you peace when you are going through your storm. He will provide His joy when you are grieved. God will supply all you need when you are willing to keep re-digging your wells.

FURTHER READING:
Psalms 18:19
Psalms 31:8
Genesis 26:19-20

April 16

Jesus is our Healer

"I have given you the authority to trample on snakes and scorpions and to overcome all the power of the enemy; nothing will harm you."

—LUKE 10:19

We live in a society that has forgotten God and His great plan for us. Our connection with God has been tampered with by Satan, who can only offer empty promises.

Jesus healed the sick and brought people back from the dead. Christ Jesus told us in John 14:12 that we would do even greater works than those.

Divine healing belongs to us today because God never changes. Healing is an established fact and was completed on the cross. Healing is the ministry of every believer—we just have to take hold of the anointing power of God (Mark 16:17-18).

Jesus healed every disease and sickness...and He still heals today! He died for us—Isaiah 53:5 says, "But he was pierced for our transgressions, he was crushed for our iniquities; the punishment that brought us peace was upon him, and by his wounds we are healed."

Let us believe today that we receive mighty miracles, deliverance and healing through the power of Christ Jesus.

FURTHER READING:
1 John 2:27
Isaiah 53:5
Psalms 107:20

April 17

Expect Blessings

"Test me in this...and see if I will not throw open the floodgates of heaven and pour out so much blessing that you will not have room enough for it."

—MALACHI 3:10

Are you always short of money or frightened that you will be without funds when you have a real need for them? Satan tries to convince us that God does not exist and that the promises He made about abundance are lies.

God wants to give you an abundant life. Jeremiah 33:3 says, "Call to me and I will answer you and tell you great and unsearchable things you do not know."

When we ask and expect Him to bless us, we allow Him to work miracles in and through us! Jesus promised, "Ask and it will be given to you; seek and you will find; knock and the door will be opened to you" (Matthew 7:7).

Give thanks that your request has already been answered through Jesus Christ. Praise God for all the blessings that He has bestowed upon you in the past. With all your heart expect Him to answer when you call.

Jesus said, "The thief comes only to steal and kill and destroy; I have come that they may have life, and have it to the full" (John 10:10). Expect God's blessings and you will receive.

FURTHER READING:
Luke 11:9
Mark 11: 23-24
John 16:23-24

April 18

Scripture Only

"Jesus answered, 'It is written: 'Man does not live on bread alone, but on every word that comes from the mouth of God.'"

—MATTHEW 4:4

Martin Luther, an Augustinian priest, ignited a reformation in 1517 with his public debates. He was troubled by the abuses of the "indulgence sellers" (those trying to sell God's forgiveness).

Luther believed that the Word of God was the only authority to which sinful man could look to for redemption or for a clear declaration of God's will.

Today the hurch is in need of reform. Too many Christians don't know what the Word of God says. They can quote the words of their favorite evangelist but they can't quote Scripture. Only the Word of God is laced with power, authority and the ability to bring miracles into existence.

As believers our motto should be the Bible first, last and always. Paul tells us to test everything against the Word (1 Thessalonians 5:21). How can we truly test everything if we do not know the Scriptures?

Take time to study the Word of God—know for yourself what God has said. The Lord said His people perish because of lack of knowledge. Study the Word for yourself!

FURTHER READINGS
Deuteronomy 8:3-4
2 Timothy 2:15
Joshua 1:8

April 19

Sacred Only

"But you are a chosen people, a royal priesthood,
a holy nation, a people belonging to God, that
you may declare the praises of him who called
you out of darkness into his wonderful light."

—1 PETER 2:9

Martin Luther believed that the priesthood is for all believers and not just for the religious elite.

Many years ago, the church system gave priests sole authority as the people's only door to salvation, forgiveness for sins, access to the Word of God or to even be heard by God in prayer. Everything started and ended with priests.

Today, many Christians do not know that they are called to be priests unto God. They do not know that God's Word has established the matter, so they look to man to intercede and intervene on their behalf when they should look only to Christ.

Calvary provided access for all believers to come boldly to the throne of grace in our times of need. There is nothing that we have to pay or do in order to get forgiveness from God except to ask (1 John 1:9). It's that simple.

Remember you are part of God's royal priesthood—you have been made sacred to God.

FURTHER READINGS
Hebrews 4:16
1 Peter 2:5
Exodus 19:6

April 20

The Bible is the Answer

"For I am the Lord, your God, the Holy One of Israel, your Savior; I give Egypt for your ransom, Cush and Seba in your stead."

—ISAIAH 43:3

No matter what you are going through or what you are facing, the Bible has a solution for you. The Bible is truly the answer for every need you may have!

Do you need to know how to discipline your children? The Bible is the answer. Do you need to know how to save your marriage? The Bible is the answer. Do you need to know how to move on from past hurts? The Bible is the answer.

Why buy a library of self-help books when you can buy a Bible—and have a permanent, eternal, God-given and approved solution?

Jesus says in Luke 8:21, "My mother and brothers are those who hear God's word and put it into practice."

Jesus faced everything we face, and He knows what you need. Take up your Bible, believe what is written there and seek the Lord in faith.

Everything you need you will find in that divinely inspired book—God's Living Word—which is your substance for life.

FURTHER READING:
Luke 6:38
Malachi 3:10
Proverbs 22:6

April 21

Fruit of Disobedience

"'You must not eat from the tree of the knowledge of good and evil, for when you eat of it you will surely die.' The Lord God said, 'It is not good for the man to be alone. I will make a helper suitable for him.'"

—GENESIS 2:17-18

When sin entered the earth through Adam and Eve's disobedience, it produced fruit...fruit that all mankind has had to reap since—the fruit of disobedience.

What is the fruit of disobedience? It is death, decay, damnation and destruction.

Romans 6:23 tells us, "for wages of sin is death" and without Jesus this is all we can reap. But God in His love for us built a bridge that covered the gap created by sin between us and Himself. The bridge was born out of His love, built on His Word and fortified by the blood of Jesus—who is our salvation. This bridge gives us life now and eternally, and it is called the "gift of God" (Romans 6:23).

You can choose to live a life of disobedience, which will surely produce its fruit. Or you can choose to live a life of obedience, which will produce the fruit of the Spirit in you: "love, joy, peace, patience, kindness, goodness, faithfulness, gentleness and self-control" (Galatians 5:22-23).

FURTHER READING:
Genesis 2:17
Romans 6:23
Galatians 5:22-23

April 22

The Well of Deliverance

"The Spirit of the Lord is on me, because he has anointed me to preach good news to the poor. He has sent me to proclaim freedom for the prisoners and recovery of sight for the blind, to release the oppressed.

—LUKE 4:18

Are you tired of living in a dry place? Are you tired of the devil holding on to your supply? Then it is time for you to re-dig the well of deliverance.

God has given you power and authority in Jesus' name. You have the ability to get the devil out of your land. You can stop him from withholding your supplies and you can get the devil's dirt out of your well!

How? Apply the assurance of the cross (Isaiah 53:5). Christ was bruised for our iniquities. Because of this, you can be free from the debt of sin and its consequences, which is death. You have been given life—physical life, spiritual life, financial life, and abundant life.

You should not be bound in any area. Christ is full of life and that is what He has given to you. He has truly come to set every captive free. Re-dig your well of deliverance and start to live the life Christ purchased for you!

FURTHER READING:
Isaiah 61: 1-2
Isaiah 53:5
Luke 4:18

April 23

The Well of Faith

"And without faith it is impossible to please God, because anyone who comes to him must believe that he exists and that he rewards those who earnestly seek him."

—HEBREWS 11:6

Do you have faith that God is, and that He rewards those who seek Him? Do you believe in an infinite God? Do you just know about God or do you know Him personally...intimately?

What you believe will affect your ability to get your prayers answered. It will also determine if you can set the enemy to flight or if the devil will dictate your life.

Faith in God is the only way to receive from Him: "And without faith it is impossible to please God, because anyone who comes to him must believe that he exists and that he rewards those who earnestly seek him" (Hebrews 11:6).

Paul makes it clear that faith pleases God. If you have been doubting the reality of God...if you have been wondering if everything that is in the Bible is true...if you have been questioning "what if"—it is time for you to re-dig your well of faith.

Romans 10:17 says, "Consequently, faith comes from hearing the message, and the message is heard through the word of Christ." Get into the Word of God. Read aloud the words of Christ—and use them to re-dig your well of faith.

FURTHER READING:
Joshua 1:8
2 Corinthians 5:7
Galatians 3:2-3

April 24

God's Universe

"The heavens declare the glory of God; the skies proclaim the work of his hands."

—PSALMS 19:1

We may never understand all the wonders of creation, but we can certainly appreciate the world God has created for us. "By faith we understand that the universe was formed at God's command" (Hebrews 11:3).

We are told in the Bible that man has no excuse for not knowing God. Romans 1:20 says, "For since the creation of the world God's invisible qualities—his eternal power and divine nature—have been clearly seen, being understood from what has been made, so that men are without excuse."

What an amazing God we have—He made His glory known in every aspect of creation so even those who have never heard the Gospel message will know of His glory and splendor.

To know the full revelation of God we must know the person of Jesus Christ, who is known as the "radiance of God's glory."

God's work can be seen through the things He has made, but the most complete picture of who He is can be found in Christ Jesus. Thank God today for His amazing revelations and the saving grace of Christ Jesus.

FURTHER READING:
Hebrews 4:13
Revelation 3:14
Psalms 145:10-11

April 25

Lovingkindness

"This is what the Lord Almighty says: 'Administer true justice; show mercy and compassion to one another."

—ZECHARIAH 7:9

Karrion was five days old, and she was dying. She was born in the south of Sudan as her mother tried to return home from the violence in the north.

Though starving, Karrion refused her mother's breast and curled against her to die. One look at Karrion's tiny face and a decision was made—we could not lose this one. We made it in time, thank the Lord!

This time the story had a happy ending, but for thousands of others in violent, anti-Christian Sudan, the ending is not as joyous. Countless will starve to death unless the Church takes to heart its God-ordained role to be a source of help to a dying world.

Micah 6:8 admonishes: "And what does the Lord require of you? To act justly and to love mercy and to walk humbly with your God." We are to show mercy to those in need—those who are starving at the hands of an oppressive regime.

It is the role of the Church to care for the needy. In their pain, they cry out for help. I believe God's people will reach out to answer their cries on His behalf when no one else will.

FURTHER READING:
Psalms 34:17
Psalms 72:12
Proverbs 21:13

April 26

Work of Faith

"The righteous will live by faith."

—ROMANS 1:17

Your faith in God is essential to walking in righteousness because it is God who produces righteousness inside of you. You don't do it yourself.

Not only that, but you will never be more righteous than you are today. You are as righteous in the eyes of God as you will ever be, from your darkest hour to when you go to be with Him.

Why? Because you have already been made righteous by God in Christ.

When you get a consciousness of your righteousness established within you, then you truly begin to act out of God's holiness. 2 Corinthians 16:7 says, "Therefore come out from them and be separate, says the Lord. Touch no unclean thing, and I will receive you."

This kind of righteousness will change your world for Christ. Nothing feels better than when temptation knocks at your door and you allow His righteousness to rise up inside of you to enable you to refuse it.

Temptation just tucks its tail and goes down the sidewalk to someone else's house—all because of the resurrected righteous One who lives inside of you!

FURTHER READING:
Genesis 15
Hebrews 10
1 Peter 2:1-17

April 27

Be Bold

"We are not of those who shrink back and are destroyed,
but of those who believe and are saved."

—HEBREWS 10:38-39

As you cultivate faith in God in your heart, it changes the way you look at life. You think and act differently.

That is why I don't acknowledge the words "quit" or "defeat." God spiritually, surgically, extracted those words from my personal vocabulary. How can you be a failure when God is still on His throne?

How can you quit when you have the Word of God that cannot fail permeating your being? How can you be defeated when you have God's presence living inside of you?

That is why, since God said in His Word that I can lay hands on the sick and they will recover...I do it! Since He said I am the head and not the tail...I believe it! Since He said I am the righteousness of God in Christ...I act like it! Since He said by His stripes I am healed...I receive it! Since He said He makes me prosper...I believe Him for that, too!

Trust all of the promises of the Lord. Many people live in the shame of the past. You need to forget the things that are behind and press forward in His victory and power!

How can you fail when God is on the throne?

FURTHER READING:
Psalms 18
Philippians 4:4-13
Hebrews 11

April 28

Jesus Redeems

"But now, this is what the Lord says—he who created you, O Jacob, he who formed you, O Israel: 'Fear not, for I have redeemed you; I have summoned you by name; you are mine.'"

—ISAIAH 43:1

The dictionary defines redemption as "buying back or recovering by payment or actions, to make up for faults or deficiencies, to save from the consequences of sin." We are of this earth and therefore we are, by inheritance, sinful.

Jesus came to earth as a man who was subject to all the temptations we face every day, but He held steadfast. He said, "Away from me, Satan! For it is written: 'Worship the Lord your God, and serve him only'" (Matthew 4:10).

He redeemed us—bought us back from our sinful inheritance and saved us from the consequences of sin. 1 Peter 1:18-19 says, "For you know that it was not with perishable things such as silver or gold that you were redeemed from the empty way of life handed down to you from your forefathers, but with the precious blood of Christ, a lamb without blemish or defect."

It is only because he was without "blemish or defect" that Christ was able to defeat death once and for all. Have you thanked Him today for this amazing sacrifice?

FURTHER READING:
Revelation 5:9
1 Corinthians 1:30
Psalms 49:15

April 29

The Well of Healing

"My people are destroyed from lack of knowledge."

—HOSEA 4:6

Did you know that there is no area in your life that should be bound—not even your health?

Many Christians go through life bound in their bodies because they do not believe or apply the provisions of the cross.

They suffer needlessly when Christ already made provisions for their healing. They choose to pop a multitude of pills on the word of their doctor, but they dismiss the Word of God about healing. They don't believe the message that "by his wounds we are healed" (Isaiah 53:5).

God says "we are healed." Look at the tense—"are" is present tense...it is currently in effect!

All you need to do is to apply it. Apply your healing by faith. Re-dig your well of healing. Claim what has been dug for you at the well of Calvary. Do not let the devil fill your well with dirt, lies, innuendos or half-truths.

Malachi 4:2 says, "But for you who revere my name, the sun of righteousness will rise with healing in its wings."

Healing is yours! Re-dig your well now. Christ did it all for you—do not allow the devil to steal part of your birthright, which is healing for your physical body.

FURTHER READINGS
Romans 4:25
3 John 1:2
Philippians 4:19

April 30

White as Snow

*"'Come now, let us reason together,' says
the Lord. 'Though your sins are like scarlet,
they shall be as white as snow.'"*

—ISAIAH 1:18

Have you ever tried to remove red fruit juice or a dark stain from a white piece of clothing?

If it is not removed, the garment is forever discolored. You can try bleach, but it doesn't always work and can ruin some fabrics. You can try other methods but chances are you will not be able to restore the fabric to its original condition. That's what our lives are like when we live in sin and ignore the Spirit's guidance and become stained by sin.

Even a small spot ruins the material and leaves the garment unwearable. No matter how we look at it, the garment is stained. We are that garment, and God sent His only Son to wipe away the stains and make us clean once more.

God wiped away all our "stains" when He sent Christ Jesus to make us white as snow—new, clean "garments" for Him. The cross is the symbol of our eternal redemption.

Even though we don't deserve it, God chose to save us and wash us clean by the blood of Jesus Christ. He died because He loves us!

FURTHER READING:
2 Corinthians 5:17
Colossians 1 13:14
Psalms 103:12

May 1

With You and In You

"The Spirit of the Lord is in me..."

—LUKE 4:18

In His first sermon, we learn what Jesus' ministry was all about... and how He wants us to follow in His footsteps.

Jesus said, "The Spirit of the Lord is on me, because he has anointed me to preach good news to the poor...proclaim freedom for the prisoners and recovery of sight for the blind... release the oppressed...proclaim the favorable year of the Lord's favor" (Luke 4:18-19).

Here at the beginning of proclaiming the Good News and praying for healing, Jesus recognized the anointing of God was on His life. What was the source of that anointing? "The Spirit of the Lord is upon me."

You and I need to recognize when the Spirit is upon us— anointing us—to do His bidding. God's Spirit is in you, waiting to be released. "I will ask the Father, and he will give you another Counselor to be with you forever—the Spirit of truth...he lives with you and will be in you" (John 14:16-17). He left us a Counselor to guide us in this life.

That is why Jesus said, "Anyone who has faith in me will do what I have been doing. He will do even greater things than these" (John 14:12). Because we have been filled with the Holy Spirit, we can do anything in His name.

FURTHER READING:
John 14
John 16
Mark 13

May 2

Lend to the Lord

"He who is kind to the poor lends to the Lord, and he will reward him for what he has done."

—PROVERBS 19:17

"Charity giving is down. The economy is bad." That's what my accountants and business consultants were telling me.

They said we couldn't afford to do a mission trip to Guatemala, but as bad as the economy was here, we were still incredibly rich compared to the people in Guatemala.

We met Isabella when we rescued her dying baby. We found her living with her children in a shack with garbage bags for a roof and walls made of sticks tied together with rags. They drank filthy water and only owned a few old plastic containers, a cooking pot and clothes that were threadbare and worn.

How could we not go back to Guatemala? People were dying there for lack of food. Nearly half of the babies born in the rural areas of Guatemala were being raised by mothers so starved that they had little or no milk to feed their infants.

How could any of my needs be more important than that? God calls us to help the poor and the needy—He does not say "If you have the time or the money." He just calls us to go in faith. Follow His command today, for He rewards those who are faithful.

FURTHER READING:
Psalms 72:12
Isaiah 58:10
Matthew 6:19-21

May 3

Break the Yoke

"In that day their burden will be lifted...
the yoke will be broken"

—ISAIAH 10:27

The anointing is the supernatural manifestation of God's creative power which destroys every yoke, every bondage in any area of your life...physically, financially or spiritually.

The anointing opens blind eyes, straightens crippled limbs and puts homes back together.

The anointing of God destroys every yoke.

"You love righteousness and hate wickedness; therefore God, your God, has set you above your companions by anointing you with the oil of joy" (Psalms 45:7).

We must realize that this day will come only when we surrender to God's anointing—we cannot do this on our own. To come under this anointing, you must return to the sovereignty of God and declare Him the center of your life.

You need to realize that He alone has the power to set you free. "The Lord is God...there is no other" (1 Kings 8:60). You must have faith that there is nothing too difficult for God—no yoke of bondage can withstand His presence and power.

The anointing of God's presence is what will set you free as you seek Him.

FURTHER READING:
Isaiah 61
Acts 28:26-27
Matthew 13:53-58

May 4

Empty Yourself

"You will fill me with joy in your presence..."

—PSALMS 16:11

God has the power to meet you at your deepest point of need.

The key is creating an environment where your faith can contact God's presence to receive your answer. You need the manifest anointing of God for a breakthrough (Hebrews 1:9). To do this, you must bring yourself to a place—physically, emotionally and spiritually—where you want nothing else but God and His anointing in your life...and will settle for nothing else than His presence.

Like the stone water pots at the wedding of Cana, God is preparing to pour out something special in your midst. But first, you must empty yourself of everything else.

You must pour out your dreams, your hopes, your plans, your family, your future, your finances—so you can become an empty vessel for God to pour His anointing into.

When Jesus saw the six stone pots sitting at the wedding, he said, "Fill the jars with water"—and likewise, Jesus is saying to you and me, "Give me what you have...and I will transform you into a vessel full of my anointing!" Filling the jars with wine was the first sign in a series of miracles to come, proving that He was the Messiah, able to change lives with His anointing!

The anointing of God turns the ordinary into extraordinary!

FURTHER READING:
John 2
John 14:9-27
Acts 1:8

May 5

Do You Really Desire God?

*"Seek the Lord while he may be found;
call on him while he is near"*

—ISAIAH 55:6

Many Christians say that they long for a closer walk with God and that they desire to hear from Him. Yet each time they need answers or they have a problem they turn to friends, relatives, therapists or talk show hosts before they seek God.

Sometimes God does not even appear on the list. Yet the answers to their problems can be found at the throne of God.

Do you really desire God? Do you seek him daily? Do you commune with Him often? Do you meditate on His Word? Do you listen when He speaks?

The proof of desire is in the pursuit!

Luke 15:8-10 tells of a woman who lost a coin. She diligently searched for it—she had an earnest desire to find it. When she did find it, she called her neighbors to rejoice with her. She delighted in finding her lost coin.

As Christians we should have this same desire for the Lord. We should seek Him daily, continually, diligently...and as we do we should delight in Him, sharing our joy with friends and family—then God will give us the desires of our hearts (Psalms 37:4).

FURTHER READING:
Matthew 6:33
Matthew 13:44-46
Luke 5

May 6

A Vessel

"...be filled with the Spirit."

—EPHESIANS 5:18

You are a vessel—God's vessel—like a blood vessel in your body. Blood vessels do not produce blood. The marrow manufactures the blood and the vessels carry it.

In the same way, you don't produce the anointing—the anointing comes from the Holy Spirit inside you. You just carry the anointing to the places and people that need it most.

That is why you need a Spirit-led life. The energy to do the things of God flows out of the spiritual source within.

Jesus said, "Whoever believes in me...streams of living water will flow from within him" (John 7:38).

In yourself, you cannot produce the energy needed to work the things of God—that comes from God's Spirit. When you are given this energy, you must get rid of every bit you have by letting it flow out of you to a depraved and destitute humanity.

A clogged blood vessel is not a healthy vessel. It has to pour out its life source to stay healthy.

The same is true of you—you need to release the anointing inside you and spread it to everyone around you.

That is why the Bible said, "These signs will accompany those who believe" (Mark 16:17).

God wants you to keep your vessel open.

FURTHER READING:
John 7
1 Corinthians 3
Romans 8

May 7

A Tangible Thing

*"They will place their hands on sick people,
and they will get well."*

—MARK 16:18

Jesus laid His hands upon the sick and they were healed (Luke 4:40). The Apostles laid their hands on people to receive the Holy Spirit (Acts 8:17) and anointed people with oil for healing (Mark 6:13).

The anointing presence of the Holy Spirit is a tangible thing. You can touch it. You can feel it. You can pass it on.

This tangible attribute of the Holy Spirit's anointing is what allowed for Peter's shadow to fall upon the sick and they recovered (Acts 5:15-16) and for handkerchiefs to be carried from Paul's body to the sick, and diseases left (Acts 19:11-12).

It is what caused a woman who had hemorrhaged for 12 years—as she reached out and touched the fringe of Jesus' cloak—to receive the miracle-working power of God.

Jesus felt the anointing flow out from Him. In that instant, despite the past failure of every treatment, diagnosis and doctor who tried to apply fleshly cures, the woman was healed.

How? Because she believed—and received the tangible transfer of His powerful anointing to meet her at the point of her deepest need. Believe in Him and your need will be met.

FURTHER READING:
Matthew 8:1-16
Acts 3
Acts 9:1-19

May 8

Anointing of God

"Handkerchiefs and aprons that had touched him were taken to the sick, and their illnesses were cured and the evil spirits left them."

—ACTS 19:12

Once a Shunammite woman asked her husband if they could build a room for Elisha to stay in whenever he passed through town. During a visit, Elisha told the woman she would bear a son. Years later, the boy died and she laid the dead child upon Elisha's bed—she knew the anointing could be transferred from Elisha through the sheets.

Similarly, Smith Wigglesworth was staying in a home where the woman of the house was saved, but her husband was not.

When Brother Wigglesworth began to leave, the woman ran out of the house yelling, "You can't go! My husband isn't saved yet!" Brother Wigglesworth shouted over his shoulder, "Don't change the sheets!" That night, her husband was asleep and suddenly sprang from the bed screaming, "My God, I'm lost! Pray for me! I need to get saved! I can feel the flames of hell licking at my feet!"

If you need healing in your life or if a loved one is not saved, believe in the power of Jesus Christ. His anointing is transferable. Believe in the power of God and do what He directs!

FURTHER READING:
2 Kings 4:8-37
Acts 16
2 Timothy 1:1-7

May 9

Mother's Day

"Honor your father and mother, so that you may live long in the land the Lord your God is giving you."

—EXODUS 20:12

One of God's first commandments to the ancient Israelites was to "honor your father and mother." Mothers in the Bible have honored roles. Proverbs 31:28 says, "Her children arise and call her blessed; her husband also, and he praises her."

Motherhood has always been one of the most important roles in a society. Without mothers to birth, nurture, and love their children, we would not have future generations.

Psalms 139:13 says, "For you created my inmost being; you knit me together in my mother's womb." Mothers, for many years, stayed in the home. Those women were truly selfless, giving up their dreams and career goals to ensure that their children were loved and well-cared for.

The Bible contains many verses that extol the virtues of mothers: patience, love, mercy and kindness. Proverbs 14:1 says, "The wise woman builds her house, but with her own hands the foolish one tears hers down."

Thank God for your mother and for the life you now have. Proverbs 23:25 says, "May she who gave you birth rejoice!"

FURTHER READING:
1 Peter 3:4
Proverbs 11:16
Psalms 127:3

May 10

Wait for the Promise

"But those who hope in the Lord will renew their strength; they will soar on wings like eagles, they will run and not grow weary, they will walk and not be faint."

—ISAIAH 40:31

The first Pentecost took place almost 2,000 years ago after Jesus had ascended into heaven. Many of his followers returned home, dejected, but more than one hundred of them did not.

They gathered together to wait in Jerusalem for the promise of the Father.

Like the disciples, don't lose heart, because Pentecost is exactly what you need in your life right now.

When the promise of the Father, the Holy Spirit, came down in the form of a mighty rushing wind and tongues of fire, He changed a fearful group of believers into intrepid disciples of the Lord who changed the world with the good news of Christ.

God has promised that same power to you. He wants to fill you with His Spirit in order that you might fulfill His purpose for your life.

Like the disciples, you need to wait for the Promise. Hunger and thirst for it. Wait upon Him, and you will taste and see the goodness of God in your life.

FURTHER READING:
Psalms 27:13-14
Acts 1:3-5
Acts 2:1-3

May 11

Happy Birthday!

"But I have raised you up for this very purpose, that I might show you my power and that my name might be proclaimed in all the earth."

—EXODUS 9:16

Do you know that God has raised you up for a purpose? From the beginning He intended to use you to help build and advance the kingdom of God.

Jesus told the disciples God's plan to save the world through His death and resurrection...and He let them know that they were included in the plan. He promised that whoever acknowledges Him publically on earth, He will acknowledge them openly in heaven (Matthew 10:32).

Paul tells us in Romans 10:9 that if we confess with our mouths that Jesus is Lord and believe in our hearts that God raised Him from the dead, we will be saved. If you have made your confession...if you have believed with your heart...then you are saved!

The day that you accepted Christ as your Savior, God opened your eyes and understanding to the knowledge of Jesus Christ— that is when you were inducted into the family of God.

You were given a new birthday...you were born again...you were raised up...and you were clothed with power from on high.

FURTHER READING:
Romans 10
Luke 24:44-49
2 Corinthians 3:16-18

May 12

Pentecost Expectations

"Suddenly a sound like the blowing of a violent wind came from heaven and filled the whole house where they were sitting. They saw what seemed to be tongues of fire that separated and came to rest on each of them."

—ACTS 2:1-3

On the day of Pentecost the prophecies of John the Baptist and the Prophet Joel were fulfilled. God poured out His Spirit on men. He baptized them with the Holy Spirit and with fire.

Pentecost marked the fulfillment of the mission of salvation. It marked the powerful transforming work of God within His people. It symbolized the spiritual birth of the Church—and the enabling of her members.

Today God is doing the same thing. He desires to baptize His children with Holy Spirit and with fire. He wants to replace our ineffectiveness with power and ability.

Like the disciples, we need to believe God and expect to receive all that He has promised. Expect equipping, expect baptism, expect to be empowered, expect the fruits of the Spirit, expect to be holy, expect to be heard by God when you pray, expect to be taught by God, expect to be led, expect to have victory...and expect God to keep His word to you.

Pentecost was about expectations that were fulfilled.

FURTHER READING:
Acts 2:16-18
John 3:8
Matthew 3:11

May 13

Hunger for Pentecost

"I am going to send you what my Father has promised; but stay in the city until you have been clothed with power from on high."

—LUKE 24:49

Throughout history, there have been men and women who have hungered after the manifest presence of God in their lives. Smith Wigglesworth was such a man.

Wigglesworth understood Pentecost as few men have. He said, "If you only knew the unspeakably wonderful blessing of being filled with the Third Person of the Trinity, you would set aside everything to tarry for this infilling."

He took literally the apostle Paul's advice to the Ephesians to be constantly filled with the Holy Spirit. Ephesians 5:18 says, "Do not get drunk on wine, which leads to debauchery. Instead, be filled with the Spirit."

This infilling enabled Wigglesworth to be used powerfully by God to bring about years of revival. Each day was Pentecost for him—God's Holy Spirit coming down to empower him.

Let the Holy Spirit empower you. God did not send the Holy Spirit exclusively for one man or only for Jesus' disciples. He was sent for every believer who thirsts and hungers for the presence of God to be manifested.

FURTHER READING:
Luke 11:9-13
Acts 1:8
Ephesians 5:18

May 14

Significance of Pentecost

"Three times you are to celebrate a festival to me...Three times a year all the men are to appear before the Sovereign Lord."

—EXODUS 23:14,17

Do you know the significance of Pentecost? Pentecost was the turning point in world history. It occurred on the 50th day after the Jewish Passover, which marked Israel's physical emancipation from Egyptian slavery and the end of the harvest season.

It was the fulfillment of God's plan and the beginning of a new age—the age of grace. It was the establishment of the Church of Christ and it was the fulfillment of God's Word.

What really happened on that day?

The Holy Spirit came to fulfill the mission of salvation (John 14: 16-17, 26; 15: 26). The disciples were baptized in the Holy Spirit and fire as John the Baptist prophesied in Luke 3:16.

They experienced a supernatural enabling. The Holy Spirit imparted spiritual fruits to each of them. They were filled with a spirit of boldness and a strong undeniable love for God.

As you celebrate Pentecost, rejoice in all that God has provided for you—power, authority, boldness and grace.

Expect great and mighty things from God...for that is the blessing that Pentecost brings.

FURTHER READING:
Exodus 19:1-8
Joel 2:15-29
John 7:37-39

May 15

Supernatural Resource

"'Not by might nor by power, but by my Spirit,'
says the Lord Almighty."

—ZECHARIAH 4:6

This life has been likened to a boxing match. There are a few moments when we can sit down and rest, but for the most part, we're engaged in conflict.

In this life, we are constantly being confronted by challenges, but we can hope, for we all have access to the power of the Holy Spirit who resides in each one of us.

On the Day of Pentecost, the Spirit of God was suddenly poured out upon the expectant disciples of Jesus. On that day, they were catapulted from ordinary to extraordinary, from the natural to the supernatural.

Whatever your need, know that God has already made provision. Ask His Spirit to guide you. Power is available to you for every circumstance you face through the indwelling of the Holy Spirit. You are able to do all things through the power of the Holy Spirit at work within you.

John 14:26 says, "But the Counselor, the Holy Spirit, whom the Father will send in my name, will teach you all things and will remind you of everything I have said to you."

Rely on the power of the Spirit and you will see victory.

FURTHER READING:
Isaiah 44:2-4
John 14:15-20
John 14:25-27

May 16

Process of Pentecost

"From wherever you live, bring two loaves made of two-tenths of an ephah of fine flour, baked with yeast, as a wave offering of firstfruits to the Lord."

—LEVITICUS 23:17

What is the process of Pentecost? To properly understand Pentecost you have to know the significance of Passover.

During the Passover season God commanded the Israelites to bake two loaves without leaven. Leaven was symbolic of sin and the two loaves represented sinful mankind, both Jew and Gentile (Romans 3:9-10). God wanted them to purge themselves of sin and be a holy nation.

The Pentecost bread, unlike the Passover bread, was made with yeast. It symbolized the replacement of sin with righteousness and truth, which is the work of God in us (1 Corinthians 5:7-8). God is calling us to a place of holiness and purity.

How is this accomplished?

First, we need to recognize that God has us in the world but we are not of the world. Second, we are to give ourselves to the purging process, which gets the leaven out. Third, we are to allow God to fill our vacant areas with the fruit of God—truth, sincerity, peace and love. Lastly, we are to give our lives as offerings before God.

FURTHER READING:
Leviticus 23:1-44
Exodus 34:18-22
Acts 2:1-4

May 17

Spirit Within

"And I will ask the Father, and he will give you another Counselor to be with you forever—the Spirit of truth."

—JOHN 14:16-17

In John 14, Jesus reveals God's plan to send His Spirit. Jesus called this Helper "the Promise of the Father" and He is to be with us forever. Our Counselor is God Himself and He dwells inside of us. He's come to guide us through every situation and every struggle we face.

Do you grasp how awesome this is? Holy men of old longed for this, yet you and I are blessed to have the very presence of God living inside of us!

Matthew 13:17 says, "For I tell you the truth, many prophets and righteous men longed to see what you see but did not see it, and to hear what you hear but did not hear it."

The Holy Spirit convicts us of sin, leads us in the paths of righteousness, teaches us how to pray the perfect prayer, gives us gifts, and produces fruit in our lives. He is our constant companion because He dwells within us.

God has stacked the deck in our favor—He wants us to overcome every hindrance and scheme that the enemy uses to keep us bound. He wants us to be free so much that He came to live within us to ensure that we live prosperous and abundant lives.

FURTHER READING:
John 14:18-20
Ephesians 5:18
Joel 2:23-29

May 18

Waiting

"I will not leave you as orphans; I will come to you."

—JOHN 14:18

How the disciples must have clung to what Jesus had told them.

There they were, their leader gone, most of their comrades gone too. They'd been given instructions to wait in Jerusalem for the promise of the Father.

The disciples must have been apprehensive, yet they waited. Is that where you are right now? Are you waiting for the promises of God to come true in your life and it seems to be taking forever?

Don't fear. He's about to make you a sign and a wonder. He's about to pour out His Spirit into your life that will make everything you've experienced until now fade away. Your heart may be broken, but if you'll just hold onto His promise, He's going to show up in a mighty manifestation of His glory with a miracle for you.

Know that you're not alone. Through the indwelling presence of the Holy Spirit given during Pentecost, you're never alone. On that Pentecost day, the disciples who'd been waiting alone in the city felt the power and the anointing in their lives as the Holy Spirit came down upon them.

Their lives were never the same after that. Those who wait on the Lord will be filled with His Spirit!

FURTHER READING:
Isaiah 30:18
Psalms 27:13-14
Luke 24:49

May 19

Desiring More

"Yet the Lord longs to be gracious to you; he rises to show you compassion. For the Lord is a God of justice. Blessed are all who wait for him!"

—ISAIAH 30:18

The disciples prayed and they waited in the days after Jesus departed. There was no other alternative for them—no way could they go back to life the way it had been before Christ.

Their prayers and their waiting reaped for them a marvelous reward in the person of the Holy Spirit.

Their lives had been changed by walking with Jesus and hearing His teachings, but now they were also changed by the infilling of the Spirit who was poured out on that Pentecost morning.

Do you hunger and thirst for more in your life? The Holy Spirit wants to anoint you with His power.

He longs to give you victory over the trials and circumstances in your life that beset you. Above all, He longs to have intimate fellowship with you.

So today, in this season of Pentecost, open up your heart and ask the Holy Spirit to inundate you with His presence. Fellowship with Him. Allow Him to guide you in all you do. Commune with Him daily—He will never leave you nor forsake you.

FURTHER READING:
Isaiah 44:3
John 16:14
2 Corinthians 13:14

May 20

Another Comforter

*"If you love me, you will obey what I command.
And I will ask the Father, and he will give you
another Counselor to be with you forever."*

—JOHN 14:15-16

The first time Jesus referred to the Holy Spirit was the night before He was betrayed. He said, "...the Holy Spirit, whom the Father will send in my name, will teach you all things and will remind you of everything I have said to you" (John 14:26).

Jesus did not leave the disciples alone without comfort—He promised to send another just like Him, one who would guide them. This other Helper, Jesus told the disciples, would be an abiding presence in their lives.

When the Holy Spirit was poured out upon them on Pentecost, their eyes were opened to the truth of what Jesus had told them that night around the Passover table.

To this day, the Spirit of Christ continues to be poured out, strengthening, counseling and ministering to those who believe.

A supernatural power and presence dwells in you and allows you to do everything Christ said you can do in His name.

He is a constant companion who will never leave you or forsake you but will bring direction and comfort to every situation of your life.

FURTHER READING:
John 14:18-21
Romans 8:9-11
Isaiah 11:2

May 21

Be Filled

"Therefore do not be foolish, but understand what the Lord's will is. Do not get drunk on wine, which leads to debauchery. Instead, be filled with the Spirit."

—EPHESIANS 5:17-18

If you have been born again in Christ, you can receive the baptism of the Holy Spirit. All you need to do is ask Him for His infilling. I have found there can be many refillings or fresh anointings of the Holy Spirit.

Smith Wigglesworth knew what it was to feel the fire of God burning in his bones—fire that caused him to preach the Gospel of Christ with boldness, fire that gave him the confidence to declare a thing and expect it to come to pass.

Set ablaze with the fire of the Holy Spirit, he impacted the world with the power of God and brought thousands to faith in Christ.

When we examine the life of the early church, we find that many believers also had a deeper, subsequent experience of the Holy Spirit. Such is the desire of the Father for every believer.

That is the reason to celebrate Pentecost. Just as the hearts of the apostles were set ablaze on that day, so He wants to set you aflame with His fire.

God will fill you to overflowing, as you ask Him in faith.

FURTHER READING:
1 Samuel 10:6-7
Nehemiah 9:19-20
John 7:37-39

May 22

The Fire of God

"Do not put out the Spirit's fire."

—1 THESSALONIANS 5:19

Are you on fire for God? Do you have a burning desire to share your testimony with people? Do you seek opportunities to share the gospel of Jesus with your friends, family, or acquaintances...or has your fire gone out?

Paul commands us in 1 Thessalonians 5:19 not to "put out the Spirit's fire." It is our job to keep the fires burning. We have the fire of God within us and we are to stir it up continually.

2 Timothy 1:6 says, "For this reason I remind you to fan into flame the gift of God, which is in you through the laying on of my hands."

Our lives should be ablaze testifying of God's ability to transform his people into the likeness of Christ.

With each act of obedience we fan the flame...with our generosity we fan the flame...when we tear down demonic strongholds we fan the flame...when we pray we fan the flame... when we spend time with God we fan the flame...and when we meditate on His Word we fan the flame.

During this Pentecost season remember to fan the flame that is within you—stir it up so that the world will know that you belong to God.

FURTHER READING:
Ephesians 4:30
1 Corinthians 2:12
2 Corinthians 13:14

May 23

Jesus Christ's Ministry

*"He said to them, 'This is what I told you while I
was still with you: Everything must be fulfilled
that is written about me in the Law of Moses,
the Prophets and the Psalms.'"*

—LUKE 24:44

When Jesus was with the Father in heaven, He was eternal, but in becoming a humble man, Jesus agreed to put aside all of His glory and power.

As you read the Gospel, you see that only after He was filled with the Holy Spirit during His baptism by John the Baptist at the River Jordan did Jesus begin His earthly ministry.

After Jesus emerged from His 40-day fast in the desert where He was tempted by the devil, He returned in the power of the Spirit: "Jesus returned to Galilee in the power of the Spirit, and news about him spread through the whole countryside" (Luke 4:14). Then He began His ministry.

He healed the sick, cast out demons and raised the dead back to life. His whole being was aflame with the power of God.

At the end of His earthly ministry, Jesus promised to endue us with this same power through the Holy Spirit.

This Holy Spirit power is sent to us to do the things Jesus did while He was on earth.

FURTHER READING:
Philippians 2:5-8
Luke 3:21-22
Acts 1:8

May 24

Living in Peace

"For God so loved the world that he gave his one and only Son, that whoever believes in him shall not perish but have eternal life."

—JOHN 3:16

In the village of Herrnhut, Germany, there is a church called the Moravian Meeting House. In the adjoining cemetery are the remains of Count Nikolous Ludwig von Zinzendorf.

Though his family wished him to become a diplomat, he loved the Lord and felt he was called to do God's work. He soon found it. A group of Moravian Christians nearby were being persecuted for believing in God. They approached Zinzendorf asking for help in founding a place for them to live in peace. Zinzendorf gave them land on his estate, established the village of Herrnhut and lead the people in their spiritual lives.

How many souls did Zinzendorf help lead to the Lord? Only God knows. More importantly, how many souls would have been lost had he chosen the way of the world, rather than to serve God?

What is the Lord leading you to do? Do not allow the ways of the world to draw you away from the path the Lord has set you on. Through Him you may accomplish great things for His kingdom. Follow Him and He will use you for a great purpose.

FURTHER READING:
1 Corinthians 1:30
1 Peter 3:18
Romans 5:8

May 25

Salvation

"I am the gate; whoever enters through me will be saved.
He will come in and go out, and find pasture."

—JOHN 10: 9

What is salvation and how can we receive it? Can we do good things and be assured of it? If we live a good life can we be part of it? If we try not to sin, are we going to receive it?

How can we be sure we are saved?

Salvation is attained only through the shed blood of Jesus Christ, who died on the cross to save mankind. Ephesians 2:8-9 says, "For it is by grace you have been saved, through faith—and this not from yourselves, it is the gift of God—not by works, so that no one can boast."

Isaac Watts wrote the hymn, *When I Survey the Wondrous Cross*. His lyrics say it all: "When I survey the wondrous cross, on which the Prince of Glory died, my richest gain I count but loss, and pour contempt on all my pride."

There is no way to salvation but through faith in Jesus Christ. It is by God's grace that we are saved and only by Him can we be redeemed from sin.

Romans 10:9 says, "That if you confess with your mouth, 'Jesus is Lord,' and believe in your heart that God raised him from the dead, you will be saved." Do you believe?

FURTHER READING:
John 14:6
Ephesians 1:13-14
1 Thessalonians 5: 9-10

May 26

God's Intent

"'Come now, let us reason together,' says the Lord. 'Though your sins are like scarlet, they shall be as white as snow; though they are red as crimson, they shall be like wool.'"

—ISAIAH 1:18

Are you reading this today because you have been born again, or are you still seeking the truth?

The saving grace of Jesus Christ is made possible only by His death and resurrection. Pray the sinner's prayer with me: "Father, I know I have broken your laws and my sins have separated me from you. I am truly sorry, and now I want to turn away from my past sinful life. Please forgive me, and help me avoid sinning again.

I believe that your son, Jesus Christ died for my sins, was resurrected from the dead, is alive, and hears my prayer. I invite Jesus to become the Lord of my life from this day forward. Please send your Holy Spirit to help me obey You, and to do Your will for the rest of my life. In Jesus' name, Amen."

Salvation is of the Lord alone, for He died on the cross to save us all from sin. He died so you could have eternal life with Him—and have a long and fulfilling life on the earth!

FURTHER READING:
1 Peter 1:8-9
Colossians 2:13-14
John 5:24

May 27

Sacrifice

"I have been crucified with Christ and I no longer live, but Christ lives in me. The life I live in the body, I live by faith in the Son of God, who loved me and gave himself for me."

—GALATIANS 2: 20

God loves us so much that He sent His son to die for us. There was and never will be a greater sacrifice than this.

Jesus didn't die because we deserved it, but because He loved each one of us so much that He was willing to sacrifice Himself on our behalf. Romans 5:8 says, "But God demonstrates his own love for us in this: While we were still sinners, Christ died for us."

Jesus Christ died on a cross so that you might have life and have it more abundantly (John 10:10). This was the ultimate sacrifice; someone dying so you might live.

The story of our salvation is made all the more powerful because it was a perfect man—God in human form—who died for the sins of us all.

Acts 4:12 says, "Salvation is found in no one else, for there is no other name under heaven given to men by which we must be saved." Only through the sacrifice of God's son are we saved and able to approach His presence.

FURTHER READING:
Romans 1:16
Romans 6:23
Romans 10: 9-13

May 28

Love Divine

"Jesus said to her, 'I am the resurrection and the life. He who believes in me will live, even though he dies.'"

—JOHN 11:25

Charles Wesley was one of the most prolific Christian hymn writers of all time.

It was said that he'd had the gift since childhood; that after he received Jesus as his Lord and Savior the words flowed freely from his pen. When we allow God to become the center of our lives, amazing things happen!

Exodus 15:2 says, "The Lord is my strength and my song; he has become my salvation. He is my God, and I will praise him, my father's God, and I will exalt him."

In one of Wesley's hymns, he expresses the sentiment of Exodus 15:2 and tells of the love of God for mankind.

The words of the hymn have a true holy feeling: "Love divine, all loves excelling, joy of heaven to earth come down! Fix in us Thy humble dwelling; all Thy faithful mercies crown. Jesus, Thou art all compassion, pure, unbounded love Thou art. Visit us with Thy salvation, enter every trembling heart."

Do you have a heart full of praise for the gift of love that is found in Jesus Christ? Give praise to Him today!

FURTHER READING:
Romans 10:9-13
John 14:1-3
1 Corinthians 1:30-31

May 29

Saved from Sin

"For Christ died for sins once for all, the righteous for the unrighteous, to bring you to God. He was put to death in the body but made alive by the Spirit."

—I PETER 3:18

The Bible says, "We have all sinned and fallen short of the Glory of God" (Romans 3:23) and "The wages of sin is death" (Romans 6:23).

If we believe the words of the Bible, we must be aware of the fact that we need cleansing and that we cannot do it ourselves. Salvation from our sins is only possible through the death and resurrection of Jesus Christ.

To accept this gift of salvation, we must believe that Jesus is the son of God and that he came to die for our sins. When we accept Him as our Lord and Savior, we need to repent and turn from our sinful ways to follow Him.

We are saved by grace, but we still need to honor the Lord with our lives. Turn away from the path of unrighteousness and allow His Spirit to guide you in all you do. In doing so, you will draw closer to God. "Seek the Lord while he may be found; call on him while he is near" (Isaiah 55:6).

Place Jesus at the center of your life today and every day. Your eternal salvation depends on it.

FURTHER READING:
Ephesians 2: 8-9
Titus 2:11-14
John 6:47

May 30

For Christ

*"Salvation is found in no one else, for there
is no other name under heaven given to men
by which we must be saved."*

—ACTS 4:12

George Williams was a godless young fellow...yet he found Jesus on the filthy, polluted streets of London, England.

In 1844 he was led by God to begin a program to win young men to Christ, which became known far and wide as the Young Men's Christian Association....the YMCA.

Walking home in Cleveland, Ohio, in 1868, Dr. Samuel Wolcott, the pastor of a Congregational church, was inspired to write a hymn titled, "Christ for the World We Sing," after attending a YMCA meeting.

It became one of the most famous hymns ever written. We never know how our actions will impact others, but God does. He can use anyone to effect change in the world and in the lives of those who have not heard His message.

Never doubt that God can work good through you. Philippians 2:12-13 says, "...Continue to work out your salvation with fear and trembling, for it is God who works in you to will and to act according to his good purpose." Open yourself to His guidance and He will use you in amazing ways!

FURTHER READING:
Acts 16:30-31
Philippians 2:12
Mark 16:16

May 31

All Things New

"Therefore, if anyone is in Christ, he is a new creation; the old has gone, the new has come!"

—2 CORINTHIANS 5:17

When you accept Christ as your Lord and Savior you become a new creature, just as the Scripture says. You feel like a different person, you act in a different manner than you did before and your thoughts are now turned Godward.

You have left your old self behind and embraced a new self in God. Ephesians 4:22 says, "You were taught, with regard to your former way of life, to put off your old self."

When we become one with Christ we need to examine what we are doing with our time. Don't hang onto the desires of the flesh or the sinful ways of the world.

Walk with those who also walk with Jesus. They will strengthen your faith and you will strengthen theirs.

We cannot say we believe God's message and still act like unsaved sinners. You have been made a new creation in Christ!

Hebrews 12:1 says, "Therefore, since we are surrounded by such a great cloud of witnesses, let us throw off everything that hinders and the sin that so easily entangles, and let us run with perseverance the race marked out for us." Throw off your old ways and embrace who Christ made you to be!

FURTHER READING:
1 Peter 3:18
John 3:36
John 4:13-14

June 1

The Well of Holiness

"For it is written: 'Be holy, because I am holy.'"

—1 PETER 1:16

As children of the most high God we are called to be holy because He is holy.

There is no middle ground. God did not tell us to try to be holy, make a resolution to be holy, or to strive to be holy. He issued a definitive command—"be holy." To abide in Him means to follow His command and make ourselves like Him.

God would never issue such a command if it were impossible for us to achieve it. There is only one way for us to be holy— and that is through the equipping of Holy Spirit: "'Not by might nor by power, but by my Spirit,' says the Lord Almighty" (Zechariah 4:6).

Are you willing to submit to the process of holiness? Are you willing to be refined by His holy fire? Are you willing for God to help you dispose of all the muck and mire that has filled your well of holiness?

Holiness has already been secured on the cross. God will be with you as you re-dig your well of holiness—He has already provided all that you need. The Lord Himself will surround you and watch over your life as you walk with Him.

FURTHER READING:
Hebrews 12:6
Malachi 3:2
Psalms 66:10

June 2

The Well of Prayer

"'It is written,' he said to them. 'My house
will be called a house of prayer...'"

—MATTHEW 21:13

Have you ever questioned why circumstances seem to be getting worse rather than better?

The answer can be found in your response. How do you respond to the attacks of the enemy? Do you complain, get frustrated, overwhelmed, disheartened, disillusioned or angry? Do you start to blame others, or do you take time to pray?

Do you pray when you have a need or when you want something from God? Are your prayers all about you?

It is time for you to re-dig your well of prayer. God allows times of adversity to strengthen us. He allows the devil to throw things at us to build our Christ-like character.

How you respond to the test is key. The devil will bombard you with distractions—financial woes, health concerns, fear and insecurity. He does not want you to become more like Christ.

God has provided fresh living water for you if you are willing to re-dig your well of prayer. Let God know you are ready to throw out worry, despair, anxiety and hopelessness.

When trouble comes, run to God in prayer, and receive the answers only He can provide.

FURTHER READING:
1 Thessalonians 5:17
2 Chronicles 7:14
Isaiah 65:24

June 3

Potter's Wheel

"So I went down to the potter's house, and I saw him working at the wheel... the clay was marred in his hands; so the potter formed it into another pot, shaping it as seemed best to him."

—JEREMIAH 18:3-4

When your thinking lines up with God's plan for your life, as Paul's did, all trials and hardships can turn out for good.

God is the Master Potter, and we must surrender to have Him shape us into the best vessel we can be. Often the shaping is painful; it's hard to give up control and allow God to form us. We can let go in faith, knowing that He knows best and he will never give us more than we can handle in life.

Paul is a good example of someone who readily yielded to the Potter's hand. He suffered many trials but still proclaimed, "I have learned the secret of being content in any and every situation, whether well fed or hungry, whether living in plenty or in want" (Philippians 4:12). He was on the Potter's wheel being transformed into the sovereign image of His Father each day.

On the Potter's wheel He will also give you the supernatural ability to grow, if you trust in His process.

Rejoice because God is forming you to be a vessel that honors God and carries His glory everywhere you go.

FURTHER READING:
Matthew 5
Acts 16:25
Jeremiah 18

June 4

Let God

"Therefore we do not lose heart. Though outwardly we are wasting away, yet inwardly we are being renewed day by day."

—2 CORINTHIANS 4:16

Quit taking situations into your own hands! Understand that you can't do it under your own power. You can never earn your own salvation. Give your fears to God and He will see you through. He longs for you to fellowship with Him in prayer.

Realize that it's not about you. Stop walking around in prideful self-pity about what you can't do. Get your mind on God, who sent His only son to save you.

When you try to do it yourself you actually shortcut the growth process. Learn the art of sweet surrender. Rest in the hope you have in Christ Jesus. He will give you strength to endure every trial so you are able to be a witness for Him.

2 Corinthians 4:11 says, "For we who are alive are always being given over to death for Jesus' sake, so that his life may be revealed in our mortal body."

Make this your prayer: "Here's my life, Lord! Here's the frailty of my human flesh. Here I am as filthy rags, poured out like a drink offering and broken bread. Lord, take my life and make it consecrated to You!"

FURTHER READING:
2 Corinthians 4
1 Corinthians 3:18-23
Isaiah 64

June 5

Growing Up

"No discipline seems pleasant at the time, but painful. Later on, however, it produces a harvest of righteousness and peace for those who have been trained by it."

—HEBREWS 12:11

God accepts us where we are and loves us too much to leave us there. Although it may be painful, He wants to refine us to remove all the impurities and make us the best we can be!

The Bible is full of God's people who were being refined.

Job was tested, and although he lost everything, he still clung to God and was eventually rewarded (Job 23:10-12).

Paul also endured many trials for the Gospel's sake...but look at the outcome! Millions may have been saved because of his letters to a handful of new churches.

Quitting is never an option for those enduring to the end. You have to follow the convictions and understandings of the Holy Spirit to gain wisdom.

Are you willing to let the battle form you or will you cower back when the world says, "You can't do that"? Will you stop witnessing when you are persecuted?

Mighty vessels of God are built in battles, forged in the fires of opposition and finished in the kiln of the Potter's fire as rock-solid examples of God's unfailing love.

FURTHER READING:
James 1:2-8
2 Corinthians 6:1-10
James 1

June 6

Giving

"Out of the most severe trial, their overflowing joy and their extreme poverty welled up in rich generosity. For I testify that they gave as much as they were able, and even beyond their ability."

—2 CORINTHIANS 8:2-3

A financial crisis is an opportune time to look at the difference between the world and the Church. It's a great time to prove that as children of the Most High, our finances do not depend on the world's economy, but on the economy of God.

We must show the devil that we are people of faith, not fear. In 2 Corinthians 8:1-5, Paul commends the churches of Macedonia for giving to the impoverished believers in Jerusalem.

Even though the Macedonians were poor as well, they pleaded with Paul for the privilege to give and they gave much more than they could afford. The greater the depth of their poverty, the greater was the abundance of their joy. Their poverty did not produce less giving but rather more!

Can we measure up to the exemplary pattern set for us by these stalwart Christians who gave out of their dedication to Christ and the joy of helping those in need? Will you have faith that the Lord will provide for you through His economy, rather than the world's?

FURTHER READING:
2 Corinthians 8:1-5
2 Corinthians 9:10
Luke 6:38

June 7

Zealous Servants

"I have fought the good fight, I have finished the race, I have kept the faith."

—2 TIMOTHY 4:7-8

Now that you have a Good Master, are you serving Him with zeal? When you fall down will you continue to get up?

Paul is the most obvious example of someone who served God with zeal regardless of the trials he endured.

He says, "Five times I received from the Jews the forty lashes minus one. Three times I was beaten with rods, once I was stoned, three times I was shipwrecked, I spent a night and a day in the open sea, I have been constantly on the move" (2 Corinthians 11:24-26).

Even though Paul faced constant danger, he still praised God and remained faithful to the end of his life.

The Bible says, "Whatever your hand finds to do, do it with all your might..." (Ecclesiastes 9:10).

God is looking for passionate people. God is a passionate God—a God of furious love; a radical God; a God that sent His only Son on a mission to save broken-down sinners like you and me.

God gave everything for the chance to gain you. What are you willing to give to gain Him?

FURTHER READING:
Ecclesiastes 9:10
Philippians 2:5-11
Matthew 26:31-35

June 8

Endurance

"We are hard pressed on every side, but not crushed; perplexed, but not in despair... We always carry around in our body the death of Jesus, so that the life of Jesus may also be revealed in our body."

—2 CORINTHIANS 4:8 & 10

The devil attacks at every point of perceived weakness, hoping to discourage us. He hopes that we will compromise, bend, yield, and stumble.

When God's people grow, Satan cowers. Satan tried to sift Peter in order to curb his spiritual growth.

Jesus explained, "Simon, Simon, Satan has asked to sift you as wheat. But I have prayed for you, Simon, that your faith may not fail. And when you have turned back, strengthen your brothers" (Luke 22:31-32).

Satan still believes that his sifting will destroy God's people even though time and time again our faith is refined by fire. When you resist the devil and his temptations, your faith will be even stronger than before.

When the heart of a devoted follower is committed in Christ, Satan has no power in that person's life.

You already have the victory—keep going through the hard times, knowing that He will strengthen you.

FURTHER READING:
Ephesians 6
2 Thessalonians 2:13-17
Luke 22

June 9

Deceit

"The great dragon was hurled down—that ancient serpent called the devil, or Satan, who leads the whole world astray. He was hurled to the earth, and his angels with him."

—REVELATION 12:9

Deceit is one of Satan's favorite weapons. He tried to deceive Peter during Jesus' trial. Satan caused Peter to be afraid for his own life and proclaim "I don't know the man!" (Matthew 26:69-75). Satan stirred up doubt in Peter's heart.

Satan attacks with lies and deceit. He plays on your fears. If the devil can sell you one lie, he will sell you a thousand. Peter calls him the "adversary" and he admonished the Church to be watchful: "Be self-controlled and alert. Your enemy the devil prowls around like a roaring lion looking for someone to devour" (1 Peter 5:8).

Peter told us to be sober and to "watch out" with a calm and collected spirit, remaining steadfast in Christ, knowing the devil is a prowler and will attack us when we are at our weakest.

On our own, we can never defeat the devil—but Christ already has. When we trust in Him and hold to His Word, the enemy cannot harm us! Be aware of the devil's strategy of deceit, and trust God to keep you on the right path.

FURTHER READING:
1 Peter 5:8-9
Acts 26:15-18
2 Thessalonians 2:5-12

June 10

Refined by Fire

"If you are ready to fall down and worship the image I made, very good. But if you do not worship it, you will be thrown immediately into a blazing furnace. Then what god will be able to rescue you from my hand?"

—DANIEL 3:15

"Open the furnace!" Nebuchadnezzar commanded. "Throw these troublemakers to their deaths for rebelling against my command. Let the world see what awaits any who refuse to bow to my honor!"

Then Nebuchadnezzar stood dumbstruck: Shadrach, Meshach, and Abednego were walking around untouched by the flames inside the furnace—and they were with a fourth brilliant figure! In the end, Nebuchadnezzar proclaimed, "No other god can save in this way" (Daniel 3:29).

These faithful men of God could have chosen to bow before an idol to save their own skin, but they had faith in the only true God and knew the right thing to do. It may not be easy to fight for what you know is right, but God will reward you for standing up in His name and refusing to yield to evil.

In the end, even Nebuchadnezzar stood in awe of the power of God! Stand fast in your faith, for He will rescue you and use your faith to proclaim His power and love.

FURTHER READING:
Daniel 3
Psalms 66:10
Isaiah 48:10

June 11

The Devil

"You intended to harm me, but God intended it for good to accomplish what is now being done, the saving of many lives."

—GENESIS 50:20

Even while the devil works his evil scheme, God works to bring good from it and further His kingdom.

Daniel was accused by Darius' counselors of breaking the king's decree and was thrown to the lions, but the mouths of the lions were shut—they couldn't harm him.

After Joseph was sold into slavery by his jealous brothers, he was faithful in Potiphar's home. He was only imprisoned because of a lie. Joseph kept an attitude of faith and he was eventually released and promoted as Pharaoh's right-hand man.

Both Daniel and Joseph knew that "in all things God works for the good of those who love him, who have been called according to his purpose" (Romans 8:28).

What a testimony we have of the commitment of these called-out, front-line warriors of God in the Scriptures. What is "good" to us may not always be what God has in mind. Unlike Daniel and Joseph, you may not understand the reason for the trials you are enduring, but trust that God is working His good and mighty plan.

FURTHER READING:
Genesis 39
Daniel 3
1 John 4:4

June 12

Prayer

"Elijah was a man just like us. He prayed earnestly that it would not rain, and it did not rain on the land for three and a half years. Again he prayed, and the heavens gave rain, and the earth produced its crops."

—JAMES 5:17-18

Prayer is the key to conforming ourselves to His image when the fires of life threaten to consume us. Only prayerful fellowship with God will always see us through and give us direction.

We are besieged daily by thoughts that try to sway us and situations that require God's wisdom to move in His ways.

Prayer is our lifeline. Elijah prayed and rain came; Moses prayed and the rock gushed water. Prayer has provided hundreds of people with miracles, even today! "Pray without ceasing," says 1 Thessalonians 5:17.

Jeremiah 33:3 says, "Call to me and I will answer you and tell you great and unsearchable things you do not know."

We serve a God who answers. Luke 11:9-10 says, "Ask and it will be given to you; seek and you will find; knock and the door will be opened to you. For everyone who asks receives; he who seeks finds; and to him who knocks, the door will be opened."

Go to Him in prayer today and seek to be like Him in all circumstances; believe that He will see you through all situations.

FURTHER READING:
Philippians 4:6-7
Isaiah 44:9-20
1 John 3:2

June 13

By Grace

"But when the kindness and love of God our Savior appeared, he saved us, not because of righteous things we had done, but because of his mercy."

—TITUS 3:4-7

I was in Appalachia recently, and in the midst of hundreds of people waiting in line to receive food for their families, one lady in particular was brought to my attention.

Not long ago, this woman had been involved in a detestable lifestyle. For years, her life spiraled out of control. She did unthinkable things—things too terrible for God to ever forgive...or so she thought. She eventually fled far from that lifestyle, but she confessed, "I don't see how God can forgive me."

There is no sin God's love cannot forgive and no sinner beyond His love. No matter what you have done, He loves you. Ephesians 2:4-5 says, "But because of his great love for us, God, who is rich in mercy, made us alive with Christ even when we were dead in transgressions—it is by grace you have been saved."

I prayed the sinner's prayer with that woman and she cried as she was overwhelmed by God's grace.

The world needs the timeless message of the Father's grace. If you know His grace, go out and share this amazing message with the world so the world might also know of His love.

FURTHER READING:
John 3:16
Romans 5:7-9
Ephesians 2:4-10

June 14

Receiving Your Miracle

"'Isn't this the carpenter? Isn't this Mary's son and the brother of James, Joseph, Judas and Simon? Aren't his sisters here with us?'" And they took offense at him."

—MARK 6:3

Why do some people receive their miracle and others do not when we serve a God for whom there is no partiality? It is by faith that people receive their miracles.

When Jesus traveled into Nazareth to bring salvation and healing to His hometown, few valued or believed His words of truth. They were amazed at His teaching and the reports of His works, but they were offended and rejected Him in their unbelief.

Jesus "could not do any miracles there, except lay his hands on a few sick people and heal them. And he was amazed at their lack of faith" (Mark 6:5-6).

Unbelief will stop the power of God. By faith the walls of Jericho fell down. The faith of men like David and Samuel subdued kingdoms, worked righteousness, obtained promises, stopped the mouths of lions and escaped the edge of the sword.

These things happened only by faith in God. He can do mighty miracles if we only have faith! Believe God for your miracle.

FURTHER READING:
Mark 6
Hebrews 11
Matthew 17:19-21

June 15

A Deal

"Again, the devil took him to a very high mountain and showed him all the kingdoms of the world and their splendor. 'All this I will give you,' he said, 'if you will bow down and worship me.'"

—MATTHEW 4:8-9

We're currently on a journey to God's spiritual Promised Land—Christ's earthly millennial reign and eternity beyond. While you are traveling, Satan will try to block your passage and keep you enslaved in Pharaoh's land.

The devil even tried to tempt Jesus—the God of the universe! Matthew 4 says, "The tempter came to him and said, 'If you are the Son of God, tell these stones to become bread.'"

Beware of the devil's modern lies. If he can't block passage into the Promised Land of the church, he will entice God's blood-washed family with a little religious sophistication that sounds like this: "You can worship God and live in Egypt. What's wrong with overcharging your customers in business? What's wrong with sensual music and entertainment? It's only a little fun." Before you know it, you've opened the door to sin.

Satan's words are all lies. Truth comes from God alone. Do what Jesus did and answer every one of Satan's lies with the Word of God: "It is written!"

FURTHER READING:
Matthew 4
John 10
Ephesians 4:25-32

June 16

Poverty and Wealth

"To the man who pleases him, God gives wisdom, knowledge and happiness, but to the sinner he gives the task of gathering and storing up wealth to hand it over to the one who pleases God. This too is meaningless, a chasing after the wind."

—ECCLESIASTES 2:26

I believe that in the day before eternity there is going to be a supernatural transfer of wealth which will literally finance the preaching of the Gospel to the ends of the earth.

However, when a preacher mentions money, many Christians clutch their wallets as though someone was going to take something away from them. As a result, many preachers never talk about money from their pulpits, and the truth about money and material things is never heard.

There are multitudes in the body of Christ who embrace poverty and regard it as a blessing. Why would anyone look at poverty as a blessing from the Lord, especially when the Bible makes it clear that God wants you to have more than enough?

The Bible says, "Give, and it will be given to you. A good measure, pressed down, shaken together and running over, will be poured into your lap. For with the measure you use, it will be measured to you" (Luke 6:38). He will always give back to you!

FURTHER READING:
Deuteronomy 8:18
John 8:12
3 John 2

June 17

Walk the Land

*"Go, walk through the length and breadth
of the land, for I am giving it to you."*

—GENESIS 13:17.

God told Abram to walk the land in every direction and to explore the new possessions God was giving him. Abram had to walk in faith believing that God was going to give him every place that his "feet of faith" walked.

And the same is true for you. Are there areas in your life that you need to have under your dominion—your family, your marriage, your job, your community?

Then take time to walk the land. Walk the land of your home, your block, your job, your mind—wherever it is that you want to possess—walk it in faith!

Deuteronomy 5:33 says, "Walk in all the way that the Lord your God has commanded you, so that you may live and prosper and prolong your days in the land that you will possess."

After Abram walked the land to possess it, he sowed seeds to possess it. Sow your seeds of faith so you can possess your land. If your seed is learning how to cast your cares on God, sow it. If your seed is learning to trust God even when things don't make sense, sow trust in God. Are you willing to walk the land? Are you willing to sow your seed?

FURTHER READING:
Numbers 13:16-25
Galatians 3:16
Genesis 12:2

June 18

Good Fruit

"He is like a tree planted by streams of water, which yields its fruit in season and whose leaf does not wither. Whatever he does prospers."

—PSALMS 1:3

Not everyone who calls him or herself a Christian is totally surrendered to Christ. Just like a fruitful tree that bears good fruit (Psalms 1:3), when you abide in Christ Jesus you can't help but bear fruit in your life.

Jesus said, "Every good tree bears good fruit, but a bad tree bears bad fruit... Thus, by their fruit you will recognize them" (Matthew 7:17 and 20).

What kind of fruit are you producing? Is your life full of praise for God and faithful devotion to His Word, or are you struggling with fear, anger or other sins? If it is the latter, you need to get planted in His Word. Jesus says all those who do not produce good fruit for His kingdom will be discarded.

Produce good fruit by spending more time in prayer with your heavenly Father. Joshua 1:8 says, "Do not let this Book of the Law depart from your mouth; meditate on it day and night, so that you may be careful to do everything written in it. Then you will be prosperous and successful." Plant yourself in Him today so you may produce fruit for His kingdom!

FURTHER READING:
Romans 11:5
John 13:31-35
John 15:1-6

June 19

New Wine

*"Neither do men pour new wine into old wineskins.
If they do, the skins will burst, the wine will run out and
the wineskins will be ruined. No, they pour new wine
into new wineskins, and both are preserved."*

—MATTHEW 9:17

"Fill the pots with water!" He instructed. "Fill them to the brim! Every one of them!" Jesus continued, and as they did, the water changed color the second it left the water pitcher's lip.

"God of Abraham, Isaac, and Jacob," whispered the bridegroom's father to his equally intrigued wife. "Do you see what I see?" "Yes," responded his astonished wife. "The water turns to new wine to properly celebrate your children's day."

This first miracle of Jesus in John 2 showed God's sanctioning of marriage and also prophesied of the infilling joy of the Holy Spirit when we open ourselves to Him.

Are you a flexible new wineskin into which the Holy Spirit can pour His presence and power in these last days?

Are you soft clay under the Potter's hand, ready to be shaped and filled? He will not work within you unless you allow it.

Allow Him to shape you into a vessel worthy of His power. Through you, He will bring about miraculous events. Trust that He has only the best for you in mind.

FURTHER READING:
John 2
Ephesians 5:17-21
Psalms 95:8

June 20

Father's Day

"My son, do not despise the Lord's discipline and do not resent his rebuke, because the Lord disciplines those he loves, as a father the son he delights in."

—PROVERBS 3:11-12

Fathers should strive to emulate the qualities of our Father above—unconditional love, mercy and loving discipline.

The Lord instructs His children lovingly and disciplines them when necessary. Likewise, earthly fathers should seek to emulate Him. The Bible says, "The father of a righteous man has great joy; he who has a wise son delights in him" (Proverbs 23:24).

Fathers in the Bible are revered for their strength and kindness. Be the kind of father Proverbs 17:27 extols: "A man of knowledge uses words with restraint, and a man of understanding is even-tempered." If you do not have a father in your life, find a spiritual father who will mentor and guide you in the ways of God. Today, far too many children are growing up fatherless. How can they understand the love of the heavenly Father without having a model of an earthly father?

Thank God today for the fathers in your life...and remember to always thank your heavenly Father for His blessings, the only eternal Father. He loves you because you are His precious child.

FURTHER READING:
Psalms 103:13
Proverbs 17:24
Hebrews 12:7

June 21

Keep Watch

"Then he began to call down curses on himself and he swore to them, 'I don't know the man!' Immediately a rooster crowed. Then Peter remembered the word Jesus had spoken: 'Before the rooster crows, you will disown me three times.' And he went outside and wept bitterly."

—MATTHEW 26:74-75

Ever since the fall of man, the devil has been actively working to sow doubt and denial in the body of Christ.

The devil succeeded in his evil work in the Garden of Eden, tempting Adam and Eve and causing sin to enter the world: "Now the serpent was more crafty than any of the wild animals the Lord God had made. He said to the woman, 'Did God really say, "You must not eat from any tree in the garden"?'" (Genesis 3:1)

Satan succeeded again with Peter on the night of Jesus' betrayal—in Matthew 26:69-75, Peter disowned Jesus.

If it could happen to Peter, one of Jesus' faithful disciples, it could happen to anyone.

The devil will try to instill fear and doubt in whatever way he can. If he can get you to doubt the power and presence of Christ, he has succeeded in his evil work.

Do not give the devil the opportunity to sow these seeds. Rebuke him in the name of Jesus!

FURTHER READING:
Ezekiel 33
Matthew 3:1-3
Matthew 10:16-20

June 22

You Are Free!

*"Why are you downcast, O my soul? Why so
disturbed within me? Put your hope in God,
for I will yet praise him, my Savior and my God."*

—PSALMS 43:5

Regardless of what life has been throwing at you, take heart—
God is still with you! David experienced despair and
hopelessness, but he did not dwell there. Instead he chose
to put his hope in the Lord. He liberated his mind from the
attacks of the enemy and walked in the goodness of God.

Disappointments will come, but how you respond to them
will determine whether you live a life of freedom or slavery.
God is the God of hope; you have the power to shake off the
chains of despair in Him! "May the God of hope fill you with
all joy and peace as you trust in him, so that you may overflow
with hope by the power of the Holy Spirit" (Romans 15:13).

In God there is freedom, for where His spirit is there is
liberty (2 Corinthians 3:17). God is good—He works everything out for the good of them that love Him (Romans 8:28).

You are free, but you have to choose to accept it. You have
to choose to believe it. How you respond to the attacks of the
enemy and how you respond to the tests will determine if you
become bound or walk in divine freedom.

FURTHER READING:
Romans 15:13
2 Corinthians 3:17
Romans 8:28

June 23

Spiritual Midnight

"Later the others also came. 'Sir! Sir!' they said. 'Open the door for us!' But he replied, 'I tell you the truth, I don't know you.' Therefore keep watch, because you do not know the day or the hour."

—MATTHEW 25:11-13

It is approaching midnight. Are you prepared to receive your Bridegroom and His blessing or will you be caught sleeping?

A greeter stands shaking hands at the church door, and an usher sees people to their seats. One is ready, one is not.

A husband reads his devotional while a wife watches her favorite television program. One may be ready, one may not. This message is both a warning and a preparation.

In these last days, the end times, you must stay prepared to do the work of the Lord. The hours tumble toward the twelfth and final hour of midnight and toward eternal life beyond this world.

A rapture is coming, and all those abiding in Christ will be swept up to join Him. As a thief in the night, the Groom will return and find some waiting and ready, while others sleep (1 Thessalonians 5:2).

Will He find you alert and eagerly awaiting His return? Or will you be left behind? Keep watch and abide in Him.

FURTHER READING:
Matthew 4:17
Matthew 25:1-13
Mark 14:37-38

June 24

Reverse the Curse

"For if the many died by the trespass of the one man, how much more did God's grace and the gift that came by the grace of the one man, Jesus Christ, overflow to the many!"

—ROMANS 5:15

The curse of sin entered the world through the Garden of Eden. Because of Adam's sin, all of humanity fell and became doomed to sin and separation from God...but our Creator wasn't satisfied with that outcome—He loved His creation too much.

God sent another man, a perfect one, to reverse the curse of sin and break the bonds of death.

Followers of God once had to offer frequent sacrifices for their sin, but Jesus Christ came into the world to be the one and only sacrificial lamb, offered on the altar for the atonement of all humanity's sin. The curse of sin has been lifted from all of us. Once you accept Jesus Christ as your Savior, you are free from the bonds that used to hold you.

Remember, "having been justified by His grace, we might become heirs having the hope of eternal life" (Titus 3:7).

Praise God for Jesus' sacrifice. It is only through Him that the curse of sin was reversed. Thank Him today for the hope of eternal life with Him!

FURTHER READING:
John 1:16-17
Romans 5:15-7
Hebrews 8:6

June 25

No One Is Perfect

*"For it is by grace you have been saved, through faith—
and this is not from yourselves, it is the gift of God."*

—EPHESIANS 2:8

The laws God gave Moses for the Israelites made them aware of their sin, because no one was able to keep the law perfectly. Each and every person broke one law or another and they had to atone for it through sacrifices.

As hard as they tried to keep the law perfectly, no onecould.

Before Jesus Christ, God's people tried to achieve righteousness through their obedience to the law—by their works, what they could accomplish on their own.

Since Christ's death and resurrection, we no longer have to atone for our sins or be subject to the law. Jesus came so we might be made clean—washed of our sins. This gift is a gift of grace—there are no strings attached and we can do nothing to earn it. It is freely given to those who believe in Him.

Being a "good" person or trying to atone for sin won't save you. The only way to eternal life is through faith in the love and sacrifice of our Lord Jesus Christ.

We can be thankful today that the only perfect being came to die for each one of us because of His immense love. You don't have to be perfect—believe you are saved by grace through faith.

FURTHER READING:
Galatians 2:21
Galatians 5:4
Ephesians 2:1-13

June 26

Thorn in the Flesh

"He said to me, 'My grace is sufficient for you,
for my power is made perfect in weakness.'"

—2 CORINTHIANS 12:9

The apostle Paul struggled with something that continually bombarded him. Is there something in your life you've struggled with for some time?

Paul took his struggle to God in prayer and proclaims, "I know what it is to be in need, and I know what it is to have plenty. I have learned the secret of being content in any and every situation, whether well fed or hungry, whether living in plenty or in want. I can do everything through him who gives me strength" (Philippians 4:12-13).

God will always give us the strength to bear the trials in life. When those around you know your weaknesses and can still see God working through you, He is magnified even more through you. Human nature is such that if we had no problems, we would never turn to Him. How quickly we would forget that He is the source of our blessings and rejoice in ourselves.

God wants us to become more dependent on Him. It is only in the grace of God through the blood of Jesus that we can boast, for His strength is made perfect in our weaknesses. Depend on Him for all your strength today.

FURTHER READING:
Proverbs 3:34
1 Timothy 1:14
1 Peter 1:13

June 27

A Strength

"If there is a poor man among your brothers...do not be hardhearted or tightfisted toward your poor brother. Rather be openhanded and freely lend him whatever he needs."

—DEUTERONOMY 15:7-8

Chuck and Vicki and their two children lost everything they owned in a house fire. Vicki was nine months pregnant and her husband and their son were both dealing with serious health problems.

When they took their three children to move into a used trailer, they melted into tears. The sellers had stripped the trailer of everything.

The Church has an obligation to take care of the poor and the needy. The Bible is full of verses instructing us to help those who have nothing. Proverbs 28:27 says, "He who gives to the poor will lack nothing, but he who closes his eyes to them receives many curses." Jesus instructed also His followers to "love your neighbor as yourself" (Mark 12:30-31).

When you follow the commands of the Lord, you help to expand His kingdom here on earth. Chuck and Vicki know the love of God in a real and powerful way because the Church followed God's Word and helped them in their time of need.

FURTHER READING:
Job 30:25
Isaiah 25:4
Psalms 33:20-22

June 28

Your Mission

"If only I may finish the race and complete the task the Lord Jesus has given me—the task of testifying to the gospel of God's grace."

—ACTS 20:24

You have been given a mission from the Lord. Your time here on earth should not be wasted—you have been called by God to testify of His grace.

Your mission is to proclaim the words of Romans 5:8, "God demonstrates His own love for us in this: While we were still sinners, Christ died for us." Are you fulfilling your mission?

We have each received this calling on our lives. We have been given different tools to complete it and different regions in which to work, but we have all been charged to testify to the world about the grace of God. What has He saved you from?

Have you been testifying to your neighbors about His infinite mercy and grace? Jesus commanded every believer to evangelize (Matthew 28). God has given you salvation freely through faith in His Son Jesus Christ and wants you to share it.

Reach those around you with the message of His grace— He loved you so much that even while you were a sinner and scorned His love, He sent His only Son to die in your place.

Fulfill your mission by sharing the good news of His grace!

FURTHER READING:
Matthew 28:18-20
1 Corinthians 15:10
Hebrews 12:1-2

June 29

Grace for Your Day

"Let us then approach the throne of grace with confidence, so that we may receive mercy and find grace to help us in our time of need."

—HEBREWS 4:16

The Lord has given you work to do today—exemplifying His love to the world and sharing the news about His gift of salvation. Make sure that you give His tasks first priority in your life.

You may feel weary because of the number of items remaining on your to-do list, but remember God's grace is sufficient for you.

As you look at your list, ask the Holy Spirit to show you which tasks are God-given and which are self-inflicted. If there are some you need to cut out, get rid of them so that you will be more effective in the tasks that deserve higher priority.

If you need more strength to accomplish what you need to do, come before His throne of grace and ask for His strength.

1 Peter 5:7 says, "Cast all your anxiety on him because he cares for you." Ask for grace to help you complete your mission.

For "God is able to make all grace abound to you, so that in all things at all times, having all that you need, you will abound in every good work" (2 Corinthians 9:8).

Grace and strength are waiting at the foot of His throne.

FURTHER READING:
Job 4:3-4
Philippians 4:13
1 Corinthians 15:10

June 30

Watch Your Feet

"What then? Shall we sin because we are not under law but under grace? By no means!"

—ROMANS 6:15

Since your sins are forgiven and you have been justified and saved through faith, should you continue to sin so that God's grace will be ever more abundant in your life?

I say with Paul, "Certainly not!"

Do not view grace as a license to sin. Brothers and sisters, stay away from this dangerous view of the grace of God. You can't have one foot in the grave and one foot in heaven. If the blood of Jesus has washed you, you have died to sin—it has no hold on you.

Watch out, those of you who continue in sin because you know you'll be forgiven—you are on dangerous ground. Grace is not a free pass to sin and behave however we want.

God freely forgives us for our sins, but He will not remove the consequences of our actions when we willfully silence the Holy Spirit's admonitions to stay on the narrow path.

Your sin has negative repercussions for your health, relationships and ministry.

Do not be led astray by Satan's lies—keep your feet on the path of righteousness!

FURTHER READING:
Matthew 7:13
John 9:31
Romans 6

July 1

Sin Separates

"But your iniquities have separated you from your God; your sins have hidden his face from you, so that he will not hear."

—ISAIAH 59:2

Sin caused the first separation in the Garden of Eden and it will do the same today. Adam and Eve were no longer able to enjoy the close relationship they had with their Creator.

"The Lord God called to the man, 'Where are you?' He answered, 'I heard you in the garden, and I was afraid because I was naked; so I hid'" (Genesis 3:9-10). The same is true for us—sin puts up a wall. That is why God made provisions through Jesus, who covers every sin and every iniquity.

First Peter 2:24 says, "He himself bore our sins in his body on the tree, so that we might die to sins and live for righteousness; by his wounds you have been healed."

As we confess our sins to God, He is faithful to forgive us. The only sin that cannot be forgiven is the one that remains unconfessed.

God decided from the beginning that He did not want to live without you—so He made provisions for you—but He left it up to you to accept the fullness of His provisions. Will you?

FURTHER READING:
Isaiah 1:15
Hebrews 9:14
Isaiah 53:12

July 2

Your Power

"But the Israelites acted unfaithfully in regard to the devoted things; Achan son of Carmi, the son of Zimri, the son of Zerah, of the tribe of Judah, took some of them. So the Lord's anger burned against Israel."

—JOSHUA 7:1

Do you know that God has destined you for greatness? God has equipped you with power and authority on the earth, but your power can be short-circuited by sin.

The Israelites were given specific instructions by God not to take any of the items set aside for Jehovah—but Achan did it anyway. Because of his sin, Israel lost the battle at Ai.

The same could happen to us—victories that should be ours can quickly turn to defeats if we disobey God's instructions and hide our sins in our tents.

Because of Achan's sin, 36 men lost their lives, the children of Israel were chased by the Ai army, lost an easy victory, and they felt shame, confusion and despair (Joshua 7:5-6).

Achan's sin cost him even more...he and his family were all stoned along with his donkeys and sheep. His tent and all that he had was burned (Joshua 7:24-25).

Whatever is short-circuiting your power...your potential... it's time to get it out of your tent.

FURTHER READING:
1 John 1:9
Psalms 32:1-5
Romans 4:7-8

July 3

Get the Sin Out

"So Joshua sent messengers, and they ran to the tent, and there it was, hidden in his tent, with the silver underneath. They took the things from the tent, brought them to Joshua and all the Israelites and spread them out before the Lord."

—JOSHUA 7:22-23

What is hidden in your tent? Is it a love of money? Is it an addiction? Is it a love of yourself—selfishness, self-centeredness, self-absorption? Whatever it is, it is time to get the sin out!

When Joshua learned who was responsible for the defeat at Ai, he and the Israelites took decisive action. They did not rationalize or excuse Achan's sin, for God said that anyone guilty would be destroyed by fire (see Joshua 7:15).

We cannot counsel ourselves out of sinning, and we can't excuse, rationalize or reason our way out of the penalties of sin... the sin has to die. It has to be nailed to the cross and covered by the blood of Jesus. It has to come out—from the root. What is at the root of your sin?

Achan probably thought he could have what he wanted and still be close to God, but he lost his life and all his possessions. Look closely at your life today.

Ask God to show you what needs to be removed from your tent. Is the cost of holding on to the sin worth it?

FURTHER READING:
Joshua 7
Matthew 5:29-30
Mark 5:43-47

July 4

Be Separate

"Therefore come out from them and be separate, says the Lord. Touch no unclean thing, and I will receive you. I will be a Father to you, and you will be my sons and daughters, says the Lord Almighty."

—2 CORINTHIANS 6:17-18

Do you have idols in your tent? Things that you value more than God, like your opinion, your need to be right, your job, your children, your spouse? Anything that occupies the place that belongs to God is an idol.

The first commandment is to love the Lord our God with all our hearts (Matthew 22:37). The Lord tells us plainly in Exodus 20:4-5 that He is a jealous God and instructs us not to make graven images of anything on this earth.

He has made a way for you to purge yourself of your idols through the blood of Jesus. Through the blood, we can get in right relationship with God. Through the blood, we can have the right mindset—the mindset of Christ Jesus. Through the blood of Jesus, every bondage that takes our focus away from God can be broken.

We must separate ourselves from that which is not of God. We must get the ungodly things out of our lives and seek to get into a right relationship with God.

FURTHER READING:
Isaiah 52:11
2 Timothy 2:19
Isaiah 1:16

July 5

Come to Jesus

"Jesus said to her, "I am the resurrection and the life. He who believes in me will live, even though he dies."

—JOHN 11:25

Why did Jesus come? What was His purpose? He wanted you to really live...not just exist, but live an abundant life. He said, "The thief comes only to steal and kill and destroy; I have come that they may have life, and have it to the full" (John 10:10).

The question is, are you ready to live the abundant life He has for you? Are you ready for the joys and the blessing of being in relationship with God? Jesus was talking about living a life of authority so that, through His power, the captive can be freed, the lame healed and the blind given their sight.

Christ was given all authority—both in heaven and on earth. As believers in Him, He has given us authority to operate in His name—to heal, deliver and to set free. By believing in Him, we have accepted our role as His heirs.

Living is more then concentrating on "me" and "mine"; it is having the heart and character of Christ Jesus. It is reflecting who He is in all you do and devoting yourself to living the life He would have you live.

Have you really chosen to come to Jesus and live? Declare that your old nature is dead and come alive in Christ.

FURTHER READING:
Colossians 3:4
Colossians 5:10-12
John 1:4

July 6

Be Set Free

"You, however, are controlled not by the sinful nature but by the Spirit, if the Spirit of God lives in you. And if anyone does not have the Spirit of Christ, he does not belong to Christ."

—ROMANS 8:9-10

Are you the master of your own life? Does that position belong to Christ, yourself, or your sinful nature? If you are not sure... look at the fruit and examine your life.

Where the Spirit of the Lord is there is liberty (1 Corinthians 3:17) but where the devil is there is bondage.

Is your life spiraling out of control? Is your family in disarray? Is your marriage on the brink of destruction? Has your peace been replaced by worry, fear, doubt or anxiety?

If so then you are in bondage—and you need to break loose by emptying your tent of the things that do not belong in there.

Take authority over your life and all your situations by the power of Jesus and through the equipping of His Spirit.

If your taskmaster is anything other than God, let it know that your true Master is Jesus and that it is time for it to die.

Break the chains of bondage and be set free—after all, isn't that why Christ came?

FURTHER READING:
Galatians 4:6
John 14:17-18
Romans 8:15-16

July 7

Get the Lies Out

"...and you may be sure that your sin will find you out."

—NUMBERS 32:23

From the beginning, man has tried to hide his sins from God.

Adam and Eve did it in the Garden of Eden. Cain did it after slaying his brother Abel. Achan did it after he stole and disobeyed God's directions. David tried to cover up his adultery.

With each act of sin, there is a cover-up; a lie that is released to hide the truth. It is time to get the lies out. Sin does not disappear; it compounds. Our sins will always be found out.

When Adam chose to rebel against God, chaos was released into the cosmos. When Cain slew Abel, his blood cried out to God. When Achan sinned, 36 men died and Israel was defeated. When David committed adultery and tried to hide it, he became a murderer and lost his son.

All sins are seen by God. Don't think you can deceive Him.

Galatians 6:7 says, "Do not be deceived: God cannot be mocked. A man reaps what he sows." He is not waiting to punish you, but wants you to confess your sin to Him, repent and walk thereafter in His light.

In Psalms 51:9, David cried out to God after his adultery was revealed, saying, "Hide your face from my sins and blot out all my iniquity." There is only one way to deal with the sin problem—Jesus, the precious blood of Jesus.

FURTHER READING:
1 Corinthians 6:9
Galatians 6:4-5
2 Corinthians 13:5

July 8

Cast it Out

"But if we judged ourselves, we would not come under judgment."

—I CORINTHIANS II:3I

When was the last time you took a good look at yourself, your life and your standing with God?

Many Christians refuse to take a hard look at what they have hidden in the tents of their hearts. They prefer to live in denial or rationalize their sin. You cannot rationalize sin, reason with it or counsel it. After a while, it will take hold of you.

Genesis 4:7 says, "If you do what is right, will you not be accepted? But if you do not do what is right, sin is crouching at your door; it desires to have you, but you must master it."

If you are in bondage to alcohol, confess it before the Lord. If you are an adulterer or engaged in inappropriate behaviors, confess it before the Lord. Apply the blood of Jesus and claim what is yours—forgiveness of sin. Then bind that sin up and cast it out. It does not belong in your life!

Do not live like a slave when you are a son of God. Do not live in bondage when you are redeemed. You are not a captive—you have liberty because Christ himself has set you free.

Cast whatever binds you out today—and live the life that Christ paid for you to have.

FURTHER READING:
1 John 1:9
Hebrews 9:14
Psalms 32:1-5

July 9

Are You Rooted in Self?

"What good is it for a man to gain the whole world, and yet lose or forfeit his very self?"

—LUKE 9:25

Did you know that you can do very spiritual things that are still rooted in self?

You can sing in the choir, lifting up songs to God, but your motive could be to be seen by men. You can become a leader or go into ministry because you want to feel important. That is why God looks at the heart and He checks our motives (1 Samuel 16:7).

Wrong motives will not please God. We can fool men who look at the outward demonstrations...but God knows the truth and He will not be pleased.

Check your motives. Ask yourself if you need to be in charge. Do you need to have your opinion followed? Then ask yourself if it is about God. Will God be pleased?

The only way to be in the will of God and to have the mind of God is to go the way of the cross. Our motives should be to please God—not ourselves—to give Him pleasure.

We were created for His pleasure, according to Revelation 4:11. God is pleased with us when our motives are selfless instead of selfish.

FURTHER READING:
Matthew 10:39
Luke 14:27
John 12:25

July 10

Crucify Him

"Those who belong to Christ Jesus have crucified the sinful nature with its passions and desires."

—GALATIANS 5:24

Have you ever tried to break a bad habit by making a resolute decision that you would never do it again? Did you find that the more determined you were, the more you did the thing you planned not to do?

Have you tried counseling to kick the habit and found that you struggled more each day...that the addiction's hold on you did not seem to diminish?

The reason is simple: your old nature cannot be managed. It cannot be compromised with. It must die...it must be crucified on the cross! God makes no other provision. We don't need reformation—we need resurrection! Memorizing scripture will not rehabilitate you, and going to Sunday school will not change you. There is only one provision for you—the cross.

Romans 8:8 says, "Those controlled by the sinful nature cannot please God." There is no middle ground if you are determined to follow Christ. You must pick up your cross daily and follow Him (Luke 9:23).

Daily you should die to your old nature...daily it should be crucified and washed in the blood of the Lamb.

FURTHER READING:
Romans 6:6
Colossians 3:5
Luke 9:23

July 11

Truth Brings Freedom

*"If anyone comes to you and does not bring this teaching,
do not take him into your house or welcome him.
Anyone who welcomes him shares in his wicked work."*

—2 JOHN 1:10-11

There are many deceivers who have been released into the world—they do not confess Jesus Christ coming in the flesh.

They are deceivers and antichrists. First John 2:18 says, "Dear children, this is the last hour; and as you have heard that the antichrist is coming, even now many antichrists have come."

As believers, we should not bless their activities, because this will make us accomplices with them that work against God. These deceivers sow fruits of bondage—false doctrine, legalism, condemnation and curses. The fruits of the Spirit are love, joy, peace, patience, kindness, goodness, faithfulness, gentleness and self-control (Galatians 5:22-23). Anything else is bondage.

Speak the truth under the anointing of the resurrected Christ. Say what needs to be said no matter who is looking... no matter what they might think about it. Tell them, "You are deceived. You need deliverance. You need Jesus." Pray for their deliverance by the power of God.

How can you know the truth? By reading the Word of God (2 Timothy 2:15). The truth will set and keep you free!

FURTHER READING:
Galatians 5:22-23
Matthew 17:20
2 Corinthians 4:4

July 12

Read Your Bible

"Your word is a lamp to my feet and a light for my path."

—PSALMS 119:105

Life can get hectic at times. Things seem to blend into one another and before you realize it, a month has gone by and you have not spent time with the Lord.

The devil tries to get us sidetracked with things that are not as important as communing with God. Why does he do this? Because he knows that each time you pick up your Bible, you hold in your hands the answer to divorce, racism, poverty, sorrow, rebellion, demonic captivity and death.

He knows that if you understand what is written in that book you will walk with power and dominion and put his demons to flight.

It is easier for him to block or bind up your blessings when you do not know your Word, your rights or know God's provisions for you. But when you know what Christ provided for you...when you know what is contained in that life-giving book...when you know and walk in it, the devil not only gets mad but he gets scared.

Take time to read your Bible daily and turn the tables on your adversary—put him to flight.

FURTHER READING:
Joshua 1:8
Isaiah 55:6-7
2 Timothy 3:16-17

July 13

Bread in the Desert

"The Lord said to Moses, 'I have heard the grumbling of the Israelites. Tell them, "At twilight you will eat meat, and in the morning you will be filled with bread. Then you will know that I am the Lord your God."'"

—EXODUS 16:11-12

In the book of Exodus, after the Israelites escaped Egypt, they could no longer do the tasks they had done all their lives in slavery. They were on a journey to a new land and had to trust God to provide everything for them.

God not only gave them water in the desert but also provided manna for them—so much manna that the ground was completely covered! There was a catch, though—the Israelites had to gather it every day. They could not store it up for the next day, and those who did found it rotted. God wanted to transform the Israelites from being independent to being dependent on Him alone for their every need.

God does the same with us today. He makes a way out for everyone who trusts Him. Do you feel like you are still in the wilderness, still on the way to your promise? Do you feel lost sometimes, like God has abandoned you? Read the story of the Israelites and remember that God will never leave you or forsake you and He will be with you wherever you go.

FURTHER READING:
Joshua 1:9
Deuteronomy 31:6-8
Genesis 28:15

July 14

Hope for the Future

"Indeed, the very hairs of your head are all numbered. Don't be afraid; you are worth more than many sparrows."

—LUKE 12:7

Back in 1929, the collapse of the stock market led to the Great Depression. Fortunes were lost overnight and men roamed the country looking for work and food.

For those whose hope lay in men, despair was their only option. Those who trusted in God were able to see beyond their circumstances and were sustained by their faith.

In the twenty-first century, we are also experiencing an economic downturn and we also need to have confidence in the One who is greater than all of us. We need to cultivate faith and trust that God is in control of everything.

Matthew 6:26 says, "Look at the birds of the air, for they neither sow nor reap nor gather into barns; yet your heavenly Father feeds them. Are you not much more valuable than they?"

Even in times of economic distress, when the world is hopeless and depressed, we as Christians can rejoice, knowing that both our future and our treasure are with Christ in heaven.

If God is watching over even the tiniest sparrow, He certainly cares for each one of us. We know that He is in control.

FURTHER READING:
Job 1:6-22
2 Corinthians 4:7-9
Psalms 84:3

July 15

Parable of the Talents

"He told them, 'The secret of the kingdom of God has been given to you. But to those on the outside everything is said in parables.'"

—MARK 4:11

In times of financial difficulty, many ministries struggle financially. Donations go down, and people stop giving because tithing seems like an extraneous expense. They want to protect what they have.

In Matthew 25, Jesus told a parable about a master who divided up his goods among his servants. While he was away, several of his wiser servants traded and gained talents for the master, but one fearful servant buried his, afraid of losing it.

When the master returned, he became angry with the servant who did not even gain interest on the talent he was given.

Jesus said, "For everyone who has will be given more, and he will have an abundance; whoever does not have, even what he has will be taken from him."

There's a lesson here for us today. Sometimes we're reluctant to give, but God gives us every good thing we have and we must take care of it wisely if we want to reap His abundance.

It is hard not to want to hold on to what we have, but if we let go and trust God, He promises that He will give us more!

FURTHER READING:
Matthew 25:14-30
Mark 4:26
Matthew 25:1-13

July 16

What is Unseen

"Sell your possessions and give to the poor. Provide purses for yourselves that will not wear out, a treasure in heaven that will not be exhausted, where no thief comes near and no moth destroys."

—LUKE 12:33

In every culture around the world, there are varying levels of the importance of outward beauty. Clothes, jewelry, cars and technology somehow determine the worth of a person...in the eyes of the world.

God's Word says, "So we fix our eyes not on what is seen but on what is unseen. For what is seen is temporary, but what is unseen is eternal" (2 Corinthians 4:18).

Owning a car or a house isn't a bad thing, but we have to remember that houses and cars, like this earth, are temporary.

What we have will fade. Your house, your car, your clothes, your furniture, everything you possess in this world will soon be worth nothing.

We need to remember that our possessions will be useless to us after we die or after Christ returns. We also need to remember that our true treasure lies with Him in heaven.

These changes in natural things are why God tells us not to focus or put our trust in them. Put your trust in the things that are not seen; the eternal things.

FURTHER READING:
2 Corinthians 4:18
Isaiah 55:2
1 Timothy 6:10

July 17

God's Economy

"The rain came down and the streams rose and the winds blew and beat against that house: yet it did not fall, because it had its foundations on the rock."

—MATTHEW 7:25

In a time of worldwide financial difficulties, many people have become fearful and prone to anxiety and even panic.

God did not plan for us to live out our earthly lives in fear and trembling. Jesus said in John 10:10, "I have come that they may have life, and have it to the full."

Some have fallen away from God and have relied on their own devices. They have built their houses on sand.

Others who call themselves Christians do not attend church to fellowship with other believers. They do not witness to the glory of God and do not revere Him in all they do.

It is time for us to put God first in our lives and give Him our talents, thoughts, actions, money and time. We who trust in God know that although the world may change and crumble, God's Word and His promises remain forever. They are the rock on which we have built our futures and our hope, and they will not fail.

When we turn to Him, the very windows of heaven will open and we will be showered with abundant blessing.

FURTHER READING:
John 10:10
John 6:1-14
Matthew 7:7-12

July 18

Destined for More

"For we are God's workmanship, created in Christ Jesus to do good works, which God prepared in advance for us to do."

—EPHESIANS 2:10

I watched as three boys—no more than five years old—scrambled to catch containers smeared with garbage. One boy peeled back the cover of a container and took a gulp. He made a face—and then nodded to the others as if to say, "Not bad."

My stomach turned and I had to look away. Didn't they know our *Bridge of Hope* team was setting up a table just 100 yards away, where we would feed them healthy, satisfying food?

But they were used to living like this. This was what the world had for them...or so they thought.

Then I thought how true this was for so many of us as well—who are so accustomed to settling for less than God's best. We point to our lack, dismissing the reality that for our sakes Jesus became poor so that we might be made rich. Psalms 107:41 says, "But he lifted the needy out of their affliction and increased their families like flocks."

Those little boys had no way of knowing any better. Will we be like those children, fighting over scraps—or will we embrace His blessings and trust Him to help us experience a better life?

FURTHER READING:
Galatians 3:13
Isaiah 53:4-5
Ephesians 2:4-7

July 19

Destroy Unbelief

"You of little faith," he said, "why did you doubt?"

—MATTHEW 14:31

Doubt is when you say in your heart, "I wonder if it could be." All statements of doubt contain an element of questioning. A questioning person usually seeks the truth, wanting to know more.

A doubter is genuinely seeking the truth in a given situation and wondering if an answer really exists. When the answer is revealed to a doubter, because of the seeking nature of his heart, he will be open to accepting the truth.

Unbelief, however, is doubt that has gone to seed. It separates you from the miracle-working manifestation of God's power. Someone with unbelief is not open to investigating or looking further. He is convinced that what he knows is absolute truth, and there could never be any other answer.

Unbelief cancels out what faith can do and prevents God from working miracles and giving blessings. When Jesus came to His hometown, the Bible says, "He could not do any miracles there, except lay his hands on a few sick people and heal them. And he was amazed at their lack of faith" (Mark 6:5-6).

Creation itself declares the mighty works of God's hand, yet there are still those who do not believe. Truth is the key for diffusing unbelief. Take up His truth today to destroy unbelief.

FURTHER READING:
James 1:2-18
Ephesians 4:13-32
Matthew 14:22-36

July 20

Step in Faith

"Faith comes from hearing the message, and the message is heard through the word of Christ"

—ROMANS 10:17

After Jesus faced the unbelief of His hometown, "Jesus went around teaching from village to village" (Mark 6:6). Jesus knew that teaching the truth destroys unbelief. Faith comes from hearing...and hearing by the Word of God.

There's no question that in order for the true miracle working power of God to be released in your life, you must have faith. To step out in faith, you need to be instructed about God's Word surrounding the situation.

Here's why: faith comes by hearing. Hearing means receiving instruction. Instruction provides information. Information produces understanding. Understanding cultivates trust. Trust is faith...and faith in God can move mighty mountains! "I tell you the truth, if you have faith as small as a mustard seed, you can say to this mountain, 'Move from here to there' and it will move. Nothing will be impossible for you" (Matthew 17:20).

Faith begins with the Word—and the Word gives us instruction for every situation. "Your word is a lamp to my feet and a light for my path" (Psalms 119:105).

Use His divine instruction manual to live victoriously.

FURTHER READING:
Psalms 119
Romans 10:8-17
Mark 9:1-29

July 21

Instruction Empowers

*"Hold on to instruction, do not let it go;
guard it well, for it is your life"*

—PROVERBS 4:13

Not long ago, I asked a young man to stand at the edge of the platform at World Harvest Church and assist me in illustrating the truth of instruction. With his back to the congregation, I explained he would fall backwards without catching himself at all—and he wouldn't be hurt.

He started to sway and I yelled, "Not now!" Oftentimes, we get ourselves in trouble like this—because we have yet to receive all the information God has for us before we step out in faith.

I called for six men to stand, their arms interlocked, behind this young man. I looked the young man straight in the eyes and told him, "When you fall, these men are going to catch you. They will keep you from hurting yourself."

What I provided the young man with was instruction... instruction produced understanding...understanding gave the man trust...which led to a leap of faith. When the time was right, he fell safely in their arms. "For these commands are a lamp, this teaching is a light, and the corrections of discipline are the way to life" (Proverbs 6:23). Listen for God's instructions and take a leap of faith when He says "Go!"

FURTHER READING:
Psalms 19
Psalms 105
Proverbs 3

July 22

Double-Mindedness

"Yet he did not waver through unbelief regarding the promise of God, but was strengthened in his faith and gave glory to God"

—ROMANS 4:20

What are you expecting God to do in your life? Do you see God as bigger than the devil? He is! God can meet you at the point of your need today. Nothing is too hard for Jesus!

Your faith must come in line with God's Word. Don't say, "I wonder if it will happen." Instead say, "My God is able!"

The Bible says of a double-minded man, "He should not think he will receive anything from the Lord" (James 1:7).

Once, Dr. Lester Sumrall walked up to Smith Wigglesworth's house with a newspaper under his arm. When Smith Wigglesworth opened the door, he said, "What's that in your hand? Keep that outside!" Wigglesworth didn't allow anything in his house that could make him double-minded.

If you want to receive from the Lord, you must understand that the devil wants to destroy you. Jesus came to set you free.

John 10:10 says, "The thief comes only to steal and kill and destroy; I have come that they may have life, and have it to the full." Encourage your faith and discourage your doubts by keeping your mind fixed on what God's Word says.

FURTHER READING:
Ephesians 3
2 Kings 13:10-18
Revelation 2,3

July 23

Christ is in You

"Christ in you, the hope of glory"

—COLOSSIANS 1:27

Jesus Christ came for one purpose: To annihilate the works of the devil in your life! "The reason the Son of God appeared was to destroy the devil's work" (1 John 3:8).

When Jesus hung on the cross, He said, "It is finished." At that moment, He destroyed the work of the enemy for eternity. Now, get this...the One who holds the authority over all the power of the enemy lives inside of you.

Paul said, "Do you not know that your body is a temple of the Holy Spirit, who is in you, whom you have received from God? You are not your own" (1 Corinthians 6:19). You and I are walking "temples" of God!

The same manifested glory that was inside the holy of holies now resides in you. If God's presence is inside of you...so is His power to deliver you and set you free from every bondage!

Romans 8:17 says, "Now if we are children, then we are heirs—heirs of God and co-heirs with Christ, if indeed we share in his sufferings in order that we may also share in his glory."

Don't let Satan deceive you into believing a lie and accepting second best.

The key for receiving the miracle you need is to take your rightful place of authority in Christ and defy the devil.

FURTHER READING:
John 15
John 17
Acts 6

July 24

Trusting God's Power

*"So that your faith might not rest on men's wisdom,
but on God's power"*

—1 CORINTHIANS 2:5

Power is available to you—power to overcome disease, despair, failure, sickness and sin...over every attack of the devil!

Some people say miracles ended when the last disciple died. The truth is, Jesus defeated death with His resurrection and gave a tag-team hand-off to the Holy Spirit for you and me!

"I have given you authority to trample on snakes and scorpions and to overcome all the power of the enemy; nothing will harm you" (Luke 10:19).

This power will allow you to walk through the fire of this life and its flames will not burn you. You will pass through the flood and it shall not drown you (Isaiah 43:1-2).

This power overcomes all the work of the enemy. "Because the One who is in you is greater than the one who is in the world" (1 John 4:4).

When Christ came to defeat death, He made us His heirs. We were created in God's image, and through Christ, we now have the power to invoke His name and overcome evil. Take your place as His heir today.

FURTHER READING:
Jeremiah 9:23-24
Isaiah 43:1-13
Philippians 3

July 25

The Cheerful Giver

"Each man should give what he has decided in his heart to give, not reluctantly or under compulsion, for God loves a cheerful giver."

—2 CORINTHIANS 9:7

Another translation of 2 Corinthians 9:7 says God is not willing to do without a cheerful giver. When you give with the proper attitude, God will actually seek you out to keep you close to Him!

The cheerful giver gives in faith, assured that God will watch over him and provide for his needs. The cheerful giver gives in gratitude because of all that God has done in him and for him.

When we give to those less fortunate or spread the Gospel of Christ, not only are we laying up eternal treasures but we also receive the immeasurable joy of knowing the blessing our gift is to someone who doesn't have much.

When you think about it, it's actually curious that there's even a description of givers as being "cheerful" givers. Ephesians 2:4-5 says, "But because of his great love for us, God, who is rich in mercy, made us alive with Christ even when we were dead in transgressions—it is by grace you have been saved."

Having received so much of God's grace and mercy, shouldn't we all give cheerfully?

FURTHER READING:
Luke 6:38
Luke 3:10-11
Acts 4:32-35

July 26

Begin at the Cross

"But God chose the foolish things of the world to shame the wise... "

—1 CORINTHIANS 1:27

There is something special about the cross. It will forever stand as a beacon, calling us out of the world and setting us apart unto God.

It gives us the life-saving message: "Without the shedding of blood there is no forgiveness" (Hebrews 9:22). The only thing that allows us to pass from death to life—from the world into the kingdom of God—is the blood of Jesus Christ.

Paul said, "May I never boast except in the cross of our Lord Jesus Christ, through which the world has been crucified to me, and I to the world" (Galatians 6:14). This "setting apart" has challenged mankind for hundreds of years. Leviticus 20:26 says, "You are to be holy to me because I, the Lord, am holy, and I have set you apart from the nations to be my own."

If water baptism could wash away your sins, then the first day your mother put you in the bathtub, you would have been redeemed. Water cannot wash away sin.

Only the blood of Jesus makes you holy and set apart to God (see Hebrews 13:12). Begin at the cross today and thank Him for His sacrifice.

FURTHER READING:
1 Corinthians 1
Hebrews 9:11-28
Matthew 16:24-27

July 27

Sanctification

"Declare the praises of him who called you out of darkness into his wonderful light."

—1 PETER 2:9

To experience the fullness of God in your life, you must understand how "sanctification" works. God calls you to be set apart from the things of this world, and holy before the Lord.

First of all, sanctification is a positional reality.

God delivered you out of the kingdom of darkness and into the kingdom of light. "Now I command you to God and to the Word of his grace, which can build you up and give you an inheritance among all those who are sanctified..." (Acts 20:32).

He saved you. You are made separate and called to be His child because of His shed blood at Calvary. You are walking in the forgiveness and freedom already accomplished at the cross and you are holy because God declares you to be holy.

In the Old Testament, the Israelites were required to offer a lamb as atonement for their sins (see Leviticus 5:6). However, Jesus became the ultimate, solitary sacrifice—bruised, battered and beaten—so we could be set free forever.

Today, understand that by His blood, you have been cleansed and made a new creature in Him. You no longer have to atone or make sacrifices for your sin. He paid the price. Hallelujah!

FURTHER READING:
Exodus 12
Hebrews 10:1-25
1 Corinthians 6:9-20

July 28

Apart from the World

"Offer your bodies as living sacrifices, holy and pleasing to God—this is your spiritual act of worship"

—ROMANS 12:1

Once you realize the cross has sanctified you, then you are ready for experiential sanctification—where you grow daily in your walk with God.

This is the process where you shed the things of the world so you can experience more of God's presence.

It's the act of offering your body as a living sacrifice, as the first verse in Romans 12 instructs us to do.

How do we do this? Paul continues in Romans 12:2, "Do not conform any longer to the pattern of this world, but be transformed by the renewing of your mind." If we do not spend significant time considering God's Word, we will not be transformed by it. We cannot become salt and light in our communities when there is no difference between us and the world in how we spend our time and what shapes our views and values.

God's love is greater than you could ever comprehend and it is important for us to spend time in prayer, understanding His will for our lives. How wonderful that God has chosen to reveal Himself in a way that we can grow to understand Him more each day. That is what experiential sanctification is all about.

FURTHER READING:
Matthew 16:13-26
Romans 12
1 Corinthians 3

July 29

Greater Things

"Blessed are the pure in heart, for they will see God"

—MATTHEW 5:8

Why does God say to the Christian, "Come out from them and be separate" (2 Corinthians 6:17)? Because the more separate you become in Him, the more pure and powerful you will be for His kingdom.

Think about it...the purer the substance is, the more power it has. For instance, do you know the difference between crude oil and kerosene? Crude oil is purified to become kerosene...kerosene is refined to become gasoline. Gasoline is purer than kerosene, so it burns stronger and more effectively.

"Blessed are the pure in heart, for they will see God" (Matthew 5:8). The purer your heart becomes, the more of God you will see—and the more of God's presence will be seen in you.

God is better than you have ever been told...better than I have ever preached...better than anything written or sung...better than you have ever imagined.

Let us not waste our lives playing with sin, but invest in ushering in the kingdom of God.

First Corinthians 2:9 claims, "No eye has seen, nor ear has heard, no mind has conceived what God has prepared for those who love Him." Do you want to know more of Him today?

Set yourself apart and you will see greater things.

FURTHER READING:
Matthew 10
John 14:9-21
Galatians 5

July 30

A New Body

"I tell you a mystery: We will not all sleep,
but we will all be changed."

—1 CORINTHIANS 15:51

As you are probably aware, this world isn't all there is to life. One day, we are going to leave this world and go to a better one where there will be no more cancer, no more hospitals, no more graveyards, no more funerals, no more fear, no more sorrow... because the Lord shall wipe away all the tears from our eyes (Isaiah 65:19).

This is what it will be like in eternity. Your body will be sanctified and you will be separated from this world and delivered into another realm...His perfect realm.

This is what the apostle Paul was referring to when he said, "The creation waits in eager expectation for the sons of God to be revealed" (Romans 8:19).

You and I have not reached this level of ultimate sanctification yet...but one day we will. Paul said, "May God himself, the God of peace, sanctify you through and through. May your whole spirit, soul and body be kept blameless at the coming of our Lord Jesus Christ" (1 Thessalonians 5:23).

Be set apart from the world now, so you may wait in hopeful expectation for the renewal of your mind and body.

FURTHER READING:
Isaiah 65
1 Corinthians 15:35-58
Romans 8

July 31

Sovereign Lord

"That the name of Jesus every knee should bow, in heaven and on earth, and every tongue confess that Jesus Christ is Lord, to the glory of God the Father."

—PHILIPPIANS 2:10-11

In the kingdom of Light, God is the One who gives the orders. He is the Lord—we are His disciples. He is the Master—we are His servants. We are called to do only what He says to do and not what we think should be done!

In the last few years, a gospel of humanism has entered the Church. It says, "March up to the throne of heaven and tell Him, 'This is what the Bible says, and what I expect!'"—as if you have the right to tell God how you feel things should be and He is obligated to do whatever you desire.

Look how ridiculous this is...the people who believe this faulty gospel are unknowingly bowing at the altar of self-indulgence and saying it is God. We, on our own, cannot know the right course of action unless we have Him guiding us there.

The truth is: God is not dependent on us. You are the one dependent upon Him. He delivered you and chose you.

He is the Potter and you are the clay. It is up to us to say, "You are the Lord and I will obey You...I will bear Your mark. Mold me and shape me."

FURTHER READING:
Romans 6
Jeremiah 18:1-6
John 5:16-40

August 1

Enemy Territory

"The weapons we fight with are not the weapons of the world. On the contrary, they have divine power to demolish strongholds."

—2 CORINTHIANS 10:4

Christian writer C. S. Lewis said, "Enemy occupied territory— that is what the world is. Christianity is the story of how the rightful king has landed in disguise and is calling us all to take part in a great campaign of sabotage."

Bridge of Hope experiences this as we bring help to territories plagued with malnutrition, disease, poverty, slavery and all the other works of the devil.

We go in to sabotage the enemy's works and to break through his strongholds, not armed with weapons of mass destruction but with food and medicine, clothing and shelter, and most of all the good news of God's love. When Jesus came, He invaded Satan's kingdom with the kingdom of God, and that is what *Bridge of Hope* continues to do. It is our responsibility as Christians to enforce the victory that our rightful King has won.

Although most people can't dedicate their entire lives to going out and helping the poor, everyone can do their part to help those who do go out. In this way, we can all be part of the great work of saving lives for His kingdom.

FURTHER READING:
Exodus 15:6
Luke 10:19
Matthew 28:19

August 2

God's Battle

"I will exalt you, O Lord, for you lifted me out of the depths and did not let my enemies gloat over me."

—PSALMS 30:1

There are some battles you are not supposed to fight! Sometimes all you have to do is hand the battle over to God and trust Him. It does not matter what your enemies plot and scheme, God has you covered. He can turn all evil into good.

You might be facing a lawsuit, struggling with addictions or fighting cancerous cells that seek to destroy your body. The devil thinks he's got you this time—but God is not going to let him triumph over you.

First Samuel 17:47 says, "All those gathered here will know that it is not by sword or spear that the Lord saves; for the battle is the Lord's, and he will give all of you into our hands."

The next time you feel you are not going to make it, you need to get up and say to the devil out loud "I'm a fighter! You've picked the wrong person when you picked on me, devil, 'cause I'll run to the ark of safety. I'll run to the Rock that cannot fail. I'm not quitting, I'm not letting up, and I'm not giving up."

Even when you are down and out and things look hopeless from the world's perspective, remember this: victory is assured for this battle belongs to the Lord!

FURTHER READING:
Psalms 18
Psalms 42:11
Isaiah 10:27

August 3

Unfailing Help

"The Lord will keep you from all harm..."

—PSALMS 121:7

God's got you covered from all sides!

Today, make this passage your own. From this moment forward, regardless of what hell brings your way, you must never give in to the temptation of feeling that you are helpless. You have spent your last helpless moment.

If I can get this to become deposited deeply within the fertile soil of your human spirit, it will cause you to bear fruit even in the middle of your winter. Take your finger and make a circle.

Let that circle encompass everything in your life. Every relationship, every situation. Your situation at work. Your situation with your family, your future, your past, your present, your everything! God's got that circle covered and protected from every side!

Psalms 91:9-11 says, "If you make the Most High your dwelling—even the Lord, who is my refuge—then no harm will befall you, no disaster will come near your tent. For he will command his angels concerning you to guard you in all your ways."

Your help is completely wrapped up in the attributes of a sovereign God. His protection will never, ever cease.

FURTHER READING:
Isaiah 54:17
Joel 2:25-26
Psalms 46:1-2

August 4

Your Enemies Will Fear

"I come against you in the name of the Lord Almighty, the God of the armies of Israel, whom you have denied."

—1 SAMUEL 17:45

Stomp your feet a little bit and let the devil know you're not only born again, you're Spirit-filled. Let him know you're full of the Word of God.

Let him know that faith abides in your heart, that you really do believe that everything is possible for him who believes. Believe that you're blessed coming in and you're blessed going out.

You don't fight your battles like the people who are of this world. The world resorts to physical violence, backbiting, slander and maliciousness, but you fight in the name of Jesus Christ.

It is time for you to exercise the authority that is in the name of Christ. You can, because you are equipped with the name of the Most High God—demons will tremble, mountains will move and sickness will flee.

Second Chronicles 20:29 says, "The fear of God came upon all the kingdoms of the countries when they heard how the Lord had fought against the enemies of Israel."

When you call on the name of Jesus, heaven will back you up! Declare today that you are a winner in Jesus Christ's name.

FURTHER READING:
Philippians 3:9-11
James 4:7
2 Corinthians 10:4

August 5

Someone is Praying

"Because He always lives to intercede for them."

—HEBREWS 7:25

Someone is praying...and that someone is Jesus Christ himself. Do yourself a favor and read the verse above again. He intercedes for you! It is mind-boggling.

You don't need to be afraid about whether you are walking in the perfect will of God, whether you will make the right decision, find the right person or have enough faith to walk through the trials of this world.

Jesus is praying for you. Yes—when the storms get rough and the clouds get dark, Jesus is praying for you. When temptation comes and you are tried on every side, Jesus is praying for you.

He's praying for you right now. You may not feel like praising, but He's praying for you that you have strength to praise. He's praying for you to have the strength to encourage somebody tomorrow.

He's praying for you that you've the ability to speak a word to somebody who is weary. Have faith; don't worry about to-morrow. He will go to the Father on your behalf so you will prosper.

"Jesus himself stood among them and said to them, 'Peace be with you'" (Luke 24:36). You will overcome whatever it is that is confronting you right now—for Jesus is praying for you. Be of good courage!

FURTHER READING:
Hebrews 7:24-26
Romans 8
John 17

August 6

A Matter of Trust!

"Don't be afraid; just believe."

—MARK 5:36

In the book of Joshua, God told the children of Israel to march for seven days and then the walls of Jericho would fall down.

Why seven days? Because God was trying to tell the children of Israel that it is only when you come to the end of yourself, your strength and your abilities, will you see the hand of God move on your behalf.

Is that your case today? You have done everything you possibly can but you still have no breakthrough. That is good news!

Why? When you get to the end of yourself, when you understand that the doctor can't help you, and the lawyer doesn't have your answer, when your husband has walked out the door, and there's nothing in the cupboard to feed your children, you know at that moment your trembling hand is going to reach out for a hand that is bigger than yours.

Do just that today—reach out for his nail-scarred hands. Do not look at your circumstances and cave in!

Joshua 6:16 says, "The seventh time around, when the priests sounded the trumpet blast, Joshua commanded the people, 'Shout! For the Lord has given you the city!'"

Trust in the Lord and you will see things beyond what you could ever imagine!

FURTHER READING:
Psalms 23
Mark 5
Luke 8

August 7

Childlike Trust...

"As for God, His way is perfect..."

—2 SAMUEL 22:31

God's plan and purpose for your life is far bigger than what you have imagined.

You may not understand what He is up to or what He is doing with your life, but trust Him, for His way is perfect. "As for God, his way is perfect; the word of the Lord is flawless. He is a shield for all who take refuge in him" (Psalms 18:30).

God consistently wants to create a life for you that makes Him necessary. God will not create a life for you that makes you independent of Him.

If you are going to walk in God's plan for your life and live in victory, you're only going to do it by faith. Faith leans and faith trusts. Second Corinthians 5:7 says, "We live by faith, not by sight."

Will you trust God today? Worry and trust cannot reside together. Worry is a joy killer, time stealer and a health destroyer.

Trust opens you up, frees you and allows God to work within you. When you start to worry, you stop trusting God. One must give way to the other. As Matthew 6:27 wisely says, "Who of you by worrying can add a single hour to his life?"

I tell you today, put your trust in Him and you will come out victorious! There is no defeat in God's plan for your life!

FURTHER READING:
Proverbs 3:5-6
Psalms 37:23
Matthew 11:28

August 8

When Tempests Rage

"He stilled the storm to a whisper; the waves of the sea were hushed. They were glad when it grew calm, and he guided them to their desired haven."

—PSALMS 107:29-30

Hurricane Ike was the third most destructive hurricane ever to make landfall in the United States. Blamed for at least 195 deaths, it left damages totaling $32 billion in the United States, Cuba, the Bahamas, and elsewhere.

Even before Hurricane Ike roared into the Texas coast, our *Bridge of Hope* trucks were on the way. We knew the scene that awaited us. We took a step of faith and loaded our trucks with diapers, fresh food, clean water and more—life-giving, life-saving, basic supplies that are rare commodities in devastated areas. I'll never forget the woman who embraced me hours after Hurricane Katrina destroyed so much of New Orleans four years ago. She wept openly, "Pastor Parsley, I knew I could count on you to be the first one here to help."

This is what the Church is supposed to be known for—it is how we will win the world for Jesus. Job 29:16 says, "I was a father to the needy; I took up the case of the stranger."

God calls us to be there for others in times of trouble. Will you answer His call today?

FURTHER READING:
Isaiah 4:6
Isaiah 25:4
2 Samuel 22:3

August 9

Heavenly Protection

*"He will cover you with his feathers and
under his wings you will find refuge."*

—PSALMS 91:4

Every born-again believer has access to heavenly protection, but not all of them enjoy it.

Wouldn't you like to be in a place where you're protected, where sickness and discouragement cannot touch you, because you're resting in God's presence and power?

When God covers you, He puts insulation between you and the hand of your adversary.

First Kings 5:4 says, "But now the Lord my God has given me rest on every side, and there is no adversary or disaster." God is covering you to survive the perils of perilous times.

God will not only cover you, He will also bring you into a place in Him where the evil one can't touch you. Psalms 5:11 says, "But let all who take refuge in you be glad; let them ever sing for joy. Spread your protection over them, that those who love your name may rejoice in you." God is covering you so that you can survive anything and everything, if you just trust in Him and hold steadfast to His Word.

Rejoice—for you've got heavenly protection from all your earthly foes!

FURTHER READING:
Psalms 91
Psalms 92
Deuteronomy 1:30

August 10

Take Out "Defeat"

"The one who is in you is greater than the one who is in the world."

—1 JOHN 4:4

Quitters never win. That's true in any arena of life. Your marriage isn't over until you have given up. Evil overcomes when you have given up.

First Chronicles 28:20 says, "Be strong and courageous, and do the work. Do not be afraid or discouraged, for the Lord God, my God, is with you. He will not fail you or forsake you until all the work for the service of the temple of the Lord is finished." Don't quit, whatever the situation. Know that you have every resource you need within you to fight the fight of faith and win the challenge against adversity. Believe that the God who is all-powerful and all-knowing lives within you.

The challenge may be bigger than you, but it is not bigger than Him. The sickness may be stronger than you, but it is not stronger than Him. Your enemies may be smarter than you, but they are not smarter than Him.

In Psalms 41:11, David says, "I know that you are pleased with me, for my enemy does not triumph over me."

You are coming out of this one as a winner. Don't quit, for God's about to bring you out triumphantly!

FURTHER READING:
Isaiah 40:31
2 Corinthians 9:8
Philippians 1:6

August 11

The God of Breakthrough

"As waters break out, the Lord has broken out against my enemies before me."

—2 SAMUEL 5:20

Some of you are discouraged and fed up with standing and waiting in faith for your breakthrough. You say you have sown but not yet reaped, asked but not yet received, sought but have not yet found!

To everything there is a season and a time! This is the season for your breakthrough.

In Luke 5:1-8, Jesus tells the disciples to let down their nets. "When they had done so, they caught such a large number of fish that their nets began to break. So they signaled their partners in the other boat to come and help them, and they came and filled both boats so full that they began to sink."

The God of the breakthrough is about to visit you and give you a net-breaking, boat-sinking harvest that will make your jaw drop! God is bigger than we have ever imagined, bigger than what we have shouted and bigger than what we have dreamed.

He is about to give you that significant breakthrough you have been waiting for all this time. God is about to do exceedingly far above all that you could ever ask, think or even dream.

Trust Him and let down your net as He directs.

FURTHER READING:
Ecclesiastes 3
Proverbs 24:10
Luke 5:1-10

August 12

Never the Same!

"Call to me and I will answer you and tell you great and unsearchable things you do not know."

—JEREMIAH 33:3

We are living in a moment in time when the supernatural intervention of God is moving in an extraordinary manner into the ordinary affairs of people.

God Himself is moving into the arena of the ordinary with extraordinary demonstration of who He is. We are living in the final moment of human history. The dawning of a brand new day is upon us. God, in this hour, is doing a quick work.

God is getting ready to take you to a higher level. He is about to set something up for you. The next time you call upon the name of your God, be ready to gain new ideas and new concepts. He might take you to a new geographical location; He may give you a new business or give you favor to find a relationship that will bless you in every area of your life.

Second Chronicles 1:7 says, "That night God appeared to Solomon and said to him, 'Ask for whatever you want me to give you.'" Solomon was wise; he could have asked for riches or power but he asked for wisdom to better govern God's people. And God gave him wisdom but also blessed him because He sought the Lord in all he did. All you have to do is ask, and when you ask, expect to receive.

FURTHER READING:
Jeremiah 29
Ephesians 3:20
Matthew 18:19

August 13

Friends in High Places

"...There is a friend who sticks closer than a brother."

—PROVERBS 18:24

Mother Theresa once said that the most common disease in this world is not cancer or AIDS or heart disease. She said the most common disease was loneliness!

Do you feel alone, lost and forsaken?

So did the Psalmist David. He often cried out to the Lord for comfort. "Turn to me and be gracious to me, for I am lonely and afflicted" (Psalms 25:16). The Psalms are full of laments and cries to God...and God always responded.

God's taken note of the tears you've shed, the prayers you've prayed and the seed you've sown. You are not alone—you are never alone! God's going to help you get through this season of trials and loneliness. He is bringing you out stronger, better and wiser than you were before!

Knowing that He will prosper you and bring you out of your despair, adopt a spirit of thankfulness today.

As Philippians 1:19 says, "I will continue to rejoice, for I know that through your prayers and the help given by the Spirit of Jesus Christ, what has happened to me will turn out for my deliverance."

Know that whatever trials you face, you are never alone.

FURTHER READING:
Joshua 1:5
John 15:15
Leviticus 20:24

August 14

Set Apart From Evil

"What fellowship can light have with darkness?"

—2 CORINTHIANS 6:14

Draw a spiritual line. "Your enemy the devil prowls around like a roaring lion looking for someone to devour" (1 Peter 5:8). Notice this verse doesn't say "the devil is a roaring lion"...it says "he walks about as a roaring lion," which means he cannot find you if you stay out of his territory.

A lady came forward during one of Dr. Sumrall's services. She was a junior church teacher and was asking for deliverance. As Dr. Sumrall prayed, a man's voice came out of that little teacher's body and said, "I don't have to leave. She wants me here. She came on my territory. She gave me the right to be here!" The voice told how she went to an R-rated movie containing pornography and profanity. She became bound because she went into the devil's territory.

We must set ourselves apart from the world. The Bible says, "Anyone born of God does not continue to sin; the one who was born of God keeps him safe, and the evil one cannot harm him" (1 John 5:18). The Word of God also says, "It is shameful even to mention what the disobedient do in secret" (Ephesians 5:12)—and yet Christians have chosen to be entertained by these things. Turn to Him and ask Him to lead you in what is pure. He will not fail you, but will honor your request.

FURTHER READING:
1 Peter 5:5-11
James 4:6-10
Psalms 26

August 15

Go Therefore

"Therefore go and make disciples of all nations,
baptizing them in the name of the Father
and of the Son and of the Holy Spirit."

—MATTHEW 28:19

Jesus was kingdom-minded. He began His earthly ministry by announcing that the kingdom of God was at hand (Matthew 4:17), and He ended it by speaking of things pertaining to the kingdom (Acts 1:3).

The expansion of the kingdom of God was in Christ's heart when He commissioned His apostles to go forth to all the nations. From America to Africa and South America, we are to deliver the message of the kingdom of God. In the midst of poverty, starvation, misery and despair, we are to lift the curtain to another world marked by abundance, wellness, joy and peace.

As Christians, we all have a responsibility to extend God's rule over circumstances and situations on earth.

Through our prayers and our giving, we can traverse borders of time and space and impact destinies of people who otherwise would never have an opportunity to know God's love and good intentions toward them. God commissioned us all to go forth; if we cannot go forth, it is our duty to help those who do.

Will you lend a hand today?

FURTHER READING:
James 2:5
Acts 14:22
Habakkuk 2:14

August 16

The Pearl of Great Price

"Again, the kingdom of heaven is like a merchant looking for fine pearls. When he found one of great value, he went away and sold everything he had and bought it."

—MATTHEW 13:45-46

There is a children's book, *The Precious Pearl*, based on the verse above. In the story, a wealthy man sees a rare pearl in a shop.

Unfortunately, it costs more than the man has—he would have to sell everything to buy the beautiful pearl. He eventually sells everything, except his favorite hat with a floppy feather, and returns to the shop. When he still comes up short, the merchant says he will sell him the pearl if the man also forfeits his favorite hat. The man hands it over and receives the pearl.

Jesus said, "If you want to be perfect, go, sell your possessions and give to the poor, and you will have treasure in heaven. Then come, follow me" (Matthew 19:21).

Jesus is like the pearl. If we want to follow Him, we can't be stuck on the things of this world. Like the precious pearl, it costs everything to follow Jesus, but once we do, we realize He is worth more than anything else. Nothing this world offers will ever fulfill you as much as a relationship with Jesus Christ.

Will you give up everything, even your most treasured possession, to have that pearl?

FURTHER READING:
Matthew 19:16-24
2 Chronicles 1:11
Proverbs 28:11

August 17

The Harvest

*"The harvest is plentiful, but the workers are few:
ask the Lord of the harvest, therefore to send out
his workers into his harvest field."*

—LUKE 10:2

Time and time again, I have seen so many miracles, so many souls saved, so much harvest. Although we have reached millions of souls around the world through our many outreaches, we are one small part of the body of Christ.

Millions of souls still don't know the saving grace of Jesus. As Jesus said in Luke, the harvest is great but the workers in His field are few.

If every church building in America was filled to capacity and overflowing on Sunday morning, it would only account for 3% of America! God has given every believer the task of evangelism. We have a big job to do, and an even bigger God to help us do it.

The Church needs to rise up and reach out. We need to let go of our complacency, our pride, and our desire to remain in what is familiar. Jesus called us to make disciples of all nations, and that is what the Church in America, and churches all over the world, must do! We must make more disciples, find more workers, to reap an even bigger harvest for the Lord!

FURTHER READING:
Matthew 28:19
2 Corinthians 9:10
Revelation 14:15

August 18

Build on the Rock

"Therefore everyone who hears these words of mine and puts them into practice is like a wise man who built his house on the rock."

—MATTHEW 7:24

There was once a man who built a beautiful house on the ocean. One day a storm came. The water rushed up the beach and into the man's home, destroying the beautiful floors and walls. The house soon began to slide away into the ocean as the sand underneath it gave way. The man survived, but wondered how his seemingly sturdy home had fallen apart so easily.

There was another man who, like the first, built a beautiful house, but this man was wiser and knew the only place to build was on sturdy rock. When the storms came, the man watched the storm from the safety of his sturdy house.

The world will tell you that you have a secure future if you've saved enough or built enough success, but what do people do when tragedies happen, when the rains begin to come and the ocean threatens to wash away their homes? The Bible tells us to build treasure in heaven and build on God, who is "a refuge for the oppressed, a stronghold in times of trouble" (Psalms 9:9).

Jesus tells us to be like the wise man who built his house on solid rock. Trust in God and He will never let you down.

FURTHER READING:
Matthew 6:19-20
Revelation 21:4
Matthew 7:24-27

August 19

The Power of Prayer

"The prayer of a righteous man is powerful and effective."
—JAMES 5:16

Sometimes it is easy to think we can do it on our own, that if we are "good enough," the Lord will smile upon us. If we do enough good works, we will "earn" our way to heaven.

We forget that sometimes all we need to do is pray. The Psalms were all about prayer: "He will respond to the prayer of the destitute; he will not despise their plea" (Psalms 102:17).

Do you have a loved one who doesn't know God? Is your marriage falling apart or have you lost a family member? Pray about it! There is nothing God doesn't already know. He knows your deepest desires, your joys, pain, and hopes and He wants you to share those with Him.

Even Jesus needed to pray. Think about the night before He died: He went away to talk to God. He understood the need for that connection with God.

Prayer is more than just a conversation with God; it is the most powerful thing on this earth! When we pray, we allow God to work in our lives, and He fills us with His Holy Spirit.

Ephesians 6:18 reminds us, "And pray in the Spirit on all occasions with all kinds of prayers and requests. With this in mind, be alert and always keep on praying for all the saints."

Go to Him in prayer today.

FURTHER READING:
John 17
Luke 18
Luke 22:39-46

August 20

Hope for Tomorrow

"Through him you believe in God, who
raised him from the dead and glorified him,
and so your faith and hope are in God."

—1 PETER 1:21

I'm sure the disciples felt hopeless the day they watched Jesus die. I'm sure they wondered, "How can this be?"

They must have despaired as they watched His body being placed in the tomb. From an earthly perspective, it was hopeless (Matthew 27:57-61).

God is more powerful than the disciples ever imagined. Jesus came back to life, taking the most frightening of human experiences—death—and turning it inside out!

Scripture is full of hope. The Psalmist writes, "May integrity and uprightness protect me, because my hope is in you" (Psalms 25:21), and says again in Psalms 43:5, "Why are you downcast, O my soul? Why so disturbed within me? Put your hope in God, for I will yet praise him, my Savior and my God."

We are called to hope for a better future, for life in death and for miracles in an unbelieving world. Put your hope in Jesus, knowing that He has conquered death to bring you life.

What better hope can you have?

FURTHER READING:
Psalms 9:18
Ephesians 1:18
1 Thessalonians 1:3

August 21

Are You Wealthy?

"But remember the Lord your God, for it is he who gives you the ability to produce wealth."

—DEUTERONOMY 8:18

In a time of iPods, fancy new cars and designer clothes, when someone asks, "Are you wealthy?" it is easy to think of bank accounts and possessions. America is the richest country on the planet! You may say, "But I only make $32,000 a year," and I will reply, "Thank you for proving my point."

You make more than what 75% of the world makes! Look at your car sitting in the driveway with gasoline in the tank. Look at your bed and the pillow you lay your head upon. Look at the clothes you have, nicely ironed and freshly-washed. You have so much to be thankful for!

Thank God for your abundant wealth! Also remember this: no matter what you have or do not have, the Bible says our focus is to be on our heavenly treasure, rather than on what we have here on earth.

Jesus says, "Do not store up for yourselves treasures on earth, where moth and rust destroy, and where thieves break in and steal. But store up for yourselves treasures in heaven" (Matthew 6:19). Your wealth lies in an unseen place, with God.

If you trust in Him, you will be wealthy beyond all measure.

FURTHER READING:
Isaiah 45:2-3
Matthew 19:16-29
1 Timothy 6:17

August 22

The Dump

"He raises the poor from the dust and lifts the needy from the ash heap, he seats them with princes and has them inherit a throne of honor. For the foundations of the earth are the Lord's; upon them he has set the world."

—1 SAMUEL 2:8

I walked through the filth and decay of a garbage dump and watched three small boys scavenging through the dump trucks for anything to eat.

I thought, "Surely, God does not want His people living in a dump. He wants to lift them out and bring them to a higher place." I felt compassion for the young ones and their families who live there.

Then my mind went to all those others who are also living in dumps. Have you considered if you might be living in another kind of garbage dump? Perhaps you're living in a situation that is less than God's best for you. Maybe it is what is going on inside you...the secret sin that has turned your spiritual life into its own dump. Maybe you've even convinced yourself that a dump is all you deserve or that you'll never have anything better. Maybe you've lived there for so long you're used to it.

Know that God doesn't want you to stay there. Today He's offering you a better life. Are you ready to move?

FURTHER READING:
1 Samuel 2:9
Galatians 4:9
Galatians 5:1

August 23

Anointing

"But you will receive power when the Holy Spirit comes on you: and will be my witnesses in Jerusalem, and in all Judaea and Samaria, and to the ends of the earth."

—ACTS 1:8

At the beginning of my ministry, I told my little congregation, "Anything that is written in the book of Acts is not only possible, it is probable."

I went on to explain the new anointing on my life and said, "Anyone who's sick, come on up here because God wants to heal you!" I barely got those words out before they started running to the altar and when they reached the front two rows, they all fell over on top of each other under the anointing!

That was nearly three decades ago and, if I've learned anything in my years of miracle ministry, it's this: with God, all things are possible!

God's people have always had to move and step out boldly in faith. In the Old Testament, the Tabernacle could be easily moved from place to place at the direction of God.

God's desire was to speak to His people, but they first had to get positioned in the right place at the appointed time. They had to move to where they could hear from God Himself.

Will you step out in faith to receive God's anointing?

FURTHER READING:
Acts 2:1-6
Acts 3
Acts 11

August 24

Open Your Hand

"'Test me in this,' says the Lord Almighty, 'and
see if I will not throw open the floodgates of heaven
and pour out so much blessing that you will
not have room enough for it.'"

—MALACHI 3:10

Recently I was in Fargo, North Dakota, in response to a devastating flood there. If you have never been in a flood, it is hard to imagine the power and the unrelenting force a wall of water can bring on the earth.

In God's Word there are only a few times the Lord makes reference to the floodgates of heaven. In Genesis 7, God's destruction of the world through a flood is one of the most well-known flood references.

By the time the rains stopped, it was not just the valleys that were underwater; the mountains were as well!

Once opened, the floodgates of heaven cannot be contained. There are few things on earth as powerful, as mighty and as unstoppable as a great flood—and no flood is as great as one that begins when the floodgates of heaven open up.

God will open the floodgates of heaven upon us and shower us with His miracles only if we open ourselves up to Him in faith and give back to the One who gave us everything.

FURTHER READING:
Genesis 7:10-12
Malachi 3:9-10
2 Kings 7:2

August 25

Standing for Purity

*"You say to God, 'My beliefs are flawless
and I am pure in your sight.'"*

—JOB 11:4

An epidemic is devastating our nation. In the 30 years I've been a pastor, I've seen how pornography can destroy lives.

One man tried repeatedly to break free from its grasp. In desperation, he threw his magazines into the cold water of a nearby creek, but days later, the power of his lustful addiction was so strong that he found himself with a hammer, chiseling through the frozen ice to retrieve the addicting images.

Unlike drugs or alcohol, where a person can stop ingesting the substance and become free, once the vile images of pornography are introduced into the mind, they cannot be erased without God's grace.

The time has come to make your voice heard! Christians aren't simply being exposed to pornography right now—they are becoming addicted to it! We must stop this epidemic and rescue another family or lost soul.

God calls us to be pure in mind and heart and we must stand against the temptations of the world (see Titus 1:15).

By standing up and refusing temptation, we can stay free and help to set others free.

FURTHER READING:
Psalms 82:3
Psalms 19:8
Proverbs 20:9

August 26

The Right Glue

Do not add to what I command you and do not subtract from it, but keep the commands of the Lord your God that I give you.

—DEUTERONOMY 4:2

What is it that unifies believers? Is it popular doctrine, our world view, or what we do not believe?

I believe that we are joined together because of what we do believe: the timeless Word of God. When God's Word is watered down, misrepresented, reasoned away or rationalized, it not only causes the Church as a whole to suffer, but also the world. We are called to be light. As believers it is our duty...our obligation...to ensure that the Word of God is presented and represented in truthfulness and accuracy—for it is the glue that holds us close to the Father.

Do you have the right glue? If you have exchanged God's Word for the ideas of man—even if they are heralded as great philosophers and writers of past ages—you do not have the right glue. We are the living epistles of God. Make sure that your binding is strong, that your pages are unfaded.

God has given us His Word, which He values above His name (Psalms 138:2)—shouldn't we also value it? Shouldn't we make sure we have the right stuff to hold us together?

FURTHER READING:
Revelation 22:18-19
Matthew 5:13-16
John 8:38

August 27

God is in the Details

*"Let love and faithfulness never leave you;
bind them around your neck, write them
on the tablet of your heart."*

—PROVERBS 3:3

My journey with the Lord has consisted of a series of small steps, taken with the abiding faith that He is in control! One of those steps led to Breakthrough's global television outreach that today reaches nearly every nation on earth with the Gospel!

God guided me to a small community outside Columbus, to a tiny TV station. I drove there once a month to tape shows with their old equipment, and the Lord moved in a mighty way! The owner of the station decided to sell and God told me to offer $17,000. Before I could offer this small amount, the owner told me that he would sell it for what he owed on it— $17,000! I have to tell you, when the coast was clear, I literally jumped up and down for joy!

Matthew 10:29-31 says, "Are not two sparrows sold for a penny? Yet not one of them will fall to the ground apart from the will of your Father. And even the very hairs of your head are all numbered. So don't be afraid; you are worth more than many sparrows." The Lord works mighty things if we have faith.

Remember, when the Lord is in the details, miracles happen!

FURTHER READING:
Psalms 25:10
Psalms 89
Psalms 100:5

August 28

Prayer Helps

"I will spread out my hands in prayer to the Lord. The thunder will stop and there will be no more hail, so you may know that the earth is the Lord's."

—EXODUS 9:29

Every year, Breakthrough receives thousands of letters from people who have been touched by God's miracles. There are so many hurting people in today's world, which is why we pray for each person who sends in a request—or even a praise report!

We have received testimonies from people like Cassandra, who received a letter from the IRS stating that she owed them over $4,000. After arguing her case in vain, she prayed for a miracle, asked us to pray for her as well...and a month later, the IRS sent a letter of apology!

We have received stories of healing miracles, financial breakthroughs, and loved ones coming to faith. God is active and working in this world, and will give us our miracle if we pray!

James 5:16 says, "Therefore confess your sins to each other and pray for each other so that you may be healed. The prayer of a righteous man is powerful and effective."

God has shown us His love and His power; all we have to do is step out in faith to receive it. When like-minded believers come together to pray, miracles happen!

FURTHER READING:
Luke 17:11-19
Psalms 54:2
2 Samuel 7:27

August 29

The Faithful God

*"Know therefore that the Lord your God is God;
he is the faithful God, keeping his covenant of love
to a thousand generations of those who love
him and keep his commands."*

—DEUTERONOMY 7:9

Alma was living near starvation on the mountainside in Guatemala a few months ago, and then came the hurricanes.

Her home and everything she and her children owned were buried in a massive mudslide. Alma told me that for months she had one prayer: "Lord give me enough to feed my children today. Just today. Tomorrow I will pray about tomorrow."

This woman was behaving in precisely the way Jesus had commanded in Matthew 6:34 when He said not to worry or be anxious about tomorrow.

As His people take small steps of faith, God honors those steps and He shows them that He is the God who is more than enough. In Alma's case, He provided her with a new home and she learned that God's love for her far exceeded anything she had imagined.

Do you know that He is a God who keeps covenant and mercy with those who love Him and believe in Him? Have faith, go to Him in prayer, and ask for what you need today.

FURTHER READING:
Matthew 6:25-34
Isaiah 41:17
James 2:5

August 30

Expand Your Territory

"Trust in the Lord with all your heart and lean not on your own understanding."

—PROVERBS 3:5

Yesterday, I told you the story of Alma in Guatemala and how she prayed for food for only one day at a time.

How about you? Is there something you are holding back? What is your heart's desire, the real need, the seemingly impossible need you have not even bothered to ask God for?

In the prayer of Jabez, the writer asks God to expand his territory. He prays, "Oh, that you would bless me and enlarge my territory! Let your hand be with me, and keep me from harm so that I will be free from pain" (1 Chronicles 4:10).

For Alma, expanding her territory meant food to feed her children for more than one day and a house strong enough to withstand the rains. What does "expanding your territory" mean for you? God wants to give you exceedingly beyond anything you could think or hope (see Jeremiah 31:14).

I want to help build your faith today and see you open your heart to the God who loves you beyond your expectations.

Don't be so lost in your personal pain and so hesitant to approach the throne of grace that you close yourself off from asking God for the blessings He wants to give you.

FURTHER READING:
Proverbs 29:25
Jeremiah 17:7
John 12:36

August 31

You Are Loved

*"A new command I give you: Love one another.
As I have loved you, so you must love one another.
By this all men will know that you are my
disciples, if you love one another."*

—JOHN 13:34-35

I have been married for more than 20 years to my best friend, Joni. Our greatest joy is our two children—Ashton and Austin.

Like everyone else, we have had our share of struggles and pain. One of our darkest hours arrived when our son was diagnosed with autism at the age of three. Here I was, a man of faith, who had seen countless people healed, and yet the doctors told us there was no cure, no treatment and no hope for our boy.

Joni and I believed in God for Austin's healing from day one—and we are still trusting Him to complete the work He has begun. Over the years, we have experienced miracle after miracle. Today, my son is a testimony to God's love. He's in high school, going to classes and has always made all A's! He loves to read and is a video game enthusiast. I'm here to tell you that God cares about His children. He cares about you!

The Bible says that nothing "will be able to separate us from the love of God that is in Christ Jesus our Lord (Romans 8:38-39). He loves you and He will never let you down.

FURTHER READING:
Isaiah 65:24
Psalms 42:8
Matthew 28:20

September 1

Listen to Him

"My sheep listen to my voice...and they follow me."

—JOHN 10:27

Are you listening to the Great Shepherd or are you following someone else's voice?

Satan may have told you that miracles no longer happen. Maybe he has told you that healing is not for today or the doctor's report is final and your life is over.

The devil is a liar! Say that out loud! If you have been listening to those lies, put a stop to it today. The solution is the Word of God! Hebrews 13:8 says, "Jesus Christ is the same yesterday and today and forever."

You are reading this today because He wants you to know beyond a shadow of a doubt that He has your best interests at heart! He has a miracle waiting for you today.

Pay no attention to what the devil tells you. His words are lies and he only wants to destroy you. He doesn't want you to know the fulfillment of a life lived in Christ.

Second Timothy 2:25-26 says, "...God will grant them repentance leading them to a knowledge of the truth, and that they will come to their senses and escape from the trap of the devil, who has taken them captive to do his will."

Fill your heart with God's Word. It will produce faith and will activate the miracle you desire! This is our victory!

FURTHER READING:
John 8:44
Deuteronomy 5:29
Proverbs 4

September 2

What is God Saying?

"Do whatever He tells you."

—JOHN 2:5

Have you received your miracle yet? You might need to go back and obey the last instruction that the Lord gave you before you receive your miracle. You might have to release forgiveness or start acting like you have already received your miracle.

Do whatever He tells you! God knows how to take you out of your mess to your miracle, from poverty to prosperity and from sorrow to joy. Sometimes the instructions God gives you may not make sense to anyone, but do whatever He tells you!

I'm sure Noah wondered why God had him build an ark in the desert. Abraham probably wondered why God would have him pick up and leave his homeland. These men remained faithful and reaped His blessings!

Faith causes you to ignore the realm of your five senses and believe what God tells you. God will always ask you to do something that requires your faith to be stretched, something that will make you trust in Him! Second Corinthians 5:7 says, "We live by faith, not by sight."

What miracle do you need today? A miracle in your family or finances? A miracle in your body or in your marriage? Whatever you need today, God sent me to tell you that you are on the verge of your miracle. Remember, do whatever He tells you.

FURTHER READING:
Exodus 14:27-30
Psalms 105:39-40
Matthew 19:26

September 3

A Miracle-Working God

"The Lord said to me, 'You have seen correctly, for I am watching to see that my word is fulfilled.'"

—JEREMIAH 1:12

Have you put your trust in God's Word? Ask God to guide you to some Scriptures to help you and give you hope.

The Scriptures are full of stories of God's amazing miracles. Job 5:9 says, "He performs wonders that cannot be fathomed, miracles that cannot be counted."

If you are waiting for God to manifest His miraculous power, I stand with you in faith today and believe that your miracle is taking place even as you read this. In fact, I believe that you are about to enter into a season of miracles.

I believe you are about to receive things that you never even prayed about. God is about to do something in your life that is completely and absolutely sovereign!

You have an incredible advantage in this world—God is on your side! Ecclesiastes 7:12 says, "The advantage of knowledge is this: that wisdom preserves the life of its possessor." God is about to take you from where you are to where you ought to be!

Put your faith in His infallible Word. His Word can never return void. God's angels are currently on assignment making sure that His promises manifest in your life today!

FURTHER READING:
Job 5:9
Psalms 77: 14
Matthew 24:35

September 4

One Word

"At that time Jesus said, "I praise you, Father,
Lord of heaven and earth, because you have
hidden these things from the wise and learned,
and revealed them to little children."

—MATTHEW 11:25

Put first things first! Your needs may be great, your trials may be fiery and your circumstances may be threatening. You have prayed and even begged God to come through for you. Yet you haven't seen the answer.

I want you to know that God is ready to deliver you, save you and set free, but God only responds to His Word—not your circumstances. So, calm down and put first things first! God's Word is immutable, forever settled in the heavens!

Don't focus on your circumstances or on your need for a miracle. It may be incredibly tough for you right now, but you have to make the Word of God your number one priority.

Spend time alone with God today, not talking, not crying, not praying and asking God to help you. Spend time in His presence doing nothing but singing and listening to the voice of the Lord. He will give you the instruction you need. He will give you the keys to your miracle!

FURTHER READING:
Proverbs 3:6
Isaiah 30:21
Psalms 73:23 -25

September 5

Settling for Less

*"Since, then, you have been raised with Christ,
set your hearts on things above, where Christ
is seated at the right hand of God. Set your
minds on things above, not on earthly things."*

—COLOSSIANS 3:1-2

My visit to the garbage dump in Guatemala touched me deeply. As I watched children digging for food, I noticed a dead animal in their midst. The vultures had picked it clean, but the bones remained. The children tripped over the carcass as they ran to get the new garbage being thrown off the truck.

A couple children fell and cried because they'd missed their chance at the "good stuff" because of the dead thing in the way.

We also live with the bones of our past in the way. We trip over them, hurting ourselves over and over again because we can't get past them. The dead things in our lives are past sins, or sins committed against us that we can't or won't forgive.

If we can't get past it, then the bones lie there for us to trip over every day. The bones of our past tell us we deserve nothing better than what we have...but that is not what God says.

God wants to lift you out of your dump and into the good life He has planned for you. Let the promises of God's Word set you free. Don't settle for less...not for another day!

FURTHER READING:
Romans 7:24
Colossians 1:12-13
Colossians 2:8

September 6

Where's Your Miracle?

"When you ask, you do not receive,
because you ask with wrong motives."

—JAMES 4:3

You may be going through a difficult time right now—perhaps you are facing some of the most incredible challenges in your life! Your prayers seem to be falling on deaf ears and you are frustrated and ready to give up.

Don't stop believing for your miracle. Remember that we serve a prayer-answering God! God also wants you to take stock of your life and your prayer requests.

The book of James tells us that there are times when we do not receive answers to our prayers because the motives of our hearts are wrong. First Corinthians 4:5 says, "He will bring to light what is hidden in darkness and will expose the motives of men's hearts. At that time each will receive his praise from God."

What's blocking your miracle? I urge you to get into the presence of God and allow the Holy Spirit to direct you so you can resolve whatever may be blocking your miracle today.

When you get your heart in the right place, you will experience the miraculous power of Christ. God is positioning you for your miracle—today!

FURTHER READING:
Matthew 6:21
Matthew 6:33
Psalms 119:1-2

September 7

Logic and Faith

"He replied, 'Because you have so little faith.'"

—MATTHEW 17:20

Faith does not come without effort. To be faith-filled you must be in a place where you are growing in God.

Without faith, there are no miracles. There are many times in Scripture when Jesus heals because of a person's faith, or does not heal because of a lack of faith.

Acts 3:16 says, "By faith in the name of Jesus, this man whom you see and know was made strong. It is Jesus' name and the faith that comes through him that has given this complete healing to him, as you can all see."

God will often speak an instruction to you that does not make sense. In Joshua 6, the children of Israel were told to march and shout for the walls of Jericho to come tumbling down. In 2 Kings 5, Naaman was told to wash himself in the river Jordan seven times to be cured of leprosy. In John 9, Jesus told the blind man to go and wash himself in the pool of Siloam to be cured from his blindness!

Don't try to wrap your natural understanding around a supernatural word from God. Wrap your faith around it and you will see God's miraculous power at work.

FURTHER READING:
2 Kings 5
Hebrews 11
John 9:1-32

September 8

What Are You expecting?

"[Jesus] asked him, 'Do you want to get well?'"

—JOHN 5:6B

Are you expecting God to work a miracle in your life? Do you live in constant and earnest expectation?

Some people are satisfied with their condition and have stopped expecting anything better. Some have become okay with the idea of compromise and being sick. Some are willing to tolerate their condition of being poor, and working more than they should just to pay their bills.

God is a God of miracles and you don't have to live that way anymore. I believe this is a year of unprecedented favor, unprecedented miracles, and unprecedented supernatural power. God is about to invade your life, your family, your city, your job and your neighborhood.

John 10:38 says, "But if I do it, even though you do not believe me, believe the miracles, that you may know and understand that the Father is in me, and I in the Father."

I urge you to expect the supernatural, believe for the miraculous and allow God to reveal His power in your life today.

I believe God is about to perform something special. Do something new and manifest something supernatural in your life. Get ready, for God is about to visit you!

FURTHER READING:
John 5:1-8
John 11:40
1 Kings 17:7-24

September 9

Refuse Fear

*"Fear not, for I have redeemed you; I
have summoned you by name; you are mine."*

—ISAIAH 43:1

The challenges in your life are real. The problems surrounding you are squeezing you from all sides. You have restless nights, sweaty palms and a wrinkled brow!

That's fear trying to assert itself on you. That's fear telling you that God will not come through, that you will be defeated and put to shame. That's fear trying to tell you that the miracle you prayed for will never manifest itself!

Hear me! This is what the Lord says to you: "You will not be afraid!" You will not be afraid, for the commandments of God are absolute. Matthew 10:31 says, "So don't be afraid; you are worth more than many sparrows." If God cares for the tiniest bird, then He certainly cares for you and will not let you fall. The commandments of God are neither optional nor flexible. The commandments of God are absolute; and this is a command: "Do not be afraid" (See Exodus 20:20). Don't be afraid, for the God of the universe is on your side and is preparing a miracle for you!

God's not going to fail you or disappoint you or allow you to be put to shame.

FURTHER READING:
Isaiah 35:4
Jeremiah 30:10
Zephaniah 3:16

September 10

Measure Your Harvest

"Give, and it will be given to you... For with the measure you use, it will be measured to you."

—LUKE 6:38

You may be in huge financial difficulty today that may require God to intervene and perform a really big miracle in your finances!

Who decides the size of your miracle or the kind of harvest you reap? God does not determine the size of your miracle or the kind of harvest you receive. You do! If you doubt me, read Luke 6:38 again.

According to Scripps-Howard News Service, more than half of the members of any given Christian church give little or nothing to the church. Is it any surprise then, to find that Christians are in debt like the rest of the world?

Do you need a miracle in your finances today? Do you need God to open the floodgates of heaven and pour out on you a blessing that you have no room to contain?

I urge you to unlock your miracle. Take a step of faith and give to the kingdom of God. Give God something to work with...and remember, the size of your seed determines the size of your harvest!

FURTHER READING:
Malachi 3:10-12
2 Corinthians 9:6
Genesis 26:12

September 11

Expect the Supernatural

"And these signs will accompany those who believe..."

—MARK 16:17

Do you expect God to supernaturally intervene in your life at any time?

These are important convictions that must be anchored in your heart if you want to go deeper in the ways of the Lord. The truth is: through the person of the Holy Spirit, the miracle-working power of God is with you right now. You may feel miracles are impossible in your life, but remember, a miracle is not a miracle to God. It's only a miracle to you. To God a miracle is a normal, everyday occurrence...and He wants to make it a normal, everyday occurrence in your life, too.

Unfortunately, so many Christians live in the "Someday Syndrome." They think, "Someday I'll have more than enough" or "Someday I will be healed" or "Someday I will walk in the blessings of God."

The Bible boldly states, "Now is the time of God's favor, now is the day of salvation" (2 Corinthians 6:2). Jesus came to proclaim liberty to the captives of the "Someday Syndrome" when He announced, "Today this scripture is fulfilled in your hearing" (Luke 4:21). Expect something today!

FURTHER READING:
Mark 16:16-18
Hebrews 2:1-4
Acts 1:8

September 12

Mercy to the Poor

"He who despises his neighbor sins,
but blessed is he who is kind to the needy."

—PROVERBS 14:21

The woman lay on a dirty cot. The wall was bloodstained, mice ran across the floor, and the toilet in the corner was rusted.

Anyone who saw her would have instinctively thought to take her to a hospital...but this was the hospital. Many went in with simple diseases that a few dollars worth of medicine would cure in America, and too many of them died because the facilities were filthy.

I can't find the words to tell you how crude, how sad, and how scary it is to go into a hospital in Haiti. I saw poverty that is beyond what most Americans have ever dreamed could be possible. How can we not help this nation right on our door-step when the Bible charges us "to do good, to be rich in good deeds and be generous and willing to share" (1 Timothy 6:18).

Think of all we have in our prosperous nation, what we take for granted, and consider how little our Haitian neighbors have.

The Lord commands us to give what we have to help those in need. You are incredibly rich and blessed, compared to the people in Haiti, Sudan and other desperate countries. Will you follow the Lord's command today and help those in need?

FURTHER READING:
1 Timothy 6:17-19
Psalms 41:1-3
Ezekiel 34:15-16

September 13

God is Able

"Now to Him who is able..."

—EPHESIANS 3:20

God is speaking to you, today. He knew you would need encouragement; He knew you would be looking for that word to direct you, comfort you and deliver you! It's not by accident that you are reading this devotional today.

God is specifically and clearly speaking to you. He wants you to know that He is able! You don't need another sign, another verse or another song—He is able.

I know you feel like you're all alone sometimes—but He is always with you! I don't know what valley you are going through, what sickness is troubling you, what bills need to get paid today.

I don't know, but God does and He has a miracle scheduled for you. Deuteronomy 1:21 says, "See, the Lord your God has given you the land. Go up and take possession of it as the Lord, the God of your fathers, told you. Do not be afraid; do not be discouraged."

Trust Him, for He is able to turn your mess into a miracle, your confusion into comfort and your test into a testimony. He is able!

So wipe your tears and flash your smile today—because God has spoken. He is able!

FURTHER READING:
Psalms 27
Psalms 121
Jeremiah 17:7-8

September 14

Master Orchestrator

"For you make me glad by your deeds, O Lord;
I sing for joy at the work of your hands."

—PSALMS 92:4

There are moments in life when you think everything is finished. Your hope is gone, your trust is shaken and your faith is lost. You may wonder if God has abandoned you.

The children of Israel felt that way when they followed Moses and then got stuck at the Red Sea. Pharoah was coming to drag them back to Egypt. There was no way out for them and they were ready to give up, give in and go down!

The Israelites said to Moses, "'Was it because there were no graves in Egypt that you brought us to the desert to die?' Moses answered the people, 'Do not be afraid. Stand firm and you will see the deliverance the Lord will bring you today....The Lord will fight for you; you need only to be still'" (Exodus 14:11-14).

Maybe you feel the same way today. The pressures of life have boxed you in and you can't seem to find a way out—until now. I tell you on the authority of God's Word that you are not going to lose this battle; you are not going down in defeat!

He is the Master Orchestrator, the Creator and the Designer of life. Don't panic, don't fear and don't give up because Christ who lives in you cannot, shall not and will not fail you—ever!

FURTHER READING:
2 Chronicles 20:6-12
1 Peter 5:7
Jeremiah 29:11

September 15

Call Me Crazy

"I have told you these things, so that in me you may have peace. In this world you will have trouble. But take heart! I have overcome the world."

—JOHN 16:33

The world is in turmoil—it always has been and always will be. How does one stay happy and calm in the midst of a global recession, a global pandemic and a global collapse of moral and rational thinking in our societies?

You serve the risen Christ. The Bible says "Take heart" and "Be of good cheer" (Matthew 9:2). Don't get influenced by what the stock market says, the news channels or what the papers print.

It's time for you to give God praise! It does not matter how dark your night is, how vicious your enemy is or how difficult your battles are. Cast your worries on Him (1 Peter 5:7) and break out in a crazy praise! Go on—turn on some good Christian music, shut the door, let your hair down and praise Him like you have never praised Him before—I dare you!

It's time for you to square your back, stick your jaw out just a little bit and walk with confidence—don't let anything or anyone rob you of your joy! Even in times of trouble, we can rejoice because we serve the God of the universe!

FURTHER READING:
Psalms 37:4-5
John 10:10
Proverbs 17:22

September 16

The Sun Will Shine

*"Weeping may remain for a night,
but rejoicing comes in the morning."*

—PSALMS 30:5

You're about to forget you ever had a sad day or a bad night. God's about to show up in the middle of your mess!

God's about to give hope to the hopeless and help to the helpless. Hope that God gives is beyond the scope of human limitation because God is a good, good God! Psalms 31:24 says, "Be strong and take heart, all you who hope in the Lord."

Through your tears, remember that the sun must shine, tomorrow must come and you will have victory! I prophesy to you that in the days that lie straight ahead you're about to see, you're about to hear the rumbling in the mulberry bushes.

You're about to see the wind of God moving in the situations of your life. You're about to know God is real. You may be going through the worst situation of your life, but stay steadfast in your faith and believe that God is about to deliver your miracle!

Job remained faithful to God even when he had lost everything—his family, his fortune, even his health.

God rewarded Job for his faithfulness (Job 42:10-11). Your miracle is coming—just hold on with hope. Today is your day for breakthrough!

FURTHER READING:
Psalms 60:12
Deuteronomy 3:22-24
2 Samuel 22:49

September 17

Joy in His Presence

"You will fill me with joy in your presence."

—PSALMS 16:11

Troubled times are upon us. This world is not going to get any better, only worse. The good news for the blood-washed and blood-bought is that although we live in this world, we belong to the kingdom of God.

The kingdom of God is diametrically opposed to the system of this world. That means when things get worse for the world, they should get better for you!

That's right! So rejoice and refill your tank of joy! The best way to do that is to spend time in the presence of God—pray constantly, read His Word daily and get to know Him intimately!

The level of your joy determines the level of your strength! The Bible is full of verses about joy. Psalms 20:5 says, "We will shout for joy when you are victorious and will lift up our banners in the name of our God. May the Lord grant all your requests."

I believe the more we're with Him, the more we learn to be like Him. The Holy Spirit will guide us and teach us to be more like Him in every way. The joy of the Lord is our strength.

When we get more of Him, we will have less of us—and that's a formula for success!

FURTHER READING:
1 Peter 1:8
Job 33:26
Psalms 5:11

September 18

Open Your Mouth

"...Open wide your mouth and I will fill it."

—PSALMS 81:10

You are supposed to let God fill your mouth with His Word—every day. Yet, there are many believers who are ready to swallow whatever the devil throws their way, and they fall for it hook, line and sinker!

You can put a stop to that by letting your mouth be filled with God's Word. Find three people today and tell them what God has done for you! Look at yourself in the mirror and say "Something good is about to happen to me today."

Don't waste another minute, another thought or another tear on what the world says or thinks of you. Your life is not measured or determined by what anybody says! God is the ruler of everything—and He loves you!

What could be better than that? Open your mouth in prayer today and let Him fill you with His Word.

Revelation 10:10-11 says, "I took the little scroll from the angel's hand and ate it. It tasted as sweet as honey in my mouth, but when I had eaten it, my stomach turned sour. Then I was told, "You must prophesy again about many peoples, nations, languages and kings."

Fill your mouth with God's Word and you will find that a successful life is inevitable!

FURTHER READING:
Joshua 1:8
Proverbs 18:21
Romans 8:1

September 19

Judgment Day Honesty

"Blessed are those who wash their robes, that they may have the right to the tree of life and may go through the gates into the city."

—REVELATION 22:14-15

There is a spirit of deception that is so pervasive today that many believers have succumbed to it. They believe they are walking uprightly before God and that a little fleshly indulgence now and again will not disqualify them from heaven. They use excuses to justify their sin, saying that "it's only a little" or "it's only one time."

God's Word on the subject is clear—the wages of sin is death. A little bit of yeast (sin) affects the whole loaf (see 1 Corinthians 5:6). You can't sin a little without it tarnishing your witness. You can't sin a little without it diminishing your power. You can't sin a little without sowing curses and death for yourself. When you sin, confess your sins and turn to the Lord who will forgive and heal your heart and your life.

You have to be honest with yourself and face your condition; you need to have judgment day honesty. If you were before the throne of Christ now, would you be confident of being welcomed in as one of His sheep? I encourage you to have judgment day honesty every day.

FURTHER READING:
1 Corinthians 6:9-10
Ephesians 5:5
Genesis 4:7

September 20

Settle the Matter

"And God said, 'Let there be light,' and there was light. God saw that the light was good, and He separated the light from the darkness."

—GENESIS 1:3-4

Many times Christians say that God gave them this or that illness. God doesn't give His children any ailments. Sickness is the work of the devil, and he alone should be blamed for it. You have no business claiming it "for God's glory."

When God gives His children things, they are good things, for He is a good God. The Bible establishes this fact from the very beginning. After each act of creation God looked it over and declared that it was good. How can a good God give out disease, illness, lack, poverty, or violence and still be a good God? He cannot.

God is good through and through, and there is no evil in Him. Whatever He does is for good, and if the enemy gives us his rotten fruit of disease, poverty or illness we can refuse to accept it in Jesus' name.

Romans 8:28 says, "We know that in all things God works for the good of those who love him, who have been called according to his purpose." We can be confident God will work all things for our good and His glory—if we believe He will.

FURTHER READING:
James 1:17
Genesis 1
Genesis 2

September 21

Do You Know God?

*"With flattery he will corrupt those who
have violated the covenant, but the people
who know their God will firmly resist him."*

—DANIEL 11:32

Do you know God, or do you simply know things about God? When was the last time you studied the Bible and sought to know God through His Word? When was the last time you prayed and sought God with all your heart?

When I talk about praying, some people immediately think of a list of needs they want God to answer. I am not talking about the prayer of petition now. I am asking you, when was the last time you got down on your knees and prayed to simply know God and His absolute power? Some of the problems you face right now would not be problems if you knew Him better!

Many years ago, I was once asked by my mentor Dr. Lester Sumrall, "Do you know what faith is?" I could have quoted Hebrews 11, but I held my peace and let him tell me. This is what he said: "Faith is simply knowing God." His answer changed my entire perspective, and I've been on an unquenchable quest to know Him intimately—not just know about Him.

Child of God—seek Him today with all your heart and you will know God better than you could have dreamed!

FURTHER READING:
Philippians 4:13
Psalms 27
Psalms 119:98

September 22

Faith Only

"For in the gospel a righteousness from God is revealed,
a righteousness that is by faith from first to last, just as
it is written: "The righteous will live by faith"

—ROMANS 1:17

Martin Luther believed that faith and not works saved man. During his time, this was a revolutionary concept because the whole church system had been built upon a saved-by-works mentality. Unfortunately today there are many who believe that they will score points with God through good works.

In our society there are many that do good works and charitable and humanitarian deeds, yet they deny God and disobey His statutes. Some even believe that their works automatically entitle them to a pass into heaven, but this is not so—they are misinformed and deceived.

Heaven is for those who have faith in God—not themselves. Heaven is for those who live their lives to please God and believe in the Son of God as Lord and Savior. It's about faith from first to last—FAITH is what matters!

Abraham had faith in God. He believed what God said to him, and even though he made mistakes, God called him righteous—because of his faith. Do you believe in God? Do you have faith in Him? This is what matters most of all.

FURTHER READING:
Hebrews 11:6
James 2:23
Ephesians 2:8-9

September 23

Shake Off the Past!

"You were taught, with regard to your former way of life, to put off your old self, which is being corrupted by its deceitful desires."

—EPHESIANS 4:22

Memories can be painful. Far too many people live miserable lives because they allow their future to be corrupted by their past. Don't keep looking back in regret.

Believers in Christ leave their old lives behind and look forward to a glorious future with Christ. Don't be like the Israelites, always looking back: "If only we had died by the Lord's hand in Egypt! There we sat around pots of meat and ate all the food we wanted, but you have brought us out into this desert to starve this entire assembly to death" (Exodus 16:3).

Jesus came to destroy all sins—past, present and future! He has already forgiven all the sins you have committed, so forget the past and look forward to a new day in Him. God is about to send something into your life that's about to drive doubt and unbelief out. Sorrow is no longer welcome in your life!

Don't look at the past no matter if the memories are painful or seem to be better than what you are experiencing today. Look toward the future and trust in the Lord. Your future is brighter than your past—embrace it!

FURTHER READING:
1 Corinthians 2:9-10
Revelation 21:4
Job 8:7

September 24

One More Shout

"When you hear them sound a long blast on the trumpets, have all the people give a loud shout; then the wall of the city will collapse and the people will go up, every man straight in."

—JOSHUA 6:5

Shout because victory is yours! Shout because the battle has already been won! Shout because Satan is defeated, death has been conquered and the grave has been denied! Shout because you have been redeemed! Shout because we have overcome by the blood of the Lamb and by the word of our testimony.

The devil just told you there is no hope for you. There's no money in the bank or gas in the tank. You've got a bad report from the doctor or a worse report from your accountant.

What do you do? SHOUT! Shout because you know victory's coming. Shout because you know the answer is already on the way. Shout like a cheerleader in the grandstands of God's arena as your enemies squeal under your feet, and the God of heaven is exalted by delivering you out of your difficulty.

Hebrews 11:30 says, "By faith the walls of Jericho fell, after the people had marched around them for seven days."

As you shout, the walls that prevent you from having God's best will fall down!

FURTHER READING:
Joshua 6
Revelation 12:11
Psalms 150

September 25

Lord, Can You?

"'But if you can do anything, take pity on
us and help us.' 'If you can'?" said Jesus.
'Everything is possible for him who believes.'"

—MARK 9:23

Many Christians are asking if God can heal, deliver or save them. What is evident is that they are not familiar with the will of God as it is outlined in His Word—the Bible.

The Bible is the expressed will of God for His children. In order to know what God says on a particular matter we must know His Word. If we fail to read the Bible we will not know what God says about healing, deliverance, blessings and walking with power and dominion. When it comes to our blessing, the true question is: Can we believe?

In Mark 9:22-25, a father asked Jesus if he could do anything to help his son who was often thrown into the fire and into water because he was demon possessed. Jesus promptly let the father know that it was not about whether He could do something for his son—but the issue was whether the father could believe.

The Bible tells us that "all things are possible for him who believes." Can you believe for your deliverance or healing? If you can believe, then all things are possible.

FURTHER READING:
Matthew 21:21
Mark 11:23-24
Luke 17:6

September 26

Lord, Will You?

*"'I am willing,' he said. 'Be clean!'
And immediately the leprosy left him."*

—LUKE 5:13

Have you ever found yourself asking, "Lord, is it Your will to heal me?" Too many Christians don't know the will of God concerning their healing. They have doubt concerning the perfect will of God to heal. Others refuse to believe that God would want to heal them.

Faith cannot exist where there is doubt. Healing will never come for those who are filled with unbelief. Faith is necessary in order to receive your healing. Acts 3:16 says, "By faith in the name of Jesus, this man whom you see and know was made strong. It is Jesus' name and the faith that comes through him that has given this complete healing to him, as you can all see."

Doubt-filled prayers lift up the problem before God but they don't anticipate the solution. Faith-filled prayers acknowledge that God is a God of the impossible and that in spite of what is seen or said, He can do it because you believe His Word.

Does the Lord want to heal you? Yes! Will you be healed? That is up to you—are you willing to believe His Word? Are you willing to walk in faith? If you are, then God's response is stated in His Word... "I am willing... Be clean!" (Matthew 8:3).

FURTHER READING:
James 1:17
Matthew 8:2-3
Mark 1:40

September 27

No Compromise

*"Everyone who has this hope in him
purifies himself, just as he is pure."*

—1 JOHN 3:3

There is a cancer running through many churches today—it is the cancer of compromise. It is the notion that we have to be like the world in order to win them to Christ. This is a ploy of the devil.

Jesus never compromised in order to win people to the Father. He presented Himself as He was and let people choose.

When Christians compromise, everybody loses. You and I have only one thing to offer the world...it is the one thing they can't get anywhere else in creation—the unchanging Gospel of Jesus Christ. Romans 12:2 says, "Do not conform any longer to the pattern of this world, but be transformed by the renewing of your mind. Then you will be able to test and approve what God's will is—his good, pleasing and perfect will."

Our message is not watered-down, secondhand, white-washed, or a finely-wrapped dead religion. It is food, life, a lamp, it is a light and it is powerful. Compromise will not cause the world to turn to Christ—but when sin-sick people see us walking in holiness and purity, and offering a way out of bondage, filth and oppression, they will want to know more.

FURTHER READING:
Psalms 119:105
Deuteronomy 8:3
1 Peter 1:15-16

September 28

Preach the Cross

"For the message of the cross is foolishness to those who are perishing, but to us who are being saved it is the power of God."

—1 CORINTHIANS 1:18

In every human heart there is embedded a "sin consciousness" and it cries out to be reunited with Father God. We all long to be reunited and justified in His sight, but the only way to be reunited with God is through the cross.

Many churches today seem to have forgotten about the cross, preferring to hear messages about seven steps to prosperity and more modern messages centered around "earning" good standing with God. Though it may not be a popular subject, without the cross we can't effectively preach the message of Christ.

Paul says in Galatians 6:14, "May I never boast except in the cross of our Lord Jesus Christ, through which the world has been crucified to me, and I to the world."

The only way that we get remission from sin is by the shed blood of Christ. Hebrews 9:22 says, "In fact, the law requires that nearly everything be cleansed with blood, and without the shedding of blood there is no forgiveness."

The message of our redemption is the message of the cross.

FURTHER READING:
1 Corinthians 1:18
Galatians 6:14
Colossians 1:14

September 29

Pray Continually

"Then Jesus told his disciples a parable to show them that they should always pray and not give up."

—LUKE 18:1

When was the last time that you faced a need so traumatic that you found yourself falling on your knees? The truth is that many people rush through their prayer time—that is, if they have a prayer time at all.

One-on-one communication with God is how we strengthen our relationship with the lover of our souls. Prayer—fellowship with God—has been the backbone of revelation, action and power since the beginning of time. Prayer can bring about cataclysmic changes in heaven and on earth (Revelation 5:8, 8:3-4) and can turn any situation around.

Prayer is the life, power and glory for the church and for its members. Prayer helps us to get into the presence of God and remain there continually. Prayer is the method that we must use in order to get anything from God.

Mark 11:24 says, "Therefore I tell you, whatever you ask for in prayer, believe that you have received it, and it will be yours."

We will hear and we will receive little or nothing from God without regular seasons spent in prayer.

FURTHER READING:
Mark 11:22-24
Psalms 2:8
Ezekiel 36:37

September 30

A Willing Spirit

"Thanks be to God—through Jesus Christ our Lord! So then, I myself in my mind am a slave to God's law, but in the sinful nature a slave to the law of sin."

—ROMANS 7:25

How often have we said the spirit is willing but the flesh is weak? We often recite that Bible verse almost flippantly, without realizing what we are saying. It becomes almost a 'cute' thing to say when we are tempted by something.

There is an old Latin proverb that says: "He conquers twice who conquers himself in victory." How true that is! To conquer our sins is one of the most difficult things we have to do in our lives on earth, because we are tempted almost every day.

General George S. Patton said, "Accept the challenges so that you may feel the exhilaration of victory."

If you accept the challenges when they come around, and take up the sword against them, you will be taking steps toward changing your history of defeat and experiencing victory! Deuteronomy 20:4 says, "For the Lord your God is the one who goes with you to fight for you against your enemies to give you victory."

Accept the challenges you face in life daily, and trust God for victory—for with Him on your side, you can defeat any enemy!

FURTHER READING:
Matthew 12:20
Psalms 13
Romans 8:35-37

October 1

Live in His Presence

"We are the temple of the living God."

—2 CORINTHIANS 6:16

Today, you need to have the Lord in your life—not just on Sunday when you're at church or singing in the choir—and live in His glory by entering His presence.

This is illustrated in the Tabernacle—the Tent of Meeting—where the presence of God dwelt with the children of Israel as they wandered the wilderness (see Exodus 40).

The Tabernacle is where you are fulfilling the purpose of God in your life—where your life becomes a sanctuary and every act is done in humble submission of priestly worship before your God. When you start living in the glory, you can't help but burst forth with thanksgiving, praise and worship (see Ezra 3:11). Praise begins to flow from your lips in spite of the circumstances surrounding you.

Then, since God inhabits the praises of His people, the Spirit of God rises up and silences your enemy along the way.

If you were to take your personal life and model it after the way the Israelites entered God's holy presence in the Tabernacle—you would never be the same.

Your adversaries would be destroyed. Your body would be healed. Your finances would be blessed. Not because of God's promises—but because of His presence being with you!

FURTHER READING:
Exodus 29:42-46
Isaiah 42:1-13
2 Corinthians 3:4-18

October 2

God's Blueprint

"Then Moses said, 'Now show me your glory.'"

—EXODUS 33:18

God gave Moses a blueprint to create a place where His glory could dwell in the very center of the Israelites' camp—and God's people could come into His presence and live. It was called the Tabernacle.

It featured three major areas: An outer court, inner court and the holy of holies—where everyone could enter into God's presence at various levels of worship. (God loves to work in threes: Father, Son and Holy Spirit. Man is made of body, soul and spirit.)

Today, God's people are looking for God to set them free by His power. The church knows a lot about getting promises, but very little—if anything—about getting presence, which releases His power into your life on a daily basis. What you need is more of His presence!

"He who dwells in the shelter of the Most High will rest in the shadow of the Almighty" (Psalms 91:1). God is calling us to dwell in that high place: the secret place of habitation in God.

Relationship makes the difference. The way we dwell in the secret place is through continuous thanksgiving, praise and worship that lead us into constant communion with Him.

FURTHER READING:
Exodus 33:12-23
Exodus 34:1-9; 28-35
Exodus 35-36:1-7

October 3

Suffer the Children

"Jesus said, "Let the little children come to me, and do not hinder them, for the kingdom of heaven belongs to such as these."

—MATTHEW 19:14

Wonsise is a little orphan girl I met in Haiti. Her mother had died in a filthy Haitian hospital when Wonsise was only three months old. Now Wonsise lives in a makeshift orphanage with nothing but a thatched roof over her head—no walls, no beds and no running water.

I thanked God for the meals we were able to deliver to feed the children in that orphanage, but there was so much more that needed to be done. It amazes me that Wonsise and her companions have to go hungry when what we would spend for one meal here in America could feed a Haitian child for a whole month.

We come to understand Jesus' instructions to take care of the orphans, the widows and the needy. In Matthew 19:21 he says, "If you want to be perfect, go, sell your possessions and give to the poor, and you will have treasure in heaven. Then come, follow me." He knew that in this imperfect world, there would be great contrasts in wealth. Who but His body of believers could He count on to help the needy in these dark times?

FURTHER READING:
Psalms 82:3-4
Isaiah 1:17
Psalms 68:5

October 4

The Outer Court

"Enter His gates with thanksgiving and His courts with praise; give thanks to him and praise his name."

—PSALMS 100:4

The outer court of the Tabernacle is the easiest level to access—it is designed to minister to the needs of your flesh in relationship with God.

Located outdoors, the outer court represents a level of prayer in which you thank Him for the things you can see and touch... such as your health, your family and your daily bread.

Scripture says you are to enter the gates of the Tabernacle with thanksgiving in your heart: "Enter his gates with thanksgiving and his courts with praise; give thanks to him and praise his name" (Psalms 100:4).

Praising Him is the first step toward entering the presence of God. Where is your relationship with God today? It may not be easy to just wake up and start praising the Lord, but that is what you need to do every moment of every day.

Take the time right now to express your gratitude to the Lord. Write it down. It doesn't matter how long it is—what matters is that you express your heart before the Lord.

If you are going to see God's glory, thanksgiving is the door that will lead you into His throne room.

FURTHER READING:
Philippians 4:6-8
Psalms 100
Psalms 103

October 5

The Art of Thanksgiving

"Give thanks in all circumstances, for this is God's will for you in Christ Jesus."

—I THESSALONIANS 5:18

Let me tell you about the power of thanksgiving.

One year, our congregation decided to line the streets and pray during a Father's Day parade sponsored by a homosexual group. More than 1,000 people showed up and I said, "We are going to go down there and not talk to anyone but God. Then, don't tell God what you want Him to do...instead, just praise Him." So that's what we did. We stood there—lifting our hands toward heaven and praising God.

One young lady in our congregation had been clinically deaf in both ears...but it wasn't because of our lack of praying. We had prayed so often for her! Many great men of God had prayed for her, but there was no audible difference.

But there we were on that day, standing on the streets of Columbus, Ohio, magnifying God with a heart of thanksgiving—when this young lady suddenly began to shout out, "I can hear! I can hear!"

God unstopped her ears through the power of praise and thanksgiving. Don't ever underestimate the power that God can release through a heart full of faithfulness and praise!

FURTHER READING:
1 Chronicles 16:7-36
Luke 17:11-19
Revelation 7:12

October 6

The High Priest is Cleansed

*"Let us draw near to God ... having our hearts
sprinkled to cleanse us from a guilty conscience
and having our bodies washed with pure water."*

—HEBREWS 10:22

The first action that occurs in the outer court is the priest cleanses himself at the laver. You might think he was merely washing his hands and feet in a brass bowl full of water, but the laver reminds us to be "cleansed ... by the washing of water with the word" (Ephesians 5:26).

Being cleansed is far more than just a lamb being placed on the altar before God at the time of sacrifice—it is a symbol of our very lives being set apart to God.

The apostle Paul said, "I urge you therefore, brothers, in view of God's mercy, to offer your bodies as living sacrifices, holy and pleasing to God ... do not conform to the pattern of this world, but be transformed by the renewing of your mind" (Romans 12:1-3).

We set ourselves apart by renewing our minds with God's Word—cleansing our minds from the filth of this world—removing the defeat, discouragement and the "dirty" images that bombard our eyes every day. You and I are priests in His kingdom. His Word cleanses us for service.

FURTHER READING:
Psalms 24
Isaiah 1:16-20
1 Peter 2:9-10

October 7

Redeeming Sacrifice

*"For the wages of sin is death, but the gift
of God is eternal life in Christ Jesus our Lord"*

—ROMANS 6:23

In the outer court was the altar of brass. At its four corners, the sin nature was dealt with, sacrifices were slain and forgiveness was received and celebrated.

The high priest would take the blood of the lamb from off the altar and put it on his right earlobe, setting himself and his life apart to hearing God's voice. He would place another drop on his right thumb—and right toe—setting apart the actions and deeds of his life unto God.

Then, forgiveness was appropriated for the people as the priest offered a lamb on the altar for their sins. This is just another example of how your forgiveness has absolutely nothing to do with you.

It's not about your good works, the church you attend or how many times a day you pray. You are forgiven only through the blood of the Lamb, Jesus Christ, our Savior and King.

All of this occurred in the outer court—reminding us of the need to put our flesh aside before going deeper into the presence of God. You could stay in the outer court if you wanted to...but God invites you to come closer.

FURTHER READING:
Leviticus 5
Hebrews 9:11-14
Hebrews 10:1-18

October 8

The Inner Court

*"Your word is a lamp to my feet
and a light for my path."*

—PSALMS 119:105

From the outer court, you step inside into the more intimate area of the inner court—moving from thanksgiving into praise—from the realm of your flesh and the world, to looking within at the deeper level of the soul.

Seven candles light this darkened room, representing the illumination of the Word of the living God through the Holy Spirit. "For the commandment is a lamp, and the teaching is light" (Proverbs 6:23). This is a place where you are in the dark, but God illuminates a promise in His Word to help you walk by faith. You have just enough light for your next step.

These are the times in your life when the check has yet to arrive in the mail, but you have a Word from God; the tumor isn't gone, but you've got a promise; the child hasn't come home, the disease is in your body or the raise hasn't come through, but it doesn't matter because you are going to praise God anyway!

So lift your hands to heaven and praise God, because you've heard the voice of the Spirit and received a promise and a Word from the Lord!

FURTHER READING:
Psalms 27
Hebrews 11
Psalms 119:129-135

October 9

Thanksgiving and Praise

"Set your minds on things above, not on earthly things "

—COLOSSIANS 3:2

In the outer court, we cleansed our flesh and offered a sacrifice of thanksgiving to the Lord. In the inner court, it's dark...and we are forced to change our focus to something more internal in nature...moving to a place of praise. This is where you praise God based not on what you see—but rather, out of a relationship with God that goes beyond what you see with your physical eyes.

Paul and Silas knew the power of praising God even in dark times. In Acts 16:19-36, they were thrown into prison after being beaten with rods. They were chained against the wall, hands bleeding and wounds unattended.

The Bible says, "About midnight Paul and Silas were praying and singing hymns to God, and the other prisoners were listening to them. Suddenly there was such a violent earthquake that the foundations of the prison were shaken" (Acts 16:25-26).

Paul and Silas may have been in prison... but they weren't imprisoned in their hearts! They never asked God for the earthquake. Instead, they chose to praise God for Who He is in spite of the circumstances...and then, God moved in power!

Follow the example of Paul and Silas; trust God in any and every situation and He will see you through.

FURTHER READING:
2 Chronicles 20:1-30
Matthew 5:19-21
Philippians 4:8

October 10

Repel the Darkness

*"For our struggle is not against flesh and blood,
but against the rulers, against the authorities,
against the powers of this dark world and against
the spiritual forces of evil in the heavenly realms."*

—EPHESIANS 6:12

We live in a time when victory over the forces of darkness has been won by Jesus Christ, but enforcement of the victory is left to His people.

Nowhere is this fight more evident than in South Africa, where more than one in every seven adults is living with HIV. Witch doctors inform those desperate to rid themselves of AIDS that having sex with a child will cure them of the disease. About 40% of infants test positive for HIV, which they contract from their mothers.

Christians have been called to repel the darkness by being beacons of God's light. John 16:33 says, "I have told you these things, so that in me you may have peace. In this world you will have trouble. But take heart! I have overcome the world."

Even though we live in dark times, we know that the battle has already been won—and we look forward to the time when evil will be banished forever.

FURTHER READING:
Matthew 11:12
Colossians 1:13
2 Corinthians 10:3-4

October 11

The Table of Showbread

"I am the living bread that came down from heaven. If anyone eats of this bread, he will live forever. This bread is my flesh, which I will give for the life of the world."

—JOHN 6:51

Your soul is comprised of your mind, will and emotions. Of the three, the will fights God the most. This is addressed at the table of showbread.

On this table are twelve loaves arranged in two rows of six. The loaves are made out of wheat that had to be threshed and ground. This is a symbol of how God separates our hearts from the chaff of the world—as He allows your life to be broken, so you can become more like Jesus, The Bread of Heaven.

Consider how the inner court is located right next to the holy of holies—which speaks of the need to bring order to your life. If you want more of the presence of God, you need to set things right. If there is disharmony in your home, you need to fix it before going into the holy place.

You must submit to the breaking—which God accomplishes through the fires of life (the tests, trials and tribulations).

God wants us all to become more disciplined, not out of ritual, but out of a desire to see more of God in our lives.

FURTHER READING:
Exodus 16
John 6:32-71
1 Peter 1:3-9

October 12

The Altar of Incense

*"The priest is to take a handful of fine flour and oil,
together with all the incense on the grain offering,
and burn the memorial portion on the altar as
an aroma pleasing to the Lord."*

—LEVITICUS 6:15

After you deal with your mind and your will in the inner court, you go before the altar of incense and deal with your emotions.

At the top of the altar of incense you will find a crown. This asks you the question: "Who is the Lord of your emotions? Are you going to react in the heat of the battle, however you feel leading you from moment to moment in life...or will you filter your feelings through the lordship of Jesus Christ, so you will respond as Jesus would have you respond?"

Four different kinds of incense were burnt on the altar. They were ground to powder before they could ever be used—symbolizing the need for our lives to be broken so our emotions can be fully submitted to the Lord.

When we praise God, it's not just because we "feel" like it. Absolutely not. We shout because the Spirit of God says to our spirit, "Shout"...and we start shouting! We hear the Word of the Lord and faith rises within us...then we start celebrating victory in the middle of our circumstances.

FURTHER READING:
Philippians 4:4-9
Revelation 5:8-10
Revelation 8:3-5

October 13

Holy of Holies

"Even though I walk through the valley of the shadow of death, I will fear no evil, for you are with me; your rod and your staff, they comfort me."

—PSALMS 23:4

In the holy of holies, you can't see and don't have a word to light your way—but you don't care because you've got the presence of the Lord with you.

You have moved from a place of praise into an area of intimacy and worship: "You will fill me with joy in your presence, with eternal pleasures at your right hand" (Psalms 16:11).

It doesn't matter if you are going through the flood or the fire, because you know God is with you. As long as you feel His arms around you, everything's all right.

Here, you come before the mercy seat of heaven—the deepest level of intercession. You have a full audience with Jesus.

The Bible says, "He who dwells in the shelter of the Most High will abide in the shadow of the Almighty. I will say to the Lord, 'My refuge and my fortress, My God, in whom I trust!'" (Psalms 91:1-3, 7).

When you are in the presence of the Lord, you have nothing to fear. The power of the presence of God will take away all despair and doubt as you fellowship with Him!

FURTHER READING:
Isaiah 43:1-3
Psalms 16
Psalms 91

October 14

The Ark of the Covenant

"Have them make a chest of acacia wood...
Overlay it with pure gold, both inside and out,
and make a gold molding around it."

—EXODUS 25:10-11

Notice where God chose to dwell on the earth: in a Tabernacle (a "Tent of Meeting") at the very center of the camp of the twelve tribes of Israel—in the midst of the holy of holies around the ark of the covenant.

The ark is a reminder for us to prepare a special place in our hearts for Christ Jesus, knowing that His presence is the only thing that can provide supernatural power to triumph over the trials of this world.

The ark of the covenant is a picture of Jesus. The wood of the ark signifies His humanity—the things of this earth. The gold represents His divinity—the heavenly realm.

On top is a mercy seat, where the blood is sprinkled and forgiveness is appropriated at the deepest level. Two cherubim look down on the top of the ark—but they see nothing but the blood: "Between the two cherubim that are over the ark of the Testimony, I will meet with you" (Exodus 25:22).

In the same way, the blood of Jesus causes all judgment to pass over our lives—so we can exist in His glory.

FURTHER READING:
Exodus 12:1-14
Hebrews 9
Hebrews 10:19-25

October 15

More of Christ Jesus!

"The Lord your God is with you, he is mighty to save."

—ZEPHANIAH 3:17

The first instructions God gave to Moses were not about the tent, but about the ark of the covenant.

This is the place where the anointing is...the power is...where the shekinah glory of God dwells. In other words, God is saying, "You find Me first, and then build everything else around Me."

What was inside this holy ark of the covenant?

First, Aaron's rod that budded—representing God's ability to take something dead and make it live again. No matter how desperate your situation may seem, there is nothing buried deep enough to keep out the resurrection power of Christ Jesus!

Second, the Ten Commandments—representing God's holy law and the living Word, brought together in Jesus Christ.

Third, a jar of manna—representing the Bread of Life who came down from heaven—Jesus Christ—our sustenance and daily provision, from whom we get our daily nourishment.

That's who you have living inside of you, right now, according to Colossians 1:27: "...Christ in you, the hope of glory."

This is the reality of His presence that God wants you to walk in every day!

FURTHER READING:
John 11:1-44
John 1
John 6:30-58

October 16

Moving Into Worship

*"God is spirit, and his worshipers must
worship in spirit and in truth."*

—JOHN 4:24

Psalms 95:6 says, "Come, let us bow down in worship, let us kneel before the Lord our Maker."

Did you know the word for "worship" is never defined in the Bible? And yet, 131 of 330 verses in the book of Hebrews alone talk about it, one-third of the Old Testament talks about it and the largest book in the Bible is a book of thanksgiving and worship!

Like the ark of the covenant, you and I are walking "temples" of God—places of mobile worship unto the Lord, where His manifest presence can move forth in power!

Psalms 29:2 says, "Ascribe to the Lord the glory due his name; worship the Lord in the splendor of his holiness." We praise the Lord because of His mercy and might, grace and power. Praise Him because His presence is inside you—and if God's presence is inside you, so is His power to deliver you and to set you free from every bondage.

Come into this place of meeting and enter into intimacy with God. Learn to acknowledge His presence, and allow Him to move forward in power.

FURTHER READING:
Genesis 22:1-19
Romans 12
John 4:1-40

October 17

Seize the Day!

"Do you not say, 'Four months more and then the harvest'? I tell you, open your eyes and look at the fields! They are ripe for harvest."

—JOHN 4:35

Although Jesus spoke the words in John 4:35 two thousand years ago, we sense the urgency He placed on preaching the Gospel and reaching the lost. At no time in history has the earth been more imperiled than it is today.

Wars abound to a greater degree than ever before, and never has the potential for the utter annihilation of the human race been more intense. If we are to discern the signs of the times according to the Bible, truly we are living in the last days.

In 23 B.C. the Roman poet Horace penned a phrase that has become a rallying cry for those impassioned with life: "Carpe Diem. Quam minimum credula postero." Seize the day. Put no trust in the morrow."

How appropriate this is. We are in the end times, and if we are to be faithful to Scripture and obedient to the mandate of Christ, we need to go all out in reaching out to the lost. There are still thousands of precious people who have been unreached by the life-changing power of the Gospel. Carpe Diem! Let us seize the day for the eternal purposes of God.

FURTHER READING:
Matthew 4:16
Ephesians 5:15-16
Revelation 5:9

October 18

In Due Season

"Let us not become weary in doing good, for at the proper time we will reap a harvest if we do not give up."

—GALATIANS 6:9

Are you struggling with a crisis? Perhaps you've lost your job or you're concerned about paying your bills. Maybe you're starting to wonder if God will ever answer your prayers and send your miracle harvest!

Sometimes we get so focused on looking down at our own circumstances that we forget to look up—to look up to God and keep walking in the light of His Word and sowing seeds in faith. Remember that before you were even born God knew you and formed a plan for your life.

Jeremiah 1:9 says, "Before I formed you in the womb I knew you, before you were born I set you apart; I appointed you as a prophet to the nations." God's plan for you is perfect, not subject to the whims of man and the uncertainty of the world.

Whatever your circumstances are today, God calls us to stand on the solid rock of His Word and take shelter in His promises. God says in His Word, "In due season we shall reap if we do not lose heart." Have faith, God is saying, keep believing.

The seeds we sow in faith today will become the harvest of blessings tomorrow—in due season, when the time is right.

FURTHER READING:
2 Timothy 4:7-8
1 Corinthians 9:24-27
Hebrews 10:35-36

October 19

Soul Harvest

"Do you not say, 'Four months more and then the harvest'? I tell you, open your eyes and look at the fields! They are ripe for harvest."

—JOHN 4:35

We are living in the closing moments of human history on this planet. These are the last days! The signs are all around us: Great economic upheaval in every nation, wars, famine, violence, wayward children and injustice on every front.

For Christians, the end times mean that the rapture is near. This is good news! But in these last moments of the world there is still much work to be done to increase His kingdom. God is looking for laborers who will go into the harvest field of the world and rescue lost souls. As every farmer knows, when harvest time arrives, workers spend long days toiling in the field. If the work is not done, everything can be lost. For Christians, the end-time harvest has arrived, and there's no time to lose! Millions are facing eternity without God, and we must do all we can to rescue them.

Won't you join me in the harvest field? The moment has arrived to "thrust in the sickle, and reap: for the time has come for us to reap; for the harvest of the earth is ripe" (Revelation 14:15).

FURTHER READING:
Matthew 9:37-38
Luke 10:2
2 Corinthians 6:2

October 20

As Man Sows

*"Do not be deceived: God cannot be mocked.
A man reaps what he sows. The one who sows to
please his sinful nature, from that nature will reap
destruction; the one who sows to please the Spirit,
from the Spirit will reap eternal life."*

—GALATIANS 6:7-8

Have you ever planted radish seeds in your garden and hoped that instead you'd produce lettuce? When you sow carrot seeds, do you hope you might end up with peas instead? No, of course not. There is a natural law to sowing and reaping: Whatever you sow will produce its own kind (Genesis 1:11). If you sow radish seeds, all you can expect to harvest is radishes.

The same principle is true with God's laws. Maybe you're saved but you're flirting with the ways of the world, pursuing earthly pleasures. If you think it doesn't matter, think again. The Bible says, "For if you live according to the sinful nature, you will die; but if by the Spirit you put to death the misdeeds of the body, you will live, because those who are led by the Spirit of God are sons of God" (Romans 8:13-14).

We need to turn away from earthly pursuits and instead sow into the kingdom of God. Seek guidance from the Holy Spirit by spending time in God's Word.

FURTHER READING:
Proverbs 11:18
1 Corinthians 6:9
Galatians 5:24

October 21

Obedience

"And without faith it is impossible to please God, because anyone who comes to him must believe that he exists and that he rewards those who earnestly seek him."

—HEBREWS 11:6

If you need a miracle harvest from God today, the secret can be found in one word: OBEDIENCE.

Every miracle performed in the Bible came about as the result of obedience. Obedience is the key to a life of reaping abundance and unspeakable joy. Plant your life in the garden of obedience, and fertilize it with the Word of God.

Only then will the divine will of God bloom through you 24 hours a day!

We serve a God who is able to do "immeasurably more than all we ask or imagine, according to his power that is at work within us" (Ephesians 3:20). But first we need to give up our way of thinking and ask God for His! Stop cluttering up the will of God with your plans, desires, dreams and goals—and let God begin to live His plan and His purpose for your life through you!

God wants to bless you with a harvest of good things! He will reward those who act in obedience to the voice of His Spirit.

FURTHER READING:
Jeremiah 7:23
Psalms 119:2
John 14:21

October 22

Bring Forth Fruit

"I tell you the truth, unless a kernel of wheat falls to the ground and dies, it remains only a single seed. But if it dies, it produces many seeds."

—JOHN 12:24

When Jesus spoke these words He was referring to His own death. Jesus used this image to describe the monumental effect that He knew His death would have on all mankind.

Through Christ, millions upon millions have been given eternal life, and generation after generation has been redeemed. With just one seed God gave life and hope to an entire world that was lost and condemned to die.

And what about the seed you hold in your hand? What would happen if you were to release it and sow it into the kingdom of God? What kind of monumental effect would it have?

Ezekiel 17:8 says, "It had been planted in good soil by abundant water so that it would produce branches, bear fruit and become a splendid vine."

As long as you hold on to it, it will be just one seed, and it will never do what seeds were meant to do—to die and bring forth fruit. Could it feed the hungry, bring life-saving aid to the sick, and help spread the Gospel of Jesus Christ? Until you release your seed, you will never know.

FURTHER READING:
John 15:8
Philippians 1:11
Genesis 1:12

October 23

Increase and Multiply

"Now he who supplies seed to the sower and bread for food will also supply and increase your store of seed and will enlarge the harvest of your righteousness."

—2 CORINTHIANS 9:10

God is the Great Provider. He provides the seed that we hold in our hands. He provides the bread to meet our physical needs. And He provides great and wondrous ways to multiply our seed so that it will come back to us!

The seed that leaves your hand will never leave your life but will only increase your blessings! "The blessing of the Lord brings wealth, and he adds no trouble to it" (Proverbs 10:22).

So let the seed go out of your hand...sow it in the kingdom of God. You can be confident that the moment it leaves your hand, your harvest of rewards is already scheduled. When you act in faith, you unlock God's store of bounty so that He can richly bless what you have sown.

Open your hand toward God, and He will open His hand toward you.

"And without faith it is impossible to please God, because anyone who comes to him must believe that he exists and that he rewards those who earnestly seek him" (Hebrews 11:6).

FURTHER READING:
Psalms 31:23
Matthew 16:27
1 Corinthians 3:8

October 24

The Same Reward

"And the gospel must first be preached to all nations."

—MARK 13:10

Much as we'd like to, not all of us can go to the mission fields in obedience to the Great Commission.

This doesn't mean, however, that we can't fulfill our role in the Commission right where we are. We can impact what happens in these nations in two ways.

The first way is through prayer. First Timothy 2 tells us to pray for all men. Particularly, we need to pray for the harvest workers as well as for the unsaved. Prayer is the secret weapon we Christians have that can cross any border and penetrate any area. Secondly, we can make giving to the missions a priority so that food, medical supplies and life-saving necessities can be brought along with the Gospel to a lost and dying world. First Samuel 30:24 promises that the share of those who stay with the supplies is to be the same as that of those who go down to the battle.

Whatever your part in the Great Commission, God's Word says that you will have the same reward as those on the front lines. Those behind the scenes are just as important as those going into battle, for they keep supplies coming in and give life-saving gifts to help those who need it most.

FURTHER READING:
1 Timothy 2:1-4
2 Corinthians 10:4
Revelation 14:15

October 25

The Shield of Faith

"In addition to all this, take up the shield of faith, with which you can extinguish all the flaming arrows of the evil one."

—EPHESIANS 6:16

Do you want to experience a miracle harvest in your life?

Then pick up your shield of faith and cast off the fears and doubts that are weighing you down. Because doubt and fear are like fiery darts of the wicked—they attempt to separate you from God, cut off the flow of the Holy Spirit, and prevent God from acting in your life!

The devil would like nothing more than to consume you with worry, fear and doubt. He wants you to think God doesn't want to bless you or reward your faithfulness. He wants you to get discouraged—but the shield of your faith will protect you! Your faith is the strongest defense you have against the fiery darts of doubt and fear that seek to destroy you.

Ephesians 6:16 says, "In addition to all this, take up the shield of faith, with which you can extinguish all the flaming arrows of the evil one."

Doubt will not produce your harvest, and neither will worry nor fear. Only your faith, and your faith alone, will ensure an abundant harvest from the Lord!

FURTHER READING:
2 Samuel 22:36
2 Corinthians 5:7
James 1:6

October 26

The Perfect Seed

"From this man's descendants God has brought to Israel the Savior Jesus, as he promised."

—ACTS 13:23

When God gave us Jesus, He gave us His perfect seed and planted Him in the garden of earth. But like a seed, in order for Jesus to produce life He had to die. And with His death, He brought forth eternal life for all mankind.

You see, God always wanted a special relationship with mankind, which is why He created Adam and placed him in the Garden of Eden. When Adam sinned, he condemned all men to die.

But through the seed of Jesus, we have been redeemed from the curse of death and our special relationship with God has been restored. When Christ rose from the dead, God showed the world that there was nothing He could not overcome. Death was no match for the King of Kings!

If you need a miracle today, remember that nothing is impossible for Him who defeated death! And if God did not spare His only Son for you, why would He withhold anything else from you? As Psalms 84:11 says: "...the Lord bestows favor and honor; no good thing does he withhold from those whose walk is blameless."

FURTHER READING:
Matthew 7:9-11
Psalms 84
Psalms 120

October 27

Set Upon A Rock

"For in the day of trouble he will keep me safe in his dwelling; he will hide me in the shelter of his tabernacle and set me high upon a rock."

—PSALMS 27:5

Are the circumstances of life pressing on you, robbing you of the peace in your life? Remember that although circumstances change, God's promises do not.

If you are caught in the winds of change, stand on the rock of His promises and take shelter under His wings until the storm passes. If you spend all your time looking down at your circumstances, you will forget to look up to God from whom all blessings flow! Philippians 4:11 says, "I am not saying this because I am in need, for I have learned to be content whatever the circumstances." The Bible tells us that the man who looks only at his own circumstances will never sow the seed he has been given because he is always too afraid to step out in faith.

"Whoever watches the wind will not plant; whoever looks at the clouds will not reap" (Ecclesiastes 11:4).

Instead, let's look beyond our current circumstances— through the clouds of misery and beyond the dark horizon— and plant our seeds in faith, knowing that the future brings a glorious harvest!

FURTHER READING:
Psalms 61:2
Psalms 18:2
Psalms 40:2

October 28

Honor God

"'Bring the whole tithe into the storehouse, that there may be food in my house. Test me in this,' says the Lord Almighty, 'and see if I will not throw open the floodgates of heaven and pour out so much blessing that you will not have room enough for it.'"

—MALACHI 3:10

God promises He will open heaven and shower us with blessings if we are faithful in our tithing. Malachi quotes God as challenging us to "prove" Him or put Him to the test on this point. In Matthew 7:9-11 Jesus says, "Which of you, if his son asks for bread, will give him a stone? Or if he asks for a fish, will give him a snake? If you, then, though you are evil, know how to give good gifts to your children, how much more will your Father in heaven give good gifts to those who ask him!"

So why wouldn't we tithe? Everything we have comes from God; He gives us the ability to prosper. So why wouldn't we return a portion to Him? Honor God by sowing your seed in His kingdom and He will return it back to you with a harvest that is multiplied many times over! Proverbs 3:9-10 says: "Honor the Lord with your wealth, with the firstfruits of all your crops; then your barns will be filled to overflowing, and your vats will brim over with new wine."

FURTHER READING:
2 Corinthians 9:6-7
Malachi 3:6-12
Proverbs 3

October 29

Bear Fruit

"This is to my Father's glory, that you bear much fruit,
showing yourselves to be my disciples."

—JOHN 15:8

Jesus commands us to be sowers and reapers of a spiritual harvest, and bear fruit that glorifies God. The Bible has some specific instructions on how we should participate in reaping souls for Christ.

The harvest of souls begins with sowing lots of the good seed of the Gospel (Luke 8:11). Then the young crop must be nurtured through the teachings of God's Word. In Matthew 4:4 Jesus says, "It is written: 'Man does not live on bread alone, but on every word that comes from the mouth of God.'" Of course, every crop needs plenty of water, which God provides. "He will also send you rain for the seed you sow in the ground, and the food that comes from the land will be rich and plentiful" (Isaiah 30:23).

At every stage, the crop needs to be strengthened and fertilized with plenty of intercessory prayer. "Brothers, my heart's desire and prayer to God for the Israelites is that they may be saved" (Romans 10:1).

The end result will be an abundant harvest of souls brought into the kingdom of God.

FURTHER READING:
John 15:16
Matthew 13:37-38
Luke 8:1-15

October 30

We Know Not How

"This is what the kingdom of God is like. A man scatters seed on the ground. Night and day, whether he sleeps or gets up, the seed sprouts and grows, though he does not know how. All by itself the soil produces grain—first the stalk, then the head, then the full kernel in the head."

—MARK 4:26-28

If you are actively laboring in the fields of the world to reap lost souls, guard against feeling discouraged if it seems your work is not yielding results. Are your loved ones shunning your attempts to share the Gospel message? Remember that God is Lord of the harvest, and He is in charge.

Our task is to sow the Word of God, but we must trust Him, depend on Him, and be patient as He perfects the results of our work. For although we are laborers together with God, we "know not" how those seeds we've sown will grow. Only God can give the increase (1 Corinthians 3:7), in His own time and in His own way, according to a definite order of development: "first the stalk, then the head, then the full kernel in the head." Only when the crop is fully developed are we expected to reap—and rejoice!

"He who goes out weeping, carrying seed to sow, will return with songs of joy, carrying sheaves with him" (Psalms 126:6).

FURTHER READING:
Isaiah 55:10-11
1 Corinthians 3:4-15
1 Peter 1:23-25

October 31

Shine Your Light

"Let your light so shine before men, that they may see your good works and glorify your Father in heaven."

—MATTHEW 5:16

It was just an old building that housed a company store decades ago, in the middle of a poverty-ridden area of West Virginia, deep in coal-mining country.

This old company store is now a place that is saving the lives and souls of countless coal-mining families in the area.

You see, this old company store houses our *Bridge of Hope* partner, the Dream Center, in Holden, West Virginia.

When I heard how devastated this area was and how the center had to stop providing hot meals to the needy because there simply was no food or money to continue, we filled two 18-wheelers with food and supplies and brought hope to the hurting in this area. Matthew 25:35 says, "For I was hungry and you gave me something to eat, I was thirsty and you gave me something to drink."

The more America hurts, the more the Church needs to step up and show God's love. When everyone else is thinking of "me, myself, and I," the Church finds its best opportunity to fulfill its role as the body of Christ and extend the strong arm of the Almighty to bring help and hope to those in despair.

FURTHER READING:
Isaiah 41:17-20
Luke 4:14-30
Matthew 25:31-46

November 1

No Longer A Slave

"So you are no longer a slave, but a son; and since you are a son, God has made you also an heir."

—GALATIANS 4:7

You are no longer a slave to sin. Isn't that wonderful news?

When you were born again, you were set free. You were delivered from the authority and the power of darkness and were brought into the light of Jesus. But salvation gives you more than your freedom—it makes you an heir.

Being an heir of God means that you have property, rights, standing, access, power, dominion, and authority in the name of Jesus. Yes, you have the right to approach the throne of God with boldness.

Hebrews 4:16 says, "Let us then approach the throne of grace with confidence, so that we may receive mercy and find grace to help us in our time of need."

You can be certain of your inheritance—because you have been bought and paid for by His blood!

Christ set you free from sin, curses and from mental, physical, emotional and spiritual bondage. It is already done. All you need to do is to apply all that Jesus did for you on the cross—by exercising your faith in God.

FURTHER READING:
Romans 6:15-23
Romans 8:1-17
Galatians 3:26-29

November 2

Share His Glory

"Now if we are children, then we are heirs—heirs of God and co-heirs with Christ, if indeed we share in his sufferings in order that we may also share in his glory."

—ROMANS 8:17

Many people wonder why they suffer, or why things seem to get worse once they have come to the Lord. I'm sure Job wondered why he kept losing family and friends—even while remaining faithful! The Bible says that if we share in the sufferings of Christ we will also share in His glory.

God wants to refine us—to develop a Christ-like character in us. God will use adversity to prune us so that we can bear more fruit. He wants us to be the best that He created us to be. If life was easy, would we need to follow Him? The things in our lives that are hindrances, stumbling blocks, or openings for the enemy prevent us from reaching our potential and purpose... and need to be discarded. But how many of us would discard them without the discomfort or the test?

Pray to become more Christlike. God in His infinite wisdom will transform your life into one that reflects more of the glory of God in Christ Jesus. When you are faced with tests—do not complain or murmur. Continue to praise God, for you know that His glory is about to be revealed in you.

FURTHER READING:
Romans 5:1-5
Hebrews 10:32-39
James 5:10-11

November 3

Who Are You?

"If you belong to Christ, then you are Abraham's seed, and heirs according to the promise."

—GALATIANS 3:29

You are a joint heir with Jesus! You have been born again into royalty! You are rich in the promises of God. You are rich in the blessings of the Lord. You are rich in the power of the Lord. You are rich in authority. You are rich in dominion. You are rich, for in Christ Jesus there is no lack.

God has already provided everything you need. Ask and you shall receive (Matthew 21:22). God will not withhold any good thing from His children. Psalms 84:11 says, "For the Lord God is a sun and shield; the Lord bestows favor and honor; no good thing does he withhold from those whose walk is blameless."

Stand in your place of authority and demand that the devil take his hand off your children, your finances and your marriage. Then ask the Lord for what you need: favor on your job, peace in your home, your health to be restored—ask Him and He will provide!

God has made the provision. He is waiting for you to take authority in Jesus' name and then to ask for what you need—and He will supply it according to His riches in Christ Jesus (Philippians 4:19).

FURTHER READING:
Ephesians 1:3-10
Galatians 3:16
Galatians 4:1-7

November 4

They Are Waiting

"We know that the whole creation has been groaning as in the pains of childbirth right up to the present time. Not only so, but we ourselves, who have the firstfruits of the Spirit, groan inwardly as we wait eagerly for our adoption as sons, the redemption of our bodies."

—ROMANS 8:22-23

The world is waiting for the manifestation of the sons of God. Your bank account is waiting for that manifestation. Your children are waiting for that manifestation. Your community is waiting for that manifestation. Your whole world is waiting for the manifestation of the sonship of God in you!

If you want to change your world, allow the sonship of God to manifest in you by accepting the inheritance God has promised to you—the inheritance of His sons! All of creation is groaning and waiting for the sons of God to rise up and take their place.

First Corinthians 12:7 says, "Now to each one the manifestation of the Spirit is given for the common good."

Today declare, "I am a child of God, an heir of God, a joint heir with Jesus. I will not live the low life. I will not take the low road. I will not sit down. I will not shut up. I am a child of God, and the whole world is waiting on me! And I'm ready!"

FURTHER READING:
Romans 8:18-27
Titus 3:33-37
Hebrews 6:13-20

November 5

Your Authority

"Because God wanted to make the unchanging nature of his purpose very clear to the heirs of what was promised, he confirmed it with an oath."

—HEBREWS 6:17

Do you know that you have Christ-given authority over everything? Over your body. Over your household. Over your mind...even over the devil!

Well, you do! And it is doubly backed by God's promise and His oath. But you have to exercise it. As a son of God, you have the right to rule in the earth.

You must bring your flesh into subjection in order to manifest being a son of God. It is time to take authority over needs, habits and bondage—to take authority by the power of the Spirit! Take authority over your tongue if your tongue has been saying what it should not say. Take authority over your mind if your mind has been thinking what it should not think. God has given you the authority to tell the devil to get out of your mind, out of your life, out of your house and out of your children! He promises that we will have the power to move mountains if we just have faith in Him. But faith is not passive—it is active! Right now, I challenge you to exercise authority by making your declaration of faith before the Lord.

FURTHER READING:
2 Corinthians 10:2-5
2 Corinthians 12:8-10
Hebrews 6:1-12

November 6

Transformed

"For you did not receive a spirit that makes you a slave again to fear, but you received the Spirit of sonship. And by him we cry, "Abba, Father.""

—ROMANS 8:15

You have been transformed. When you were born again, you became a new creature (2 Corinthians 5:17). Your spirit was reborn—completely transformed by the power of the risen Savior.

But you still have to work out your salvation—you have to contend with killing your old nature—your old emotions, old thought patterns (2 Corinthians 10:5), old relationships and old fleshly desires. God will help you if you only ask!

If you find yourself still struggling with your emotions, feast on the Word of God. If the enemy is condemning you, apply the blood that wipes out all his charges. When you are plagued with despair and hopelessness, ask God to give you the same mind and attitude of Jesus.

Call on God and He will send help! He will send ministering angels to help the heirs of salvation (Hebrews 1:14). You are an heir because of Christ Jesus!

You have an eternal hope, for you have received the Spirit of sonship (Titus 3:7). You are blessed... for you have been transformed by the power and the blood of Christ Jesus.

FURTHER READING:
Galatians 4:1-7
Ephesians 1:3-6
Romans 8:28-39

November 7

Setting Things Right

"The Lord laughs at the wicked, for he knows their day is coming. The wicked draw the sword and bend the bow to bring down the poor and needy, to slay those whose ways are upright."

—PSALMS 37:13-14

Perhaps few people need to hear the message of divine justice as much as the Christian Sudanese. They are victims of a war of genocide, perpetrated against them by a government that wants to force them into a totalitarian way of life.

All of us have suffered injustice to one degree or another. Whatever the form of injustice we've experienced, it's plain to see that the world doesn't work the way it's supposed to. We all yearn for a time and a place when things will work the way they're supposed to, a world where good is rewarded and evil punished. In the meantime, we want assurance that, regardless of how things seem in our bleakest moments, Someone is watching out for us. We need to hear that the things we are going through are not meaningless, that somehow they will be transformed into good.

This is the message *Bridge of Hope* has been delivering to the Christian Sudanese. It brings the guarantee that God weeps with them now but that someday they will laugh with Him.

FURTHER READING:
Psalms 37:28-40
Isaiah 11:1-9
Revelation 21:1-4

November 8

Unlock the Door

"And the prayer of faith will save the sick, and the Lord will raise him up. And if he has committed sins, he will be forgiven."

—JAMES 5:15

Have you ever been on the wrong side of a locked door? Maybe you've left your keys in the car or locked yourself out of the house. The door is in your way; you want be on the other side of that door.

Perhaps you feel that way when you pray. You know God is there; you know He's powerful enough to heal the sick and make the blind see, but your words seem to bounce off a door between you and God. You know the power that is available on the other side of the door, yet you can't access it. Faith is the hinge on which the door swings. It is the essential element, the one inescapable condition of successful prayer. Hebrews 11:6 tells us that everyone "who comes to God must believe that He is, and that He is a rewarder of those who diligently seek Him."

To pray in faith is to know beyond the shadow of a doubt that God is real, that He cares deeply about everything that concerns you, that He's listening intently to everything you have to say and that He is able to move mountains to provide a miracle for you.

FURTHER READING:
Psalms 118:19-21
Luke 11:5-10
Luke 18:1-8

November 9

God Answers Prayer

"You do not have, because you do not ask God.
When you ask, you do not receive, because
you ask with wrong motives, that you may
spend what you get on your pleasures"

—JAMES 4:2-3

Many believers are disheartened because they believe that God doesn't answer prayers. This is simply not true.

God tells us in His Word what His will is for us, but we must ask first (Ezekiel 36:37). He tells us that if we ask it shall be given to us. Luke 11:9-10 says, "So I say to you: Ask and it will be given to you; seek and you will find; knock and the door will be opened to you. For everyone who asks receives; he who seeks finds; and to him who knocks, the door will be opened."

God tells us in Luke 11 of both our need to spend time in prayer and His response when we pray. If we come to God in prayer with the right motives, putting first the kingdom of God, and if we live for Him, He will give us the desires of our hearts (Psalms 37:4).

He will answer our prayers, provide for our needs, rescue us in the time of danger, and pour out His favor upon us.

We serve a God who answers prayers...why not give Him the opportunity today?

FURTHER READING:
Mark 11:22-24
Psalms 2:8
Ezekiel 36:37

November 10

Spare Tire

"And pray in the Spirit on all occasions with all kinds of prayers and requests. With this in mind, be alert and always keep on praying for all the saints."

—EPHESIANS 6:18

How often do you think about the spare tire in your car? If you're like most of us, you think of it only when you're on the side of the road and your car won't move without it. Many people treat prayer the same way. They don't pray until that's all they can do. Do you treat prayer as a last resort?

That's not the model the Bible gives us for prayer. Jesus prayed constantly, even as His ministry was exploding and followers were waiting for Him to speak (Luke 5:15-16). He didn't wait until He was betrayed to pray to the Father, but spent the last night before He was betrayed praying in the garden (Luke 22:42).

Prayer is about spending time seeking God, getting to know Him and strengthening our relationship with Him. Psalms 32 tells us, "Therefore let everyone who is godly pray to You while you may be found; surely when the mighty waters rise, they will not reach him." We are told to pray before the storms of life come, before the tire blows out, at all times and in all situations.

Prayer is not a spare tire, but a constant in our lives.

FURTHER READING:
Luke 22
Acts 1:14
Acts 2:42-47

November 11

Tap into His Power

"With this in mind, we constantly pray for you,
that our God may count you worthy of his calling,
and that by his power he may fulfill every good purpose
of yours and every act prompted by your faith."

—2 THESSALONIANS 1:11

Deborah recently had to have emergency surgery. Her hospital bills totaled $30,000—an amount she couldn't pay. She lifted her bills to the Lord, praying that He would rescue her. Soon afterward, she received a letter from the hospital—her bills had been miraculously paid in full. She owed nothing!

Prayer is able to change any situation. Like Deborah, we need to connect to God's awesome power by praying in faith. We need to step out in faith, believing that He has heard us and has already provided what we need. "Do not fear, little flock, for it is your Father's good pleasure to give you the kingdom" (Luke 12:32). Our God is the mighty creator of a vast and complex universe, yet He cares deeply about every aspect of your life and wants to shower you with blessings. Praying in faith is essential in releasing God's mighty power.

Ephesians 3:20 tells us that He is able to do exceedingly more than we can ask or even imagine. Call on Him today, and He will show you great and mighty things.

FURTHER READING:
2 Samuel 22:33
Matthew 21:22
Mark 11:24

November 12

Holy Spirit and Prayer

"But the Counselor, the Holy Spirit, whom the Father will send in my name, will teach you all things and will remind you of everything I have said to you."

—JOHN 14:26

People tell me all the time they're struggling with prayer. If you're struggling in your prayer time, remember that the Holy Spirit is there with you.

You need to listen and receive what the Spirit is teaching you. If you're praying for something outside of God's will for your life, you aren't going to see the answers you want.

If you want to know if you're praying in God's will, you need to consult His Word and the Holy Spirit. He has given us over 1,000 pages of His will. Thank God for the blessed Holy Spirit who reveals the Word to our hearts, to our spirits, to our minds, and gives us exactly what we need to live every day in victory.

If you find yourself struggling as you enter the throne room of the Most High, remind yourself that the Holy Spirit is with you, guiding you as you pray.

Trust Him and allow Him to fill you as you pray. The Lord knows what is best for you and He knows your heart. Go to Him in prayer openly and honestly. We receive power when the Holy Spirit comes upon us (Acts 1:8). With your faith and the Holy Spirit's power, your prayer life will be transformed.

FURTHER READING:
Acts 1:1-8
Jude 1:20-21
John 14

November 13

Does He Hear Me?

*"But God has surely listened and
heard my voice in prayer."*

—PSALMS 66:19

You may wonder, when you're down on your knees petitioning God, whether or not your prayers have been heard.

You may wonder if He's listening. You may be in a situation similar to Jennifer and Eric, a couple who tried for 10 years to conceive and could not. Dear friends, He is listening and He has heard your prayer. It doesn't matter what time of day you pray, whether you're in your car or at the mall—He hears you. The Bible assures us of this over and over again.

Elizabeth and Zacharias in the New Testament had prayed for a baby for years, until her child-bearing years were long past. Then, long after they had given up hope, an angel appeared to Zachariah in Luke 1:13 and says, "'Do not be afraid, Zacharias, for your prayer is heard; and your wife Elizabeth will bear you a son.'" Their son, John the Baptist, came at his appointed time to prepare the Jews for the coming of their Savior.

God heard Jennifer and Eric's prayer also, and Jennifer recently delivered a healthy baby girl. We must continue to pray earnestly and vigilantly (Colossians 4:2) with full confidence that God hears our prayers.

FURTHER READING:
Psalms 102:17
Jeremiah 29:12
Luke 1:5-25

November 14

A Praying Church

"Whoever serves me must follow me; and where I am, my servant also will be. My Father will honor the one who serves me."

—JOHN 12:26

Too many preachers spend more time in marketing meetings, strategy development seminars and business workshops than they do in prayer.

They try to run the Church as a corporation instead of as the Church of God with the guidance and administration of the Holy Spirit.

Because of this, many members run their lives the way they see the pastor running the church—disconnected from God. You cannot have an abundant life without having a prayer life. You cannot be victorious without spending time with God—for it is in those private moments that God reveals strategies, plans and tactics that will assure your victory.

In John 12:23 Jesus says, "The hour has come for the Son of Man to be glorified."

We need a praying Church, not a playing Church—a Church that ministers with the fires of prayer in our hearts, a Church that is willing to humble herself and inquire of the Lord—a Church that is willing to keep watch.

FURTHER READING:
Ezekiel 36:37
Matthew 26:41
John 12:23-27

November 15

The Power of Thanksgiving

"This service that you perform is not only supplying the needs of God's people but is also overflowing in many expressions of thanks to God."

—2 CORINTHIANS 9:12

If you want to live a life of abundance, start by thanking God.

Colossians 4:2 says, "Devote yourselves to prayer, being watchful and thankful." Before you can begin to receive more blessings you must look around and see the blessings God has already brought to you!

God knows all that we need even before we pray for it, and He is waiting to pour gifts and blessings down upon you. Your thoughts and prayers do not have to be constantly on your mind for God to fulfill them—God is big enough for all of the trials and problems you face today.

Look around you and give thanks for all that you have today. Give thanks in faith, for God not only provides the basic needs of those who thank and praise Him, but pours abundance upon their heads as well.

Make every day a day of thanksgiving and praise! Praising God publicly is one way we can take the light from beneath the bushel and shine for the unsaved around us. Do it as an expression of love for your heavenly Father who provides for you.

FURTHER READING:
Luke 8:16-18
Philippians 3:10-13
Colossians 1:12

November 16

The Wrong Things

"The Pharisee stood up and prayed about himself, 'God, I thank You that I am not like other men—robbers, evildoers, adulterers, or even like this tax collector.'"

—LUKE 18:11

Do you ever find, like this Pharisee, that you are thanking God for all the wrong things?

Do you ever pray to God with a sense of superiority, thanking Him for the fact that you've done the right things and that you're better than all those "sinners" out there? Don't be like the Pharisees, whom Jesus called "a brood of vipers" (Matthew 3:7) and "sons of hell" (Matthew 23:15).

It is right to give thanks and praise to God, but we should do it remembering always that He is the source of all goodness.

John 15:5 tells us, "Without God, you can do nothing." There is nothing good or praiseworthy that comes through us, but only through the grace of God. Remember that we are called to be an example to non-believers. Second Corinthians 5:20 says, "We are therefore Christ's ambassadors."

As you sit down for your time with God today make sure you are praising Him with the right heart and the right attitude. He has allowed you to be a light for Him in the world and has allowed you to hold His hand as you do good together.

FURTHER READING:
1 Corinthians 1:26-29
Luke 5:31-32
Romans 1:21

November 17

Come into His Presence

*"Let us come before him with thanksgiving
and extol him with music and song."*

—PSALMS 95:2

What is praise and thanksgiving? Psalms 95 teaches us that it is an act of "shouting joyfully." Psalms 95:6 calls on us to "worship and bow down" after we have praised. Thanksgiving is nothing less than the proper prelude to worship! This psalm also places thanks before worship. We cannot properly worship without a joyful, thankful heart towards our Lord.

Hebrews 4:16 says, "Therefore let us come boldly to the throne of grace, that we may obtain mercy and find grace to help in time of need."

What a blessed privilege we've been given! Even if you're stressed, you can shout for joy and be thankful, for the Maker of heaven and earth has invited you to come boldly before His throne. Thanksgiving is the act of dressing properly to be in God's court. Don't go into the presence of God without praise.

Psalms 69:30 says, "I will praise God's name in song and glorify him with thanksgiving."

Even when you are crying out to Him in pain, crying brokenly for Him to reach out to you, you can still be grateful in the knowledge that He is there to listen and He will respond!

FURTHER READING:
1 Chronicles 16:8-12
2 Chronicles 5:13-14
Philippians 4:4

November 18

Prayer of Thanksgiving

"'Give thanks to the Lord, for his love endures forever.'
As they began to sing and praise, the Lord set ambushes
against the men of Ammon and Moab and Mount Seir
who were invading Judah, and they were defeated."

—2 CHRONICLES 20:21

Jehoshaphat stood before the people and commanded their attention. He told them to have faith in God—which is the essential ingredient for prayer to work.

He assured them that if they had faith in God they would be upheld, and if they believed the word of the prophets they would have success. They could not have doubt.

After Jehoshaphat spoke to the people he appointed men to sing to the Lord and to praise Him for His holiness. As a result of this, God set ambushes against their enemies and God's people were victorious.

The prayer of thanksgiving, praise and worship brings about miracles. It opens the door for God to set ambushes. Ezra 3:11 says, "With praise and thanksgiving they sang to the Lord: "He is good; his love to Israel endures forever."

In the midst of the battle...take time to lift up your songs of thanksgiving, praise and worship—have faith in God, believe His Word, and you will be upheld and have success.

FURTHER READING:
Isaiah 7:9
1 Chronicles 16:29
1 Chronicles 16:34-35

November 19

Prayer in the Spirit

"But you, dear friends, build yourselves up in your most holy faith and pray in the Holy Spirit"

—JUDE 1:20

Many misinformed teachers have told their students that Paul did not encourage the people to speak in tongues—but that is not so. Paul encouraged them to speak in tongues but he asked that they do it in decency and in order when in public meetings.

Praying in the Holy Spirit builds us up with our most holy faith—this type of faith is pure and holy because it comes directly from God.

When we pray in tongues it is a prayer that we do unto God—it is not for men to understand. When God prays through us we are praying mysteries that no man can understand except God, who gives the interpretation.

Paul tells us in 1 Corinthians 14:18 that he spoke in tongues more than the other believers—this indicates that he did it often.

He says, "I thank God that I speak in tongues more than all of you." In our private time we should allow God to pray through us so we will pray His perfect will. And because it is God doing the praying, we know that His Word will accomplish all that He sent it forth to do.

FURTHER READING:
1 Corinthians 14:2-4
Isaiah 55:11
Mark 16:17

November 20

Anxious About Nothing

"Be anxious about nothing, but in everything by prayer and petition, with thanksgiving, present your requests to God."

—PHILIPPIANS 4:6

The Bible often commands us to avoid anxiety and fear. God tells us that He will supply for our every need. Even though we may not see the fruits of our faith immediately, we should always thank God, knowing He will bring them when the time is right. Philippians is very clear on this point—prayer and petition must be accompanied by thanksgiving.

In Philippians 4:19 God's Word promises that He will supply "all your needs in accordance with His riches." Picture for a moment what the riches of God must look like! There is no need to fear that these boundless blessings will ever run out. God has promised you the abundance of His riches!

Be of the same mindset as David in Psalms 118:6, "The Lord is with me; I will not be afraid. What can man do to me?"

Don't look down at the ground in discouragement—look up to heaven and praise Him for the great gifts He has promised you! Then get up and go, believing and expecting that God will supply for all your needs.

Today is the day to stand on those everlasting promises!

FURTHER READING:
Matthew 6:31-34
1 Samuel 1:19-20
Luke 13:10-13

November 21

Open the Prison Doors

"About midnight Paul and Silas were praying and singing hymns to God, and the other prisoners were listening to them. Suddenly there was such a violent earthquake that the foundations of the prison were shaken. At once all the prison doors flew open, and everybody's chains came loose."

—ACTS 16:25-26

The act of thanksgiving and praise opens impossible doors and shakes loose all chains! Sometimes we find ourselves constrained by our circumstances. Don't be afraid when that happens—perhaps the reason is so that you can be a blessing to those around you.

In the passage from Acts 16, we sometimes forget that Paul and Silas were not the only ones freed from prison—all the prisoners' chains were shaken loose. Then the keeper of the prison himself gave his life to Jesus Christ. The one who was responsible for holding all of these men in bondage repented and came to Christ because Paul and Silas did not ever give up and did not ever fail to give thanks. That is the power of gratitude and thanksgiving to God our heavenly Father.

Keep giving thanks—He is big enough to deliver you from your circumstances and to do a great work through you.

FURTHER READING:
Genesis 39:20-23
Daniel 3:24-29
Daniel 6:16-27

November 22

Simple Praise

*"From the lips of children and
infants you have ordained praise."*

—MATTHEW 21:16

Thanksgiving is the prelude to Christmas, the season in which
we give thanks for the greatest gift ever given—Jesus Himself.

But for too many of us, thanksgiving means the beginning of
a season of stress and worry. Meanwhile our children's prayers
and thanks are simple: "God is great, God is good, let us thank
Him for our food."

This time of year is also when many families feel a lack and
a need they cannot fulfill themselves. Yet we know that God's
strength is perfected in our weakness.

Whatever your situation is this Thanksgiving, I hope you will
stop and listen to these children as they are praising the Lord.
I hope you will listen to how they don't put qualifiers on their
thanks or praise, how there is no doubt in their prayer, and how
they pray in simple faith.

First Chronicles 29:13 says, "Now, our God, we give you
thanks, and praise your glorious name." If any sort of stress is
following you through this season of praise, relinquish that
to God. Take a step back and become as a trusting child once
more, knowing that Father will take care of every detail.

FURTHER READING:
Hebrews 11:32-34
2 Corinthians 12:9-10
Matthew 19:13

November 23

Prayer of Agreement

"Again, I tell you that if two of you on earth agree about anything you ask for, it will be done for you by my Father in heaven. For where two or three come together in my name, there am I with them"

—MATTHEW 18:19-20

The prayer of agreement is one that is prayed with another believer. It is a prayer that has the power to fill us and anoint us to speak with boldness.

In Acts 2, God gives us irrefutable evidence that the prayer of agreement works. As the believers gathered together there was a sound from heaven that filled the house where they were meeting. Tongues of fire rested on each of them and everyone was filled with the Holy Spirit.

When we stand in agreement, the Lord manifests Himself and everyone receives from God. All too often, we will agree with one another about how bad the situation is, yet we do not pray a prayer of agreement believing God that He will show up and He will enable us to reap a harvest of victory even while we are in the clutches of defeat.

The prayer of agreement is for those who believe that Christ Himself is in our midst when we pray—and that what we ask in faith will be done.

FURTHER READING:
Acts 4:31
Matthew 7:7
Mark 11:24

November 24

Prayer of Commitment

"Do not be anxious about anything, but in everything, by prayer and petition, with thanksgiving, present your requests to God."

—PHILIPPIANS 4:6

The prayer of commitment, consecration and dedication is a prayer that sets us apart unto God. This is the type of prayer that Christ offered in the garden of Gethsemane in Matthew 26.

We, as believers, need to pray this prayer often—setting ourselves apart from the world and consecrating ourselves unto God.

In life there are so many distractions that it can be difficult at times to focus and to press into the presence of God. These are the times when we have to separate ourselves as Christ did.

Too often we give up, believing that it is useless to continue to contend for what we are seeking from God or what He requires of us. But God will give us victory in every area if we do not give up.

The prayer of commitment, consecration and dedication requires a commitment to God and to doing His will—even when it is uncomfortable and painful. It helps us to put our flesh under subjection to our spirit and to do what God has called for us to do.

FURTHER READING:
1 Peter 5:7
Matthew 6:25
Matthew 26:39

November 25

Prayer of Authority

"I will give you the keys of the kingdom of heaven; whatever you bind on earth will be bound in heaven, and whatever you loose on earth will be loosed in heaven."

—MATTHEW 16:19

As a believer in Jesus Christ, you have the keys to the kingdom of heaven. You have the authority to bind things on earth which will also be bound in heaven, and if you loose anything on earth it will be loosed in heaven.

Yet so many go through life defeated, oppressed and bound because they don't pray with authority. We have the authority to defeat all evil through the power of God!

Matthew 21:23 says, "Jesus entered the temple courts, and, while he was teaching, the chief priests and the elders of the people came to him. 'By what authority are you doing these things?' they asked. 'And who gave you this authority?'"

To pray with authority you have to learn how to "bind and loose" in the name of Jesus. The prayer of authority refuses to take no for an answer. It is knowing how to speak the law of the Lord. It is taking hold of your God-given right to speak the Word of the Lord to the devil knowing he has to obey.

Don't let anything stop you!

FURTHER READING:
Psalms 2:7
Isaiah 22:22
Matthew 18:18

November 26

Prayer of Faith and Petition

*"'Have faith in God,' Jesus answered. 'I tell
you the truth, if anyone says to this mountain,
"Go, throw yourself into the sea," and does
not doubt in his heart but believes that what
he says will happen, it will be done for him."*

—MARK 11:22-24

The main ingredient for a prayer of faith and petition is "faith in God." Many Christians have faith but it is rooted in self, luck, the right formula or strategy—but faith in God is not included.

Mark 11:24 says, "Therefore I tell you, whatever you ask for in prayer, believe that you have received it, and it will be yours."

Jesus told them to have faith in God. He did not suggest that they do it. He did not say it was optional. He commanded them to "have faith in God"—and then what they said without doubt in their heart would manifest.

Luke 17:6 says, "He replied, "If you have faith as small as a mustard seed, you can say to this mulberry tree, 'Be uprooted and planted in the sea,' and it will obey you."

We are to speak to the mountain—the devil and the obstacle, and tell it to move. We need to stop talking to everyone else and start to tell the mountain to cast itself into the sea—and believe it will happen because we have faith in God.

FURTHER READING:
Matthew 17:20
Matthew 7:7
2 Corinthians 10:5

November 27

Prayer of Intercession

"In the same way, the Spirit helps us in our weakness. We do not know what we ought to pray for, but the Spirit himself intercedes for us with groans that words cannot express"

—ROMANS 8:26

The highest form of prayer that we can pray is when we surrender to the Spirit of God who dwells in our heart. This type of prayer usually moves beyond prayer in our native language and even beyond prayer in "unknown tongues." It is groaning that cannot be uttered.

Romans 8:27 says, "And he who searches our hearts knows the mind of the Spirit, because the Spirit intercedes for the saints in accordance with God's will."

When you reach the point where the Spirit of God so fills you that He Himself is praying through you, you will experience great success. Your prayer will be according to God's will, since it will be guided by the Spirit.

Hebrews 7:25 says, "Therefore he is able to save completely those who come to God through him, because he always lives to intercede for them." Prayer is not an option—it is as essential to our spirits as breathing is to our physical bodies. Prayer is mandatory for those who desire to please God and live a godly life.

FURTHER READING:
1 Samuel 1:10-15
1 Corinthians 14:18-19
Hebrews 7

November 28

Faith Comes By Hearing

*"Consequently, faith comes from hearing the message,
and the message is heard through the word of Christ"*

—ROMANS 10:17

When you first heard the Word of God, you received faith from God. Sadly many Christians are struggling with lack of faith. Why is this? I believe that it is because they have allowed tradition to steal their faith.

Matthew 6:30 says, "If that is how God clothes the grass of the field, which is here today and tomorrow is thrown into the fire, will he not much more clothe you, O you of little faith?"

Tradition steals faith in three ways—first, tradition takes doubt and produces unbelief. Second, tradition nullifies the Word of God, because it trivializes the power of Satan and causes believers to be ignorant of their own power in Christ Jesus. Third, tradition steals your faith and hope which causes barrenness in every season.

In order to reclaim what is rightfully yours you must do it in faith. John 8:54 says, "Jesus replied, "If I glorify myself, my glory means nothing. My Father, whom you claim as your God, is the one who glorifies me." You have to know the Word of God, believe the Word of God, apply the Word of God, stand on the Word of God and fight with the Word of God in FAITH.

FURTHER READING:
Galatians 3:2
Galatians 3:7
Galatians 3:5

November 29

Prison Bars

"...To open eyes that are blind, to free captives
from prison and to release from the dungeon
those who sit in darkness."

—ISAIAH 42:7

Sometimes we need to be rescued from things that hold us captive—things like debt, addictions or relationships we can't escape from under our own power. But Jesus has come to set every prisoner free.

In Acts 12, Peter was in jail after James' execution—and King Herod was planning to execute Peter as well. But the Church came together to pray and miraculously, though he was chained between two prison guards, Peter's chains were loosed and he was set free through the power of prayer. He went immediately to the prayer meeting and knocked on the door while they were still praying for him.

Prison bars can't hold fast against the power of God. If you or someone you love is in bondage to the world, pray fervently! Never underestimate the power of prayer! Our God is a mighty God who can and will break the strongest chains!

Even if you can't see a way out, the Lord has already planned one for you—you have been set free. Claim Jesus' victory in your life and walk in the light! Like Peter, you will be liberated.

FURTHER READING:
Genesis 39-41
Isaiah 42:1-9
Acts 12

November 30

Miss the Mess

*"But whoever listens to me will live in safety
and be at ease, without fear of harm."*

—PROVERBS 1:33

You may not even realize it as you go about your day, but the devil is out to discourage you. He lays traps and snares for you, hoping to catch you, to trip you up, to make you fall. He is working against God's people all the time.

First Peter 5:8 tells us to "be sober, be vigilant; for your adversary the devil walks about like a roaring lion, seeking whom he may devour."

It's easy to feel powerless to protect yourself and your family. With the power of prayer, however, we can go boldly out into the world, knowing the protection and peace that comes through faith in Jesus Christ. He has already conquered evil, and because of that we are able to live without fear.

We can stand on Jesus' promise in Luke 10:19 "I have given you authority to trample on snakes and scorpions and to overcome all the power of the enemy; nothing will harm you."

When we pray, we draw upon the strength of the Lord to claim victory over the evil one.

Be on your guard today. Keep praying that the Holy Spirit will reveal traps and temptations the enemy has laid for you.

FURTHER READING:
Psalms 141:8-10
Proverbs 3:23
1 John 4:4

December 1

Our High Priest

"When all the people were being baptized,
Jesus was baptized too. And as he was
praying, heaven was opened."

—LUKE 3:21

When Jesus prays, heaven opens. And He is now sitting at the right hand of God, praying for us. Jesus petitions God on our behalf daily.

In the Old Testament, people with prayer requests had to offer a sacrifice at the temple and have a priest intercede for them before God. When Jesus died on the cross, however, He changed everything. "Therefore...He always lives to make intercession for them. For such a High Priest was fitting for us, who is holy, harmless, undefiled, separate from sinners, and has become higher than the heavens" (Hebrews 7:24-26). We need only to come to Him, and our prayers will be answered. Jesus is on our side, praying with us and for us, and the Holy Spirit also intercedes for us with groans that words cannot express.

Isn't that amazing? Even when we can't find the words to pray, the Holy Spirit is there, taking our requests before God Almighty. I want you to understand the team you have on your side as you pray. Claim Romans 8:31 today: "If God is for us, who can be against us?"

FURTHER READING:
John 17:20-26
Hebrews 4:15
Hebrews 9:24

December 2

Incense

"May my prayer be set before you like incense; may the lifting up of my hands be like the evening sacrifice."

—PSALMS 141:2

God loves to hear our prayers. It says in the Word that the prayers of the saints are like bowls full of incense (Revelation 5:8), a pleasing aroma to the Lord.

Maybe you've been led to believe that your prayers about everyday things are too small for God and you don't want to "bother" Him. Many people justify not bringing their prayers to the Lord because they don't want to bring Him "little things."

Hear me on this: He wants us to pray constantly (1 Thessalonians 5:17) and to pray about everything in our lives (Philippians 4:6). He cares about every detail! He wants us to bring everything before Him so that He can heal us, teach us, and demonstrate His love for us. Our prayers glorify Him.

God treasures our prayers; each one is important to Him. He hears them all, and He will answer. Don't be caught up in a lie, believing that your concern isn't worth His time. Your prayers are precious to Him. The next time you pray, imagine your prayer as a sweet fragrance drifting up to heaven.

When you come to God, you please Him, and He wants to bless you in return.

FURTHER READING:
2 Samuel 24:24-25
Ezra 6:9-11
Revelation 8:3-4

December 3

Weapon of Victory

"In addition to all this, take up the shield of faith, with which you can extinguish all the flaming arrows of the evil one."

—EPHESIANS 6:16

We have the ultimate weapon in the war of good versus evil. As we suit ourselves for battle, we need to put on the whole armor of God, which will keep us safe from the devil's arrows.

As you get dressed today, remember to put on your armor: the belt of truth, the breastplate of righteousness, the gospel of peace on your feet, the shield of faith, the helmet of salvation, and the sword of the Spirit (Ephesians 6:14-17).

But keep reading; don't forget the most important weapon we have—our direct connection to God. Verse 18 goes on to tell us to pray continually.

First Kings 8:44-45 says, "When Your people go out to battle against their enemy, wherever You send them, and when they pray to the Lord...then hear in heaven their prayer and their supplication, and maintain their cause."

When we're in the midst of battle, we always need to be praying. Prayer will keep us on the right course and keep our feet steady in the fight. Are you making use of prayer in your battle?

FURTHER READING:
1 Samuel 2:9
Isaiah 54:17
Ephesians 6

December 4

Send Help

"And what does the Lord require of you but to act justly and to love mercy and to walk humbly with your God?"

—MICAH 6:8

Do you know that you have the power to send help to the ends of the earth? Your prayers for God's people all over the world set miracles in motion.

We need to pray the prayer of agreement on behalf of others. In Matthew 18:19 Jesus said, "...if two of you on earth shall agree on anything you ask for, it will be done for you by my Father in Heaven." If you and I pray in agreement for people we've never even met, God moves, and He moves in mighty ways. Today, send help to the ends of the earth with me.

Pray with me in agreement for your brothers and sisters around the globe. Pray today for children like Elvira, a two-month-old in the depths of the Guatemalan forest, severely malnourished and weighing only three pounds.

Pray for missionaries who work with children like Elvira and their parents and show them that they have a reason to hope. Pray today for our *Bridge of Hope* ministries; pray for the people that run them and the people that are being ministered to.

The power of prayer can change the world; will you go before the Lord today? A life may rest on your fervent prayers.

FURTHER READING:
Exodus 22:22-25
Galatians 2:9-10
James 2

December 5

Need Only to Ask

"In that day you will no longer ask me anything. I tell you the truth, my Father will give you whatever you ask in my name."

—JOHN 16:23

Why do we hesitate to bring our requests before God? We have Jesus' word that whatever we ask in His name, the Father will give to us. Do you believe His promise?

Too often we try to fight our battles on our own. But why not leave it to the awesome power of the Almighty God?

Jesus Christ promises us over and over again that He will give us what we ask Him for. Liza, a woman from Florida, prayed that her son would be saved. As an act of faith, she tucked her prayer cloth behind his picture and asked God to bring him to salvation. Her son, his girlfriend, and his friends have now all been saved and marked for eternal life.

God wants to grant any request you lay before Him (1 Chronicles 4:10). No matter how big your mountain is, remember that nothing is too big for God! Do you need healing in your life? Are you trying to get out of debt? Have you lost your job? Ask Him for help. No request is too small or too large for Him. Give Him your cares and burdens (1 Peter 5:7) and believe that He will do as He has promised.

FURTHER READING:
John 5:16
John 16:23-24
James 4:2-3

December 6

Staff to a Shadow

"The Spirit of the Lord is on me,
because he has anointed me..."

—LUKE 4:18

The Bible's pages are filled with accounts of how God's anointing was present upon everything from a staff to a shadow.

The anointing rested on Moses' staff as it swallowed the snakes of Pharaoh (Exodus 7:8-13) and upon Elijah's cloak as he parted the Jordan and walked on dry ground (2 Kings 2).

The anointing rested upon Elisha's bones—and, when a dead man was thrown into his open tomb, the dead man's eyes popped open and he became alive again (2 Kings 13:21).

The anointing will cause what was once dead to come alive again! It is the life force of Almighty God!

Romans 8:11 says, "And if the Spirit of him who raised Jesus from the dead is living in you, he who raised Christ from the dead will also give life to your mortal bodies through his Spirit, who lives in you."

The anointing of God was in the mud Jesus placed upon the blind man's eyes and upon Peter's handkerchiefs and aprons. The same anointing that resurrected Jesus is still at work in our lives today for God's glory and for the furthering of His kingdom.

FURTHER READING:
2 Kings 6:1-7
Mark 7:31-37
Mark 8:22-26

December 7

Jubilee Anointing

*"'Not by might nor by power, but by
my Spirit,' says the Lord Almighty."*

—ZECHARIAH 4:6

In Jesus' first sermon, He declares the anointing for Jubilee: "The Spirit of the Lord is on me, because He has anointed me to preach good news to the poor. He has sent me to proclaim freedom to the prisoners and recovery of sight to the blind, to release the oppressed, to proclaim the year of the Lord's favor" (Luke 4:18-19).

The anointing of Jesus' ministry—the Jubilee anointing— brings liberty to captives, healing to those broken in body and in heart, recovery of sight (physically and spiritually), and illuminates the message of good news to the lost!

Jubilee means rejoicing and celebrating! David said, "I know that the Lord saves His anointed; He answers him from His holy heaven with the saving power of His right hand" (Psalms 20:6). There is nothing too big for God to change with His power.

Whatever you are mourning over today, God wants to bestow a "crown of beauty instead of ashes, the oil of gladness instead of mourning, and a garment of praise instead of a spirit of despair" (Isaiah 61:3). This is the Jubliee anointing of Jesus in our lives. This is your season of restoration!

FURTHER READING:
Isaiah 60:1-5
Isaiah 61
Luke 19:1-10

December 8

Stand Against the Devil

"Jesus returned ... in the power of the Holy Spirit."

—LUKE 4:14

There is an anointing of the Holy Spirit that will propel you through every line of Satan's defense. Jesus walked in it as He withstood the onslaught of the devil while fasting in the wilderness and received power from on high (Matthew 4:1-11).

Jesus was baptized in the river Jordan prior to praying and fasting 40 days and 40 nights. At the end of the fast, Satan came and tempted Jesus to sin against God in spirit, soul and body. (Note that after Jesus was baptized and had fasted, then the enemy attacked. When you draw near to God, that's when Satan takes notice.) But Jesus resisted Satan's tactics and refuted what he said (Luke 4:4-10). From there, Jesus returned in the power of the Holy Spirit into Galilee and word of Him went through the entire region.

If Jesus needed the anointing to speak God's Word and stand against the schemes of the devil, how much more do we need the power of the Holy Spirit? "But you will receive power when the Holy Spirit comes on you; and you will be my witnesses in Jerusalem, and in all Judea and Samaria, and to the ends of the earth" (Acts 1:8). Even the Son of God needed the anointing—and we must follow in His footsteps.

FURTHER READING:
1 Peter 5:1-11
James 4:1-10
Acts 17:16-34

December 9

Preach Good News

"He has anointed me to preach good news to the poor..."
—LUKE 4:18

"Jesus went through all the towns...teaching in their synagogues, preaching the good news of the kingdom" (Matthew 9:35).

Imagine Jesus walking from village to village and proclaiming the good news of His kingdom to anyone who would receive it. "Set your minds on things above, not on earthly things" (Colossians 3:2). Jesus came to bridge the gap between man and God.

Today, we have the advantage of looking back to the cross. On Calvary, Jesus saved us from an eternity spent in Hell and brought us into the glorious kingdom of God... and that's good news. The message of the cross never changes.

Because of sin, there was an enormous breach between God and His creation. But God built a bridge through the cross. Now, instead of being separated from God by the chasm, we can have a personal relationship with Him. Galatians 3:13 says, "Christ redeemed us from the curse of the law."

When you share the good news, you are sharing truth already accomplished. God's love will never change. All you have to look for is God's anointed time for people to hear.

"For it is by grace you have been saved, through faith—and this not from yourselves, it is the gift of God" (Ephesians 2:8).

It's the most wonderful gift anyone could hope for—share it!

FURTHER READING:
Romans 8
Acts 8
Acts 26

December 10

Set Free

"He has anointed me ...
to proclaim freedom to prisoners."

—LUKE 4:18

The anointing of Jesus Christ frees you from the devil's grasp. If he has disrupted your life—in your finances, health, marriage or home—we can tell him, "Hands off!" and make him put it back in order. "Submit yourselves, then, to God. Resist the devil, and he will flee from you" (James 4:7).

During a World Harvest Dominion Camp Meeting, Dr. Lester Sumrall told a story in which he was staying in a village deep in the jungle after preaching the gospel and casting out devils.

While he lay on his bed, it suddenly began to shake and dance across the middle of the floor. Dr. Sumrall recounted, "I recognized immediately it was the devil, so I jumped up and said, 'I rebuke you!' and the bed stopped shaking." Then, Dr. Sumrall commanded the devil, "Now, put it back!"

The bed began shaking across the room and came back to rest against the wall.

Today, by the anointing of Jesus, we are not only going to tell the devil to set you free in those areas where you feel bound... but we are going to tell him to "put it back!" He will have to restore whatever he has stolen from you!

FURTHER READING:
Mark 5:1-20
Matthew 17:14-21
Romans 7:21-8:13

December 11

A Faith That's Effective

"He has anointed me ... [to bring]
recovery of sight to the blind."

—LUKE 4:18

In the Gospels, Jesus walked from village to village, healing every sickness and disease that came across His path. "Jesus went throughout Galilee ... preaching the good news of the kingdom, and healing every disease and sickness among the people" (Matthew 4:23).

To me, this is the true ministry of the Gospel. People become open to the good news after they have seen an answer to prayer. People long for something real—a faith that's effective. We in the Church need to believe for something more. Signs and wonders validate the Gospel message and cause it to spread. Look for opportunities to pray—God will prove Himself faithful. Matthew says, "News about Jesus spread all over Syria" (Matthew 4:24). This is evangelism at work. When people hear there is a God who will meet them at their point of need, they will come looking for Him.

As times get tough, the Church in America needs to seek God's anointing, and preach the old-fashioned, heartfelt, Holy Spirit, sin-eradicating, life-changing, healing message of Jesus Christ ... the whole Gospel. The world is longing for it!

FURTHER READING:
Matthew 11:2-6
Mark 16:15-18
Luke 9:1-6; 10:1-24

December 12

Deliverance

*"The Spirit of the Sovereign Lord is on me, because
the Lord has anointed me to preach good news to
the poor. He has sent me to bind up the
brokenhearted, to proclaim freedom for the
captives and release from darkness for the prisoners."*

—ISAIAH 61:1

Do you know what deliverance means? Deliverance is defined as "rescue from bondage or danger." This is what Christ did for us on the cross...He delivered us from the bondage of sin...from the curse of death...from the clutches of the devil.

Yet so many believers live in bondage...they live in the prison camp of Satan. Why? They may live by the dead letter of the law or perhaps they minimize the power of the Holy Spirit to change and deliver people. Ignorance is also a factor—many Christians are ignorant about their rights as God's children.

They don't know that they have been fully delivered and all they need to do is walk out of their place of captivity.

"You are a chosen people, a royal priesthood, a holy nation, a people belonging to God, that you may declare the praises of him who called you out of darkness into his wonderful light" (1 Peter 2:9). If you want to be free from bondage, drink from the well of deliverance and start living your life of freedom!

FURTHER READING:
Matthew 16:18
Mark 16:17
Luke 10:19

December 13

Heal the Brokenhearted

"He has anointed me ... to release the oppressed"

—LUKE 4:18

Have you poured out your soul during a time when you felt you couldn't go on? Have you faced a tragedy when you didn't know what to speak or pray? The Psalmist declared, "He heals the heartbroken and bandages their wounds" (Psalms 147:3).

I've experienced this in my own life. When my son Austin was a child, the doctors handed him to us with the report: "No cure. No treatment. No hope."

Joni and I knew there was no way our Lord, Jesus Christ, was going to abandon us in these dire circumstances. With tears in our eyes and faith in our hearts, we pressed on, believing for a miracle. Our hearts felt shattered in a million pieces... but God didn't leave us alone (see Matthew 28:20).

God hears your cry. Austin's progress has been remarkable, and he has continued to grow and check one thing after another off the list of things the doctors said he would never do.

Our God specializes in hopeless situations, and He gives grace to the humble.

"Humble yourselves, therefore, under God's mighty hand, that he may lift you up in due time. Cast all your anxiety on him because he cares for you" (1 Peter 5:6-7).

FURTHER READING:
Isaiah 43:1-5
2 Corinthians 1:3-4
Psalms 23

December 14

Like a Child

"Let the little children come to me, and do not hinder them, for the kingdom of God belongs to such as these."

—MARK 10:14

Jesus told the disciples that the kingdom of God belongs to those who are like children, but what does it really mean to be like a child? Are we to be immature and naïve as children? Are we to be helpless and dependent?

Children have an unshakable trust in their parents. They walk in faith daily, believing that their parents will keep their promises and will keep them safe. They wake with an air of expectation. They have a tendency to see good—even when their parents fall short. They have an innate ability to hold on to hope.

Jesus said, "I tell you the truth, anyone who will not receive the kingdom of God like a little child will never enter it" (Mark 10:15). God wants us to be like them.

He wants us to trust Him, to have an expectation that He will answer our prayers, provide for our needs, deliver us from evil, heal our bodies, and lead us in the paths of righteousness.

He wants us to have an unshakable faith in our God. For unlike parents who may break promises and make mistakes, He is infallible. All that He promises He does... and it is always good.

FURTHER READING:
Matthew 18:3
Mark 10:15
1 Peter 2:2

December 15

Your Seeds

"Sow for yourselves righteousness, reap the fruit of unfailing love, and break up your unplowed ground; for it is time to seek the Lord, until he comes and showers righteousness on you."

—HOSEA 10:12

Did you know your life is a seed and that you have the ability to produce fruit? God has given each of us the ability to produce spiritual fruit. Our harvest is determined by the seeds we sow.

What types of seeds have you been sowing—seeds of righteousness or seeds of deception? As believers, our seeds should be holy, pure, true, righteous, loving, kind, gentle, honest, peaceful and meek. Unfortunately, many have eaten from the fruit of deception and allowed their lives to produce seeds of wickedness, lies, rebellion and self-reliance.

Romans 7:6 says, "But now, by dying to what once bound us, we have been released from the law so that we serve in the new way of the Spirit, and not in the old way of the written code."

If you desire to plant seeds of righteousness so you can reap the fruit of unfailing love, break up your unplowed ground, pull up the crops of the enemy and plant the seeds of God in your life through Holy Spirit. If you plant it, He will water it and bring forth an abundant harvest.

FURTHER READING:
Proverbs 11:18
Isaiah 45:8
2 Timothy 2:11

December 16

Power and Authority

"If you have any encouragement from being united with Christ, if any comfort from his love, if any fellowship with the Spirit, if any tenderness and compassion, then... Do nothing out of selfish ambition or vain conceit, but in humility consider others better than yourselves."

—PHILIPPIANS 2:1-3

When Jesus Christ came to earth as a man, He left behind everything He possessed in glory. He came to earth as a man like you and me. He was tempted in every way as we are, and yet was without sin. He had to rely on the Holy Spirit just like we do. When He shed His precious blood on Calvary and went back to heaven, it was only then that God gave Him everything as an inheritance. How did Jesus get His godly power and authority back? The Father gave Jesus a name above every name as part of His inheritance, "that at the name of Jesus every knee should bow, in heaven and on earth and under the earth, and every tongue confess that Jesus Christ is Lord, to the glory of God the Father" (Philippians 2:10-11).

Have faith in that name! Jesus said, "Until now you have asked nothing in My name. Ask, and you will receive, that your joy may be full" (John 16:24). All you need is in the name of Christ Jesus.

FURTHER READING:
Philippians 2:5-11
John 16:23-24
Hebrews 1:1-4

December 17

Praise Him

"Praise the Lord, O my soul; all my inmost being, praise his holy name. Praise the Lord, O my soul, and forget not all his benefits."

PSALMS 103:1-2

Friend, do you know what you have in Jesus? Do you really know what God has provided for you? Do you know your God-given rights?

Sadly, too many believers do not know what they have in Christ Jesus. Too many do not realize that they are mighty in the Lord, that they have power and dominion over evil forces, and that they have creative ability to speak forth those things that are not as though they were.

When I think about all that God has provided, I rejoice. I can't help but praise Him!

We already have everything that we need from God. That is why Paul didn't pray that believers will get things from God... he prayed that they will understand what they have already received from God. Too many of us are asking God for what He has already provided.

If we had the proper understanding we would be praising Him, for every need has been met though His riches in Christ Jesus (Philippians 4:19).

FURTHER READING:
Psalms 16
Psalms 103
Ephesians 1:15-23

December 18

God's Perfect Gift

"For God so loved the world that he gave his one and only Son, that whoever believes in him shall not perish but have eternal life."

—JOHN 3:16

We all love gifts. They make us feel special, treasured and appreciated, but they all pale in comparison to the gift that God gave us in Jesus—God's perfect gift.

In Jesus, God has provided His children with many gifts: Redemption, forgiveness, perfect love, blessings, favor, victory, freedom, adoption, provision, healing, deliverance and relationship. God has thought of and provided us with everything we will ever need...and He provided it 2,000 years ago in the form of a little baby, sent to save the world.

Luke 2:13-14 says, "Suddenly a great company of the heavenly host appeared with the angel, praising God and saying, 'Glory to God in the highest, and on earth peace to men on whom his favor rests.'"

So many live as if God has not provided for them. God sent us His only son, Jesus, because of His perfect love toward us. He wants us to enjoy all that is wrapped up in His Son.

He wants us to live abundant lives. Are you ready to enjoy the fullness of your perfect gift?

FURTHER READING:
Romans 5:8
Romans 8:32
1 John 4:9-10

December 19

A Gift of Shoes

"Suppose a brother or sister is without clothes and daily food. If one of you says to him, 'Go, I wish you well; keep warm and well fed,' but does nothing about his physical needs, what good is it?"

—JAMES 2:15-16

Little Leslie bounced and smiled as she proudly walked me through the tiny two-room concrete house our mission partners had built for her family. She was oblivious to the dire circumstances that enveloped her family, even in what to her was a wondrous new house.

In this village in Guatemala, there was no running water. The ground where they lived was infected with parasitic worms that could penetrate into the children's skin and live in their intestinal systems. "Oh Lord," I prayed, "please help us get some shoes to protect these children." God is a God who answers prayers. He answered my earnest prayer with 10,000 pairs of shoes.

God commands us to help those who have nothing, and He promises to reward us if we do. Hebrews 6:10 says, "God is not unjust; he will not forget your work and the love you have shown him as you have helped his people and continue to help them." It is our Biblical responsibility to look after the weak, the needy and the poor. God will reward us when we do.

FURTHER READING:
Mark 9:36-37
Luke 3:10-11
3 John 1:2

December 20

Begin with Faith

"'I am the Lord's servant,' Mary answered. 'May it be to me as you have said.' Then the angel left her."

—LUKE 1:38

When the angel came to Mary she was "greatly troubled at his words and wondered what kind of greeting this might be." But she accepted the angel's message and declared: "I am the Lord's servant. May it be to me as you have said."

Mary accepted the angel's words in faith; but when the angel appeared to Zacharias, he was fearful and he could not accept what the angel was telling him.

Therefore the angel said to Zacharias: "And now you will be silent and not able to speak until the day this happens, because you did not believe my words, which will come true at their proper time" (Luke 1:20).

Hebrews 11:6 says, "And without faith it is impossible to please God, because anyone who comes to him must believe that he exists and that he rewards those who earnestly seek him."

Faith is the basis—the foundation for our walk with God. You must believe that He is a rewarder of those that seek Him.

Mary believed and was blessed; Zacharias didn't believe and was silenced until God had completed His purpose. Will you begin with faith?

FURTHER READING:
Luke 1:20
Hebrews 11
Matthew 1:18-25

December 21

Christ's Victory

*"I have given you authority to trample on snakes
and scorpions and to overcome all the power of
the enemy; nothing will harm you."*

—LUKE 10:19

You may not look like or feel like much, but there is great power in you. The power that raised Christ from the dead resides in you.

Jesus was born not only to be the perfect sacrifice but also to declare victory over death, hell and the grave. Paul said, "And if Christ has not been raised, our preaching is useless and so is your faith" (1 Corinthians 15:14).

Jesus Christ rose from the dead, so death no longer has dominion over Him. And since you are in Him, death no longer has dominion over you.

Christ's victory over death is also yours if you are born of Him. Right now you live in hope of your redemption, but the promise is sure and you can rest in Him knowing He is faithful.

Colossians 1:13-14 says, "For he has rescued us from the dominion of darkness and brought us into the kingdom of the Son he loves, in whom we have redemption, the forgiveness of sins." You may not feel powerful, but there is great power in you—power to defeat death through the resurrection of Christ Jesus!

FURTHER READING:
1 Corinthians 15
Romans 6
Matthew 27

December 22

Rejoice!

"The shepherds returned, glorifying and praising God for all the things they had heard and seen, which were just as they had been told."

—LUKE 2:20

In Luke 2, we are told that the angel of the Lord told the shepherds about the Savior's birth. The angel told them that is was a great occasion for rejoicing for everyone and told them where they would find the Messiah and how they could recognize him. The angels sang songs of praise to God. But then they left.

The shepherds had to make a choice—were they going to go and see if what the angel said was true? Or would they stay where they were? They chose to act on what they heard... they moved in faith—for they believed what the Lord had said through His messenger.

As the shepherds returned to their fields, they glorified and praised God for what the angels had told them and because they had seen Jesus. "The shepherds returned, glorifying and praising God for all the things they had heard and seen, which were just as they had been told" (Luke 2:20).

Do you praise God for all that you have heard about Him? Do you praise God for Jesus? Do you rejoice in the good news of salvation? It's time to rejoice!

FURTHER READING:
Isaiah 55:10-11
Hebrews 6:18
Genesis 12

December 23

God Is Light

"When Jesus spoke again to the people, he said, "I am the light of the world. Whoever follows me will never walk in darkness, but will have the light of life."

JOHN 8:12

Are you walking in light? Or are you walking in darkness? Jesus said that if we follow Him we will never walk in darkness because God is light...there is no darkness in Him. As believers, we are children of light.

Can we belong to God and still walk in darkness? First John 1:6-7 tells us, "If we claim to have fellowship with him yet walk in the darkness, we lie and do not live by the truth. But if we walk in the light, as he is in the light, we have fellowship with one another, and the blood of Jesus, his Son, purifies us from all sin."

Light has no fellowship with darkness. If we walk in the "light of life" we have fellowship with one another and the blood of Jesus purifies us from sin.

In John 12:36, Jesus said, "Put your trust in the light while you have it, so that you may become sons of light."

If you desire to walk in the light of Jesus, decide to follow Him all the way. His light will purify, cleanse and transform you...so you will reflect the light of His glory.

FURTHER READING:
1 John 1
Romans 13:12
Ephesians 5:11-15

December 24

Sweet Perfume

"Be imitators of God, therefore, as dearly loved children live a life of love, just as Christ loved us and gave himself up for us as a fragrant offering and sacrifice to God."

—EPHESIANS 5:1-2

As children of God, we are to follow His example in everything we do. We are to love one another because God so loved us that He gave His only son for us. We are to follow the example of Jesus because He willingly sacrificed His life so that we could live and have forgiveness of sin.

We are called to live lives full of love for others following the life of Christ. We are to live lives that are pleasing to God...lives that are sweet perfume to Him...lives of sacrifice, putting others before ourselves.

Romans 12:1 says, "Therefore, I urge you, brothers, in view of God's mercy, to offer your bodies as living sacrifices, holy and pleasing to God—this is your spiritual act of worship."

God gave us His best on that first Christmas day 2,000 years ago...Jesus gave us His all...and we are called to do the same.

Let us lift up our lives before God as sweet aromas...let us spread the perfume of Christ throughout the world...let us demonstrate that we are His...let us show the world His love by the lives we choose to live.

FURTHER READING:
Ephesians 5: 1-14
John 8:12
Romans 13:12

December 25

Goodwill

"Suddenly a great company of the heavenly host appeared with the angel, praising God and saying, 'Glory to God in the highest, and on earth peace to men on whom his favor rests.'"

—LUKE 2:13-14

Did you know that when God sent Jesus to earth it was the greatest act of benevolence ever? It was an act of unprecedented generosity. God gave us the person that He loved most...and Jesus laid down everything for us—His position, His wealth, and eventually His life.

Why? Because of love! God loved us so much that He did not consider the cost. He did not say, "Well, since only some will come to me it is not worth the sacrifice." God gave His best in spite of the number who would accept His gift. God showed us favor in our fallen condition. Jeremiah 29:11 says, "'For I know the plans I have for you,' declares the Lord, 'plans to prosper you and not to harm you, plans to give you hope and a future.'" He showed us love though we were separated from Him and gave us a gift that cost Him what He treasured most.

Luke 19:38 says, "Blessed is the king who comes in the name of the Lord! Peace in heaven and glory in the highest!" As you celebrate Christ Jesus' birth, rejoice in the benevolence of God.

FURTHER READING:
Psalms 139
John 3:19-21
John 14:27

December 26

My Neighbor

"But he wanted to justify himself, so he asked Jesus, 'And who is my neighbor?'"

—LUKE 10:29

There is a crisis erupting in America's streets. The need is desperate and overwhelming, and pastors are sounding the alarm for help.

It's a sad but true fact that many who were once among the middle class are now among the poor and the homeless. People are losing jobs and homes. Sadder still is that shelters are starting to shut down at a time when they're most needed, leaving thousands of families out on the street.

The Bible tells us repeatedly to show kindness to those less fortunate and to love our neighbors as ourselves. Mark 12:33 says that the two most important commandments are "To love [God] with all your heart, with all your understanding and with all your strength, and to love your neighbor as yourself is more important than all burnt offerings and sacrifices."

When the pilgrims first arrived in this country, they formed communities like the first churches. Without each other and the communities they formed and the help of their neighbors, these brave pilgrims would not have survived. Today we must follow this same idea of community and help the needy.

FURTHER READING:
Deuteronomy 15:11
Job 22:5-11
James 2:8

December 27

Walk in Faith

*"Blessed is she who has believed that what the
Lord has said to her will be accomplished!"*

—LUKE 1:45

When the angel appeared to Mary and told her she would bear
the son of God, Mary chose to believe God and the result was
the conception by the Holy Spirit—the Son of God.

An angel visited Joseph in a dream, saying, "Joseph son of
David, do not be afraid to take Mary home as your wife, because
what is conceived in her is from the Holy Spirit. She will give
birth to a son, and you are to give him the name Jesus, because
he will save his people from their sins" (Matthew 1:20-21).

Joseph rose up and did exactly as the angel had commanded.

It will always be a walk of faith. By faith, Noah prepared an
ark for the saving of his household; by faith, Abraham obeyed
when he was called to go to the place which he would receive
as an inheritance; by faith, Sarah received strength to conceive
seed, and she bore a child when she was past the age.

This life we are called to live is not the result of blind faith.
Faith is, as my mentor Dr. Lester Sumrall said, simply knowing God. When you know God, it is not hard to believe Him.
When you believe Him, you will see the fulfillment of the
impossible, for with God all things are possible (Mark 10:27).

FURTHER READING:
Matthew 2
Hebrews 11
Mark 10:23-31

December 28

God's Covenant

"But the ministry Jesus has received is as superior to theirs as the covenant of which he is mediator is superior to the old one, and it is founded on better promises."

—HEBREWS 8:6

Since the beginning of time, God has sought to be in covenant with man. He tried with Adam, but he reached for a piece of forbidden fruit. He tried with David, but he coveted another man's wife and then murdered her husband.

So in order to restore man into a right relationship with Himself, God decided to send His perfect son—Jesus Christ— to save the world from sin. Jesus was born to climb Golgotha's hillside and become the sacrificial offering—the only solution for sin-infected humanity.

The covenant was sealed and ratified. Mercy had paid the price! Here is the good Gospel news: You are in covenant with God through the blood of His Son, Jesus, and therefore, you are in covenant with perfection! How can you fail? God lives inside you!

Christ in you has become the hope of glory (Colossians 1:27). You cannot fail. When the adversary comes knocking at your door, faith will answer! Redeemed! How I love to proclaim it. Redeemed by the blood of the Lamb!

FURTHER READING:
Psalms 107:2
Colossians 1:24-29
Hebrews 9:23-28

December 29

Looking at the Unseen

"So we fix our eyes not on what is seen, but on what is unseen. For what is seen is temporary, but what is unseen is eternal."

—2 CORINTHIANS 4:18

There's hope for you beyond the scope of human limitation, but you're not going to get it just by looking at the natural all the time and being dictated by your feelings.

Get ready: things are going to get shaken up. You may be required to walk through the lonesome valley. Satan has a plan. It doesn't matter if it's a fever, a bad report or some kind of destruction, his plan is to take you out. But, when the devil's got a plan to take you out, God's got a plan to keep you in. So fix your eyes on the unseen. Have you read of the perseverance of Job? God rewarded Job with double for all the pain he faced (see Job 42:10-17).

Fix your eyes on Jesus in this new year, because He went into the grave and came out the other side victorious.

You're going through; don't quit in the middle of the storm. Grab the reins of life, hold on and steer the wild wings of the wind toward hope—pursue the things of eternity. God will reward you for your faithfulness to His everlasting Word.

FURTHER READING:
James 5:11
Job 42:10-13
Hebrews 12:25-29

December 30

What Is Left

"The words 'once more' indicate the removing of what can be shaken—that is, created things—so that what cannot be shaken may remain."

—HEBREWS 12:27

What can we count on in perilous times? What rock are we to build our lives on? When everything else has faded, three things will remain: Faith, hope and love (1 Corinthians 13).

We have inherited a kingdom that cannot be moved, cannot be shaken and cannot fall apart. It is going to endure.

Lift up your eyes. Quit looking at what you can see, and focus on what you can't see—angels walking all around you, the fiery hosts of heaven surrounding you in everything you do.

Look! See that blood covering you? That's the blood of Jesus! You're in a kingdom that can't be moved. The only reason you have to fear is that you've stepped outside that kingdom. The devil's a thief; he doesn't have to be strong. He just has to wait until you are not paying attention, not holding steadfast to God's Word.

Purpose in your heart not to be entangled again with a yoke of bondage. Walk in the Spirit! Build your life on the sure foundation of the Word of God and when everything else around you is being shaken, you will remain standing.

FURTHER READING:
Galatians 5:1
Romans 8
Hebrews 12:1-2

December 31

A Life of Change

"We were therefore buried with him through baptism into death in order that, just as Christ was raised from the dead through the glory of the Father, we too may live a new life."

—ROMANS 6:4

Jesus died to pay for your sins and to make you a new creation. You come into your new life for one purpose: to make you more like Jesus.

What should this new life look like? "And these signs will accompany those who believe: In my name they will drive out demons; they will speak in new tongues; they will pick up snakes with their hands; and when they drink deadly poison, it will not hurt them at all; they will place their hands on sick people, and they will get well" (Mark 16:17-18).

You have a new language with which to commune with God. You have power from another realm over all the works of the enemy. You will heal the sick. You will walk in love. Step into the newness that God has for you.

Continue to grow from glory to glory, and from one manifested presence of the Lord to another. As you begin the New Year, meditate on God's Word so you might live abundantly in Him and become all that you are meant to become for Him.

FURTHER READING:
2 Corinthians 3:16-18
Luke 24:49
2 Corinthians 5:17-19

In 1985, God gave Pastor Parsley a revelation he called **Resurrection Seed.** It was a defining moment in the ministry, and the beginning of hundreds of documented testimonies from around the world. The revelation was this: **Easter is when God planted His Best Seed—His Only Son—on Earth.** From that miracle came our eternal life. How can we give less than our best this season?

Next to the Lord, his wonderful family and dear friends, Pastor Parsley loves the company of his dogs, Balko and Gita.

On November 26, 1992, Dr. Lester Sumrall presented Pastor Parsley with a sword, a symbol of the mantle that was passed to Sumrall from Smith Wigglesworth (and from Howard Carter to Wigglesworth) and was now being placed on Pastor Parsley's ministry.

Every day, the Breakthrough broadcast reaches the four corners of the world with the message of the Gospel.

In July 2004, Pastor Parsley founded The Center for Moral Clarity with a goal to impact the culture and the government according to Biblical principles and values.

As founder of *Bridge of Hope*, the missions outreach of Breakthrough, Pastor Parsley travels to third world nations and places devastated by disaster. The *Bridge of Hope* team brings help, hope and the message of the love of God. Through the generosity of partners and friends of Breakthrough, the team has been able to bring life-saving supplies to millions.

Pastor Parsley enjoys his walks in God's creation with his dogs.

The Parsley family (from left): Ashton, Joni, Austin and Pastor. Their dog, Balko, is also pictured here.

Teacher, preacher, evangelist...Pastor Parsley is all these and more. An anointed messenger for these troubled times, Pastor Parsley preaches the Gospel around the world to as many countries as the Breakthrough broadcast will allow him to reach.

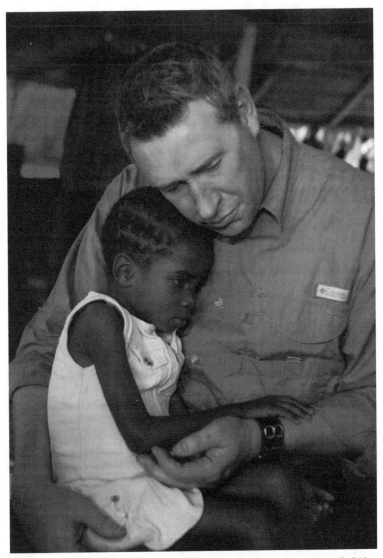

In Haiti, Pastor Parsley visited orphans whose home at the orphanage had been destroyed by a hurricane. The food, medical supplies and love that *Bridge of Hope* was able to bring comforted the little ones.

REMIXED

A Collection of Classic Illustrated Sermons

> ## "I was born to preach; it's in my DNA!
> It's who and what I am! Over the years, there have been set times when God has given me specific prophetic words to deliver to His people. I believe many of those words are even more relevant today than when I first released them."

Rod Parsley has prepared a very special collection of eight of his most life-transforming landmark illustrated sermons—each one updated with relevant Gospel truth for a new generation, and re-preached under a fresh anointing—just for you.

Rod Parsley ReMixed . . . A Collection of Classic Illustrated Sermons

- Repairers of the Breach
- Holiness: Living Leaven Free
- Raise the Standard Part 1
- Raise the Standard Part 2
- The Tangible Touch
- No More Crumbs
- Hidden InTents (Part 1)
- Hidden InTents (Part 2)

Don't miss this limited opportunity to receive this very special ministry collection. And remember your generous gift is helping keep the worldwide ministry of Breakthrough proclaiming the Gospel of Jesus Christ to a suffering world.

Order the complete collection—just $79.

Order the single-DVD, *Repairers of the Breach*, one of Pastor Parsley's most requested illustrated sermons for only $15. You'll learn vital Biblical truths that can help you and your family experience divine health, glorious freedom and power over the schemes of the enemy.

Order the 8-DVD ReMixed Sermon Series by Pastor Rod Parsley today! Call 1-866-241-4292 or visit us online at www.rodparsley.com.

Other products from Pastor Rod Parsley you may enjoy:

SKU	TITLE	DESCRIPTION	PRICE
949	Ancient Wells, Living Water	Draw from the ancient wells of God's truth.	$20.00
953	At the Cross: Where Healing Begins	Understand the gift of healing.	$10.00
BK365	Blessed Assurance	A collection of scriptures and quotes to encourage you.	$10.00
BK401	Breakthrough Moments	Learn to live each moment in breakthrough.	$10.00
348	Breakthrough Sword and Shield	Lead the lost to Christ.	$20.00
BK419	Culturally Incorrect	Understand different worldviews and break the divisions.	$15.00
WK419	Culturally Incorrect Workbook	An accompanying study guide to the book.	$10.00
957	Don't Look Now: Thriving, Not Just Surviving in Today's Troubled Economy	Reap a harvest in the midst of famine.	$10.00
BK412	Family Beyond Limits	An empowering book for you and your family.	$10.00
941	He Came First	Destroy obstacles by following in Jesus' footsteps.	$15.00
BK373	Healthy Country Cooking Cookbook		$10.00
BK352	It's Already There	Learn how obedience to His Word will bring victory.	$15.00
BK378	It's Showtime	Walk in the power of our covenant with God.	$10.00
921	No Dry Season	A prophetic message for the end-time church.	$15.00
BK307	Preparing for the Glory: Living Leaven Free	How to keep vigilant in your walk with God.	$10.00
RBIBLE	Reformation Bible	The renewing, restoring Word of God.	$30.00
409	Repairers of the Breach – Revised Edition	Rebuild the bridge back to God.	$15.00
BK355	Silent No More	This book expounds upon the issues of our day.	$15.00
WK355	Silent No More Workbook	An accompanying study guide to the book.	$10.00
BK912	Ten Golden Keys	God's prescription for never-ending abundance.	$10.00
BK358	Touched by the Anointing	Allow your need to be touched by His anointing.	$10.00
BK308	Tribulation to Triumph: God's Vision, Your Victory	The tools needed to prepare you for victory.	$10.00
BK357	Your Way Out	Focus on Him as He provides your way out.	$10.00